Cataloguing-in-Publication
Conomos, John.
Mutant media : essays on cinema, video art and
new media.
Bibliography.
Includes index.
ISBN 9781920781323 (pbk.).
1. Multimedia communications – Social aspects.
2. Multimedia (Art) – Social aspects. 3. Visual sociology.
4. Mass media – Social aspects. I. Artspace
(Woolloomooloo, N.S.W.). II. Title.
302.23

Copy editing: Alexandra Kaufman, Reuben Keehan
and Sarah Shrubb
Design: Ricafeli Design
Printing: Green and Gold Printing

Co-published by Artspace Visual Arts Centre and
Power Publications, Sydney, 2007.
text © John Conomos.
edition © Artspace and Power Publications.
Artspace Visual Arts Centre
43-51 Cowper Wharf Road
Woolloomooloo NSW 2011
Sydney Australia
T +61 2 9356 0555
F +61 2 9368 1705
www.artspace.org.au

Power Publications
The Power Institute Foundation for Art & Visual Culture
RC Mills Building, A26, Fisher Road
University of Sydney NSW 2006
Sydney Australia
T +61 2 9351 6904
F +61 2 9351 7323
www.arts.usyd.edu.au/departs/arthistory/power/institute

ARTSPACE SYDNEY WWW.ARTSPACE.ORG.AU **POWER PUBLICATIONS**

Mutant Media

ESSAYS ON CINEMA, VIDEO ART AND NEW MEDIA

John Conomos

ARTSPACE / POWER PUBLICATIONS
Sydney 2007

AUTHOR'S ACKNOWLEDGMENTS

I am gratefully indebted to Nicholas Tsoutas for asking me to do this book. It was Nick who patiently waited, in his former position as Executive Director of Artspace, for the appearance of the book some time ago. Many sincere thanks to Nick. However, it was also the late Nicholas Zurbrugg who since the early 1990s kept insisting— as a fellow 'yobbo' critic—that I collect some of my essays for book publication. In this critical sense *Mutant Media* is dedicated to him as it is to the late Edward Said.

I am, truth be told, indebted to many different people for their advice, friendship and encouragement. First and foremost, many thanks go to Brad Buckley and Helen Hyatt-Johnston who kept reminding me of the pressing deadline to publish the book. Both Brad and Helen in this context were consistently conscientious in their personal commitment to see my book published within the given deadline. I should also thank Blair French, the current Executive Director of Artspace, for his advice, friendship and invaluable editorial suggestions. It was Blair who, after Nick's departure from Artspace, took up the project with such grace and conviction.

I also wish to express my deep appreciation to Laleen Jayamanne and Tina Kaufman who encouraged me, so many years ago, to publish my first efforts in critical writing. Many thanks. In particular, I wish to sincerely thank the following people who have given me their advice, friendship and support over the years: George Alexander, Brad Buckley, Robert Cahen, Alessio Cavallaro, Su Baker, Chris Caines, Lino Caputo, Jon Cattapan, Jon Cockburn, Jean-Paul Fargier, Jason Gee, Phillip George, John Gillies, Lynne Roberts-Goodwin, David Haines, Joyce Hinterding, Barrett Hodsdon, Eddy Jokovich, Stephen Jones, Craig Judd, Brian Langer, Robert Lloyd, Helen Macallan, Gary Manson, Adrian Martin, Salvatore Panatteri, Nikos Papastergiadis, Eugenia Raskopoulos, Glenn Remington, McKenzie Wark and Geoff Weary. Many apologies to my other friends who I have not included above. They know who they are and my gratitude and thanks go to them for their companionship over the years.

A special thanks goes to Sarah Shrubb for her consummate copy editing skills and to Eddy Jokovich for his much-appreciated help in getting the manuscript into some acceptable shape. I am also deeply grateful to Sydney College of the Arts Librarian Jennifer Hayes and her supportive staff for their constant assistance and understanding in tracking down books and articles essential to my book. In this context I wish to single out the Inter Library Loans Officer, Dominica Lowe, for her patience and unstinting support. Finally, I wish to express my many sincere thanks and appreciation to Carolyn, Joel and Mahla for their patient understanding, support and love. Many heart-felt thanks for your enduring empathy and companionship.

Earlier versions of these essays have appeared in previous publications. 'Cultural difference in contemporary Australian cinema' originally appeared as 'Cultural difference and ethnicity in Australian cinema' in *Cinema Papers*, 90, 1992, pp. 10-15. 'Documentary surrealism: on Luis Buñuel's *Land without Bread* (1933)', originally appeared as 'Prisoners of the documentary: revisiting Buñuel and his only non-fiction Film', *Metro*, no 124/125, 2000, pp. 106-107. 'Art, cinema, Hitchcock', originally appeared as 'The vertigo of time', a conference paper prepared for *For the Love of Fear*, Museum of Contemporary Art, Sydney, 31 March-2 April 2000, and later published in *Senses of Cinema*, 2000. 'Collage, site, video, projection', originally appeared as 'Video installations as spatial collage: inside the white cube with Shigeko Kubota and John Gillies and the Sydney Front', chapter 6 of my MA thesis *Video as Electronic Collage and as Writing*, University of Technology, Sydney, Department of Humanities and Social Sciences, 1994, pp. 65-86. 'Border crossings: Jean-Luc Godard as video essayist', originally appeared as 'Only the cinema', *Senses of Cinema*, May 2001. 'Australian new media arts: new directions since the 1990s', originally appeared as 'A view from the antipodes' in Phillip George and Yu Wei-Cheng (eds), *Art and New Media*, Taiwan, Digital Art Centre, Tainan University and COFA, UNSW, October 2004, pp. 147-154, as did 'Entering the digital image: Jeffrey Shaw and the quest for interactive cinema' as 'Jeffrey Shaw, virtual voyager', pp. 85-93. 'Framing Australian video art' and 'The spiral of time: Chris Marker and new media' were written specifically for this book.

Contents

Introduction

Filmmaking seems to me a transitory and threatened art. It is very closely bound up with technical developments. If in thirty years or fifty years the screen no longer exists, if editing isn't necessary, cinema will have ceased to exist. It will have become something else. That's already almost the case when a film is shown on television: the smallness of the screen falsifies everything. What will remain, then, of my films?

Luis Buñuel, *Pessimism* (1980)

The cinema is always as perfect as it can be.

Gilles Deleuze, *Cinema 2: The Time Image* (1985)

I await the end of cinema with optimism.

Jean-Luc Godard, *Cahiers du cinéma* (1965)

Today, anyone who is interested in cinema and new media technologies will be used to frequently encountering mournful pronouncements concerning the impending death of cinema itself and the demise of cinephilia. It is argued, in certain circles, that old media (painting, cinema and photography) will soon become passé—that cinema will end because the emerging digital media will replace it or so radically reconfigure it that we, as filmmakers, critics, and spectators, will not be able to recognise it. This is one of the more spurious techno-utopian perspectives concerning the increasing interface between cinema and the new digital media.

The shape of cinema to come has always been open to question, despite the hype and hysteria colouring debates about it during the last decade or so. To some, it is a scenario of either nostalgic disaster (cinema will end as we know it or will be substantially impoverished) or utopian technological determinism (cinema will irreversibly mutate into cyber-cinema). Both scenarios are equally problematic, for many complex reasons.

What we are witnessing, in so many different contexts, is the definition of cinema expanding to include the new audiovisual media. This has been ongoing since the 1960s. Through the writings collected here I attempt to address this continuing fragmentation of cinema in the context of the increasing ascendancy of new media in our private and public lives and the very recent phenomenon of visual artists resorting to cinema, its icons, narratives, genres and history in their artworks in the art gallery world.

Mutant Media gathers together a selection of my essays across the years and broadly across the areas of cinema, video and new media. Thus, it charts my own trajectory in terms of my cinephilia since the 1960s and my ongoing interests in film criticism and theory as well as in video art and new media since the 1980s. In other words, this book is, in a modest way, an autobiography of sorts, of someone whose eclectic life as an artist, writer and educator centres around cinema's grand, unpredictable adventure since its inception in the 1890s.

The various essays of *Mutant Media* reflect the many paths I have crossed over the years as an image-maker and critic engrossed in cinema in all its different contexts—art cinema, genre cinema, experimental cinema, etc.—including its more recent 'in between' links with video and media art and its explosion into the art gallery context. Therefore *Mutant Media* also traces the mutation of the moving image via video and the new technologies across our cultural and media landscape. Indeed, the book's three sections document in their respective ways the complex 'criss-crossing' connections between cinema, video art and new media. Following Raymond Bellour's passionate enquiry into the 'in between' images, sounds, forms and textures of the ever-present collision of cinema with video, TV and photography, as a collection of discrete essays written across time and context *Mutant Media* attempts to show, in its cross-disciplinary acategorical emphasis, the value of seeing film and the screen arts as a continuing long conversation between these various media art forms.[1] The collection is also informed by the belief (advanced by critics such as Bellour, Raymond Durgnat, Serge Daney, Manny Farber, Adrian Martin, Sylvia Lawson and Jonathan Rosenbaum, amongst many others) that there is great aesthetic, cultural and historical capital to be obtained by going beyond the traditional academic analysis of film as an aesthetic form and into the broader context of exploring images and their intricate, kinetic connections and relations in a convulsing image culture.

For me—someone who, like my 'baby boomer' peers, experienced cinema as celluloid-cinema in the 1960s and 1970s, and saw and heard its subsequent thematic, formal and stylistic changes and shifts over the following three decades—Jean-Luc Godard, as a (post)modernist voyager of the moving image, stands at the centre of the book's theoretical architecture. Godard's poetic probing of the medium's future in his films and criticism since the 1950s is a testament to the developing convergence between cinema, literature, painting and video. He remains one of cinema's greatest innovators and theorists, always exploring the archaeology of cinema as the expression of the memory and history of the 20th century.

The essays collected here represent my life's role as an artist-critic, and always as a cinephile, as a form of 'aesthetic vagabondage' (Jean-Louis Schefer).[2] Here, I believe, is criticism that still believes in the fragility and poetry of the moving image, and self-reflexivity, and does not succumb to any authoritarian meta-narratives of grand, totalising film and media theory. Criticism that is speculative, historically informed, modest and intimate with the dancing textures of image, sound, space and style of a movie in all its fleeting suggestiveness. Nothing less than what Manny Farber, whose own film writings are a kind of jazz-inflected film criticism and so acutely conscious of that multifaceted imagistic, sonic and especially spatial encounter between the film and the spectator, once said: that a critic—worthy of the name—needs to find the right kind of language to best describe the 'struggle to remain faithful to the transitory, multisuggestive complication of a movie image'.[3] This is poignantly registered when Chris Petit meets Farber in his absorbing video essay *Negative Space* (1999), which is a homage to Farber and his idea of a 'termite cinema' and to Robert Mitchum as a cool noir icon performer in Jacques Tourneur's 1947 noir classic, *Out of the Past*.[4]

When we speak of 'the death of cinema', we need to remind ourselves that since its beginnings as a popular cultural art form, cinema was always described as a medium without a future. Witness Louis Lumière's fatalistic statement that cinema was 'an invention without a future'. But cinema is still with us today in all its splendid multiplicity. Reading cinema's 'tea leaves' and seeing a single doomed future is myopic and unhelpful, for the same was said when photography first appeared apropos of painting, or when the Internet first appeared apropos of mail and newspapers. So it is more productive to speak of how cinema, already the bastard form of other hybrids (architecture, theatre, music, literature, radio, etc), something which is constantly underlined in Durgnat's gloriously open-ended film criticism, actually has multiple futures in multiple forms due to its unpredictable encounter with the new technologies. This, now, is a commonplace statement to make, but 20 years ago that was not the case. Then it amounted to heresy: cinema having other futures than the one defined in its classical form as a mass art form projected in a darkened auditorium? Back in the 1970s and 1980s, to even suggest to your cinephilic friends that video was a creative medium of expression would create moral panic.

But to people such as Raymond Bellour, Jean-Paul Fargier, Jean-Luc Godard, Thierry Kuntzel and Chris Marker, amongst others, video and cinema were not mutually exclusive art forms: instead, as Darke puts it, '"cinema" could provide a way of looking at the moving-image as it mutates across media'.[5] Thus, 'cinema' became, as I discovered in the last two and a half decades, a speculative and rhizomatic way of reading across film, video and new media. Being always suspicious of 'border patrol' orthodoxies, embracing video as a cross-disciplinary collage form of techno-creativity was a positive thing to do in the context of my cinephilia and film criticism, for it generated an anti-ghettoised critique of official culture and monocultural thought.

To have a lifelong passion for seeing and hearing cinema means that it quickens your heart and provides a 'pillow-text' road map for relating to the world at large and everything in it—it is a multifaceted phenomenological adventure giving form and substance to one's personal life in a shared experience of spectatorship. Alas, what we are now seeing is that shared mass experience of film viewing undergoing severe changes—best epitomised by the sentiments of the above opening quotes. Because of corporate cinematic culture, media technology, changing demographics and globalisation, our opportunities to see classical cinema are becoming rarer by the day. Contrary to the conventional wisdom, cinema is not dying, as

Rosenbaum argues in his sharp polemic *Movie Wars* (2000), despite the contempt that industry shows towards the spectator and how what parades itself today as film criticism and reviewing is nothing less than vapid 'consumer guide' rhetoric, cinema is alive and well beyond the multiplex theatres. It is living in other sites, such as *cinémathèques*, film festivals, museums and other national cinemas.[6]

Therefore, as a consequence of the rapid convergence in the digital media and the related countless image systems of delivery and reception, classical cinema as we have known it over the last 100 years, with its clearly delineated Aristotelian dramaturgical and narrative form, is undergoing severe aesthetic and cultural anxiety. Critically, cinema, as defined by Jean-Luc Godard in his long-awaited (but rarely seen) autobiographical pun-encrusted *Histoire(s) du cinéma* (1988–97)—film plus projection in a dark room—is being graphically problematised by the increasing use of film in the art gallery and the museum. Cinema space, cinema venues, cinema experience are all—to reiterate—being significantly affected (in a range of ways) by the computer, video, virtual reality, computer graphics, computer games, CD-ROMs, rock videos and the Internet. New meanings, new contexts of distribution, production and reception, and new audiences are being formed. But this does not mean, as some of us may think, that the proverbial baby is being thrown out with the bathwater.

On the contrary, we are being challenged by these new developments in cinema and the emergent digital media culture to critique our own understanding of cinema as text and as an institution. This also means that we need to question our ability to analyse, interpret, observe and evaluate in a non-judgmental and sceptical manner. What we need to do is become curious, inventive, self-questioning and open-minded about our emergent audiovisual culture.

We have to be careful that we don't impose aesthetic and cultural judgments on the new media that are more relevant to older media forms, just because we have as yet to establish accepted codes and conventions of 'reading' these new media works. We need to be alert to the 'unforeseen encounters' (Deleuze), the new regimes of signs that will come through the daily visible collision between cinema and new media. To do this we should address this new intertextual phenomenon in our camera-based arts in real time, in cultural, historical and social contexts.

Let us now reconsider the future of cinema in its familiar classical definition apropos its intricate relationship with the appearance of television in the late 1940s and 1950s. Cinema has been reinventing itself ever since. To some of us, the cinema in its nostalgic, warm and communal form of movie-going, movingly described by Roland Barthes in his extraordinary essay 'Upon leaving the movie theatre' as a curious cocoon-like hypnotic activity taking place in the dark anonymous ambience of a movie theatre, is being radically reconfigured today.[7] There are some who believe that it may vanish forever: time will tell, but I suspect it will remain with us for some time yet. It is interesting to note that for Barthes, who was not a film buff as such, and who once described film as 'that festival of affects', speaks of cinema as 'that dancing cone which pierces the darkness like a laser beam'.[8] However, in telling contrast, television (which also shows films), for Barthes, has no compelling attraction, as the 'darkness is erased, anonymity repressed; space is familiar, articulated [by furniture, known objects], tamed'.[9] Barthes's evocative essay succinctly delineates the complex issues surrounding cinema's fate during the latter half of the last century in terms of its increasing entwinement with the televisual and digital media.

Cinema and its uneasy complex dialectic with television is germane to a post-New Wave cinephilia: to some of us, cinema will always be our shared kingdom of shadows, where we dream our lives before the large screen of projected flickerings and shapes, whilst television and film-on-video are something quite different. Chris Marker quotes Godard in his CD-ROM *Immemory*: 'Cinema is that which is bigger than we are, what you have to look up at. When a movie is shown small and you have to look down at it, it loses its essence ... What you see on TV is the shadow of a film, nostalgia for a film, the echo of a film, never a real film.'[10]

Serge Daney, who became interested in the 1980s in exploring television's impact on cinema, was intrigued by the silent immobility of movie spectators—the way they sat and watched, in a state of 'frozen vision' which has its own history.[11] Both Barthes's and Daney's observations about movie-going relate to the cinema we have known since the advent of the talkies. Now we live in an epoch where cinema is said to be fragmenting, mutating, via the rapid expansion of the new audiovisual media in our daily lives. As indicated earlier, cinema audiences, distribution and exhibition are changing, and the mixing of analog and digital technologies is now altering the colour, definition and grain of the cinematic image itself. Popular discourses about films, particularly those that belong to the so-called theme park cinema of spectacular digital special effects, morphing and the hyper-kinetic synthetic cinematic body, are dominated by the fetish of big box-office numbers. The digitalisation of cinema in the last three decades, as Alex Horwath reminds us, may be attributed (amongst other things) to 'visual experiences that stretch from the TV image of the first man on the moon to hip alienation effects in rock video, a kind of fungus or virus [that] has been eating into the once transparent movie image'.[12]

But we are also witnessing, as Victor Burgin articulates in his recent fine study of how cinema has been scattered across a variety of media, plus fantasy and memory, the emergence of the 'cinematic heterotopia'.[13] This follows Michel Foucault's essay 'Of other spaces', with its valorisation of the concept 'heterotopia', a place of incompatible, juxtaposed sites.[14] Therefore, the 'cinematic heterotopia', according to Burgin, 'is constituted across the variously virtual spaces in which we encounter displaced pieces of films: the Internet, the media and so on, but also the psychical space of a spectating subject that Baudelaire first identified as "a *kaleidoscope* equipped with consciousness"'.[15]

Once, a film was experienced in a particular site, localised in space and time as a finite projection of a narrative; now, as we all know, film is no longer—as Burgin reminds us—something simply that may be 'visited' in the way one might attend a live theatrical performance or visit a painting in a museum.[16] In other words, a 'film' may be encountered as isolated iconic images, fragments or scenes in our everyday lives, in magazines, posters, on TV, on the radio, on the Internet, in advertisements, newspapers, video clips, trailers, and now on our mobile phones, etc. Thus in the course of daily life we encounter a kaleidoscope of film fragments, which suggests vast aesthetic, cultural and technological implications for our understanding of cinema in the context of the new media technologies. And now, with a rapidly changing definition of 'film', film studies is confronting a heterogeneous 'object' which is equally confounding, as Burgin claims—photography and television studies.[17]

Of course nowadays, the fragmentation of cinema offers a substantial challenge to academic film and media theory to eschew its past dogmatic theoretical fashions in order to come to terms with the notion that cinema today is something more than what is identified as the 'classic' narrative film. As Francesco Casetti puts it in his informative analysis of a half-century of film theory: 'Now cinema is not even identified exclusively with movies ... Experiences that cinema made known return in the form of exotic mass-vacations, in video clips, in the special effects of business conventions ... Further, cinema in turn follows publicity, magazines, games, television. It no longer has its own place, because it is everywhere, or at least everywhere that we are dealing with aesthetics and communication.'[18]

Critics such as Bellour have been at the forefront of going beyond the limits of academic analysis of film as an aesthetic form. He has explored—in a broader context than celluloid-based cinema—images and their intricate relations in a transformative image culture. For Bellour, this has explicitly meant nothing less than a commitment to 'saving the image'.[19] Meaning that we need to find new ways of talking about the image and new ways of seeing. And to seek to understand the diverse orders of hybrid images, structures and contexts that exist beyond classical cinema. In other words, we need to try to come to terms with the possibility that maybe film is 'verging on obsolescence', and that its values are vanishing with the rapid encroaching of the cinematic into contemporary art.

One of the essential reasons why cinema has been so radically reconfigured since the 1970s has been the ability of the VCR to allow us to personally manipulate the order of film's narrative. This meant that for the first time one could accelerate and/or slow down a film. One could therefore 'freeze' a frame of film, view one's favourite sequence or scene of film repeatedly, or simply, as Burgin notes, fixate upon an image.[20] Thus, Burgin argues, just as André Breton and Jacques Vaché hopped from one cinema to another in Nantes in an afternoon—soon to become a favourite pastime of the French surrealists—one could now, with digital editing and personal computers, 'zap' through films shown on television and engage in a 'sedentary version of Breton's and Vache's ambulatory *dérive*'.[21]

Consequently, Bellour's attempt to find a new understanding of cinema's transformation in contemporary screen culture and its new modes of spectatorship and participation in the context of its exploding diverse hybrid progeny in the art world is primarily based on (after Christian Metz) the recognition of the 'still'.[22] Bellour was one of the first critics to probe what it means to 'arrest' the image; to stop the motion in order to unravel a film intricately, frame by frame, thereby, as Pavel Bucher and Tanya Leighton point out, making films 'open to the critical means that [had] long been applied to still images'.[23]

The power to slow down a film or freeze its pace for textual analysis was once reserved to academics and professionals who had access to 16 or 35mm flatbed editing tables, as Laura Mulvey reminds us in her fascinating article on the paradoxical tension between celluloid and new technology and its focus on the stillness of the movie image.[24] For Annette Michelson, cited in Mulvey's eloquent article, these editing tables elicited in the user 'the sense of control, of repetition, acceleration, deceleration, arrest in freeze-frame, release, and reversal of movement ...'[25] Nowadays, thanks to new technologies, one can experience Michelson's 'heady delights of the editing table' in exploring stillness as a property of celluloid cinema, and in the process become an inquisitive, 'curious' spectator—this, as Bucher and Leighton correctly suggest, is today's artist, excavating historic cinema for its buried utopian fragments, forms, textures and spaces.[26] The curious spectator, for Mulvey, is therefore someone who realises—at the touch of a button these days—that time itself 'can be discovered behind the mask of storytelling', and that the new digital technologies are able to manifest the beauty of the cinema in the context of a new spectatorial experience that implies (by definition) a displacement 'that breaks the bond of specificity'.[27] Following Bellour's lead, Mulvey argues that a new paradoxical fascination comes into being when the movie image is stilled.

Thus artists working in video or multimedia installation are now, in the context of Mulvey's argument for the emergence of the 'curious' spectator, exploring the possibilities of film—as an image, as a reference, and as a source of material—by affirming the 'bond of specificity' as it is being displaced in their new art forms, highlighting the distinctive time properties of video at the forefront of their mixed-media artworks.

Godard and Marker are two seminal filmmakers who experimented with the intertextual dialectics of the 'still image' and the moving image in their films and videos. Marker, like Godard, is a nimble 'go-between' between the cinema, video, photography and the digital media, and is adaptable to the convulsing new landscape of postmodern techno-creativity. Marker is concerned with the task of producing a small personal cinema—continuing the tradition of Alexandre Astruc's notion of a *camera-stylo* cinema, but made possible by today's digital tools. In other words, a cinema that is not like the grand auteur of the last century, but is nevertheless possibly a cinema of intimacy and solitude.

Marker's oeuvre of the 1990s—including video and media installations such as *The Zapping Zone* and *Silent Movie* and CD-ROMs such as *Immemory*—is a fine illustration of specific artworks that have been exhibited in a number of different forms. Of course Marker is not alone in contributing to the mixed-media zeitgeist that prevails in the contemporary art world, aptly defined by Raymond Bellour as 'the aesthetics of confusion'. Numerous filmmakers, new media and video artists and installation artists, such as Chantal Akerman, Peter Greenaway, Wim Wenders, Stan Douglas, Sadie Benning, Mona Hatoum, Gary Hill, etc., have in their respective ways contributed to this new aesthetic of mutating mixed-media artworks and presentation systems.[28]

As the recent proliferation of electronic media challenges cinema's autonomy, what exactly is happening with the filmic in art reasserting itself in the 1990s in the museum/gallery world? In other words, as Bellour puts it, when filmmakers such as Raul Ruiz, Raymond Depardon, Atom Egoyan and Harun Farocki, etc., agree to make installations, what is it that they are surrendering to?[29]

How do we critique and relate to these new hybrid dynamic artworks of analog and digital media? And where is cinema in this vertiginous cultural landscape? Arguably, what we have been experiencing in the last 40 odd years is cinema and the emerging new technical media moving towards being part of the same developing multilayered narrative of audiovisual creativity. But at the same time, we need to be careful not to bypass analog media through the excessive valorisation of digital media. Promoting one without the other would be tantamount to creative myopia.

We need to remember that cinema, from its early funfair origins in the 19th century till the 1960s, uses numerous concepts, effects and techniques that were first articulated in that art form and are not necessarily evident in the new media arts. The question of cultural amnesia and ahistorical thinking is central here. How many of those who embrace video, film and interactive media installations know the significant film installations of the avant-garde cinema of the 1960s (Michael Snow, Paul Sharits, etc.)? And, indeed, how many know that the experimental cinema of the 1950s through to the 1970s, because of its collaborative multi-disciplinary nature and its modern modes of distribution and production, can (arguably) serve as a model for the digital arts of the last decade and a half?

What is critical to grasp, now more than ever, is the key notion that the screen arts in this digital age seem to be part of the one single system where each artwork consists of varying combinations of different art forms and media. Various commentators, including Bellour, Philippe Dubois and Heinrich Klotz, to name but a few, have argued this kind of transgeneric point of view of old and new media.[30] For Bellour, contemporary cultural production is characterised by the proliferation of computer-mediated, non-binary 'in between' images, sounds and texts suggesting a particular reflexive, hesitant and fragmentary style of image-making indicating the legacy of the essay (Theodor Adorno, Roland Barthes, Michel de Montaigne, and Friedrich Nietzsche) as much as the 'border-crossing' aesthetics of *camera-stylo*-inspired cinema and video (Jean-Luc Godard, Thierry Kuntzel, Chris Marker and Orson Welles). It is a highly fertile cross-disciplinary concept of late 20th century media culture encapsulating an open relationship between creativity, speculation and risk-taking that is alert to the elaborate kinetic connections between the various art forms.

This particular self-reflexive, transgeneric form of image-making can also be best described, as Steve Fagin reminds us, as a 'Northwest passage' art form (after Michel Serres's evocative 'two cultures' metaphorical description of travelling through the Davis Sound, which connects the Atlantic and Pacific Oceans), where the artist can travel freely across borders 'without a passport'.[31] Indeed, it is essential to appreciate the intertextual alchemy that is occurring between old and new media on the same plane of multimedia creativity. We live in a post-computer epoch which is notable for its increasing, virtual life of simulation, high-speed information and global networks and it is important to adopt an interdisciplinary approach to the exact and human sciences—we need to remember Serres's multifaceted comparativism, which is based on the zigzag pattern of a fly.[32] This means having the ability to traverse many spaces of interference, located between many different things, making different connections. Serres's distinctive indifference to temporal distance suggests that he can make unpredictable connections (all within the same timeframe) between numerous authors, texts, genres and myths.

For Serres, the past is never out of date, and nor is an art form such as classical cinema or video art: like Hermes (the operator who brings diverse things together), Serres's provocative concept of a rapid time machine scanning texts and signs across different artistic, cultural and temporal contexts implies a fluid capacity to treat complex subjects with lightness, speed and simplicity.

This is one of the most critical tasks facing anyone who is interested in the screen arts today. We need to become switchboard operators across culture, space and time, and between analog and digital media; and we need to always question our own cultural baggage. This means becoming more 'empirical' and less theoretically certain of ourselves, letting go of our dogmatic certainties about the Cartesian method of philosophising and becoming more intuitive, self-critical and non-authoritarian, more alive to Wittgenstein's challenge: 'Don't think, look.'[33] To which we may also add, 'and listen'. In other words, we need to become—in Nietzsche's apt term—'experimentors'.[34]

Bellour's imaginative critique of the 'crisis' in the image in late 20th century culture, with its speculative emphasis on the different aesthetic, historical and technical 'passages' that are taking place between old and new media, is indicative of his fecund ability to explore film in the broader context of art, culture and technology. As a critic, Bellour's work is exemplary, in that it focuses on understanding the ongoing fragmenting 'unspeakable images' that cut across film, video and the gallery. Thus Bellour, who was one of the first critics to see that cinema, video and photography were rapidly becoming inextricably linked to each other, was also one of the first to realise that cinema, in Darke's words, had lost 'its autonomy and is now one more station through which the image circulates'.[35] For Bellour, 'the mixing, the contamination, the passage or movements between images that have accumulated at the convergence of three techniques and three arts: photography, cinema and video', indicate that video is primarily 'the agent of three passages between images'.[36] These mixed passages that are occurring in today's dramatic computer-mediated collision between the camera-based art forms form the curatorial architecture of the 1990 *Passages de l'image* exhibition—which was curated by Bellour, Catherine David and Christine van Assche. The exhibition also points, as the curators suggest, to Walter Benjamin's 1930 study of the arcades or passages of 19th century Paris and the beginnings of modern visual culture, as well as to Henri Michaux's book of essays, *Passages* (1950), a work which vividly evokes (as Christopher Phillips puts it) 'the fluid transitional zones of human consciousness'.[37]

In order to appreciate the intertextual dialogue that is ensuing between traditional and new media it is crucial to note that they exist, in Klotz's expression, 'side by side', in a non-mutually exclusive spirit.[38] More and more, we are aware of the significance of the intersections between the different forms of audiovisual representation and value seeing one media form through another. This is central to Philippe Dubois:

> I have come to believe that it is no longer possible in today's audiovisual and theoretical landscape to speak of art in and of itself, as if it were autonomous, isolated and self-defining ... I think that we have never been in a better position to approach a given visual medium by imagining it in light of another, through another, by another, or like another. Such an oblique, off-center vision can frequently offer a better opening onto what lies at the heart of a system. Entering from the front door, where everything is designed and organised to be seen from the front, seems to me to be less sharp, less pertinent, less prone to yield discoveries than slipping in *from the side*.[39]

It is precisely this non-purist point of view, this seeing of all media forms, that Dubois, along with Godard and Serres, amongst others, notes, that forms the developing narrative of audiovisual creativity. It is crucial to observe this, because it underlines how undesirable bypassing analog media for the valorisation of digital media would be. Godard is alive to the transgeneric wisdom of Dubois's words. Regardless of the medium—film, TV, video and writing—Godard's dazzling multifaceted oeuvre suggests an artist who is prepared to start from scratch, from zero, in making sense of the multiplying and fragmenting signs that surround him. Godard is prepared to think aloud, to stutter, and to see and hear what exactly is taking shape in front of him.

One critical reason, amongst many others, why Godard's work is relevant today is that it raises far-reaching questions about cinema's fate. Is it possible to make cinema in the age of the digital? Can cinema hold its own in the public spaces of spectatorship? Do cinema, video, television and digital media belong to each other? Does 'digital cinema' exist? These questions are essentially related to 'the death of cinema' debate of the last 40 odd years and salient to Godard's art.

To speak of 'the death of cinema' as a collaborative popular industrial art form is, not after all, such a new thing. Anyone who cares for cinema and its historical evolution will immediately recognise this: cinema in all its splendid multiplicity, from the silent era to our present Internet era of global media, will probably acknowledge this. Strictly speaking as, Michael Witt has recently pointed out in his lucid analysis of Godard's wistful views on 'the death of cinema', cinema has died many 'deaths' since the 1910s.[40] Briefly, they include (a) the suppression of the vitality of the silent cinema by the 'talkies'; (b) the failure of cinema in the face of the Holocaust; (c) the May 1968 critique of cinema as a reactionary cultural form; and (d) the disintegration of cinema by the omnipresent debilitating contagion of the televisual.

But also, there is some truth in Nicole Brenez's idea that for certain filmmakers (such as Godard), 'the death of cinema' theme was a necessary and neat melancholic formula that helped them become productive as artists.[41]

Brenez's observation is significant because we need to remember that Godard, who has always championed, in Timothy Murray's words, 'the cinematic screen as an ontological foundation of the twentieth century', was also one of the first to explore video innovatively—as early as *Numero deux* (1975).[42] Thus Godard's oeuvre is profoundly emblematic of cinema's fate in its convergence with digital technology. Further, what Godard is lamenting is not, as Murray points out, videotech being 'the debasement of the screen and its complex machineries of projection'.[43] It is cinema's illuminated rectangular screen and the attentiveness of the cinematic gaze that are, for Godard, passing into today's electronic screens of digital distraction.

When we speak of 'the death of cinema' we need to make a vital distinction between cinema as a social and industrial institution and the medium of film as art. In other words, we need to be precise about the fact that cinema and film are not the same thing. Film, for someone like Hollis Frampton, who was an eloquent practitioner of film as art and saw film as 'verging upon obsolescence' in 1975, is what takes form on the projected screen.[44] Frampton realised as early as the late 1960s, according to Bucher, how fragile film was: he maintained that 'film is, first, a confined space ... it is only a rectangle of white light.'[45] Everything about film as an art form, including its limits, for Frampton, flowed from this illuminated rectangle and the film projector.

Today's 'death of cinema' debate does not imply cinema's imminent death. Far from it. This is a too simplistic view of cinema and its complex and shifting relationships with other media. When you hear suggestions of 'the death of the novel', 'the death of painting', 'the death of photography' etc., you can always be assured that there is some life left in the supposed corpse. It is naive, for a range of elaborate aesthetic, cultural and technological considerations, to believe that new media will automatically replace the old media.

What is interesting to observe is how many artists' use of film in the 1990s—particularly Hollywood film, according to Chrissie Iles—is partly to do with their desire to connect to the idea of film as a socialising medium of communication.[46] Following Marshall McLuhan's prediction in the 1960s that where the 19th century had been obsessed with privacy, the 20th century would be obsessed with communication, Iles argues that artists are seeking to engage with 'the connective tissue that film creates'.[47] But the relationship between film and art is, by and large, a one-way street: artists love film, but the film world is often indifferent to this fact. Thus the art and film worlds have always represented (in Anthony McCall's fitting words) 'a double helix, spiralling closely around one another without ever quite meeting'.[48]

Let us now return briefly to the essays in *Mutant Media* and see how they aggregate to develop the major theoretical framework for the collection—the delineation of the ongoing convergence between cinema and other media and its vast implications for contemporary art practice, and how cinema itself, as a collective experience and as a medium, is undergoing profound aesthetic, cultural and technological changes..

In the first section, 'Then and now: cinema's passing shadows', chapter 1, 'Cultural difference in contemporary Australian cinema', looks at the complex representation of ethnicity in Australian cinema since World War II and the development of certain non-Anglo-Celtic filmmakers who were germane to the examination of this significant theme in their particular marginalised oeuvres. The essay, aside from its brief autobiographical section concerning the author's diasporic experience as spectator of Greek cinema in an inner-city cinema in the 1950s, also notes the many other filmmakers who were concerned with the inscription of ethnicity, class, gender and history in their works. Chapter 2 discusses Luis Buñuel's only documentary, *Land without Bread*, which to some is one of the first examples of the personal essay documentary form, and is a critical work in that it registers the intricate intersection between film modernism, surrealism and the essay documentary. The work is an emblematic example of the lyrical and anti-clerical surrealism that spanned the entire career of Buñuel, one of the key surrealist auteurs from the 1920s to the 1970s.

Finally, chapter 3 in this section probes the elaborate links between contemporary art, cinema and the classic modernist works of Alfred Hitchcock. This essay endeavours to create an overview of the recent mutating convergence between art, cinema and the gallery in terms of Hitchcock's oeuvre.

To some, such as Godard and his *Cahiers du cinéma* associates, Hitchcock was *the* modernist filmmaker of the last century. Why is Hitchcock so attractive to contemporary artists working in photography, installation, painting and projection? And how significant is the role of art itself in Hitchcock's oeuvre? Like Buñuel, whom Hitchcock admired a lot, Hitchcock spanned both the talkie and the sound eras.

This essay encapsulates some of the recurring critical concerns of the collection overall: what is 'cinema', and why is it rapidly converging with other media? Addressing such important questions equates to nothing less, amongst other things, than engaging with the prophetic truth of Godard's utterance: 'We're born in the museum; it's our homeland, after all …'[49] Why, after all, are we now—at this historical juncture—witnessing the increasing rich and overlapping convergence between film, video, new media and the gallery?

The second section, 'Video art: from the margins to the mainstream', concentrates on the role of video art—a much misunderstood medium of techno-creativity, particularly in terms of its elaborate histories, effects and genres—in the latter half of the 20th century. Video is, as Bellour has eloquently argued, time and again, perhaps the medium that has been most responsible for the proliferation of complex 'in between' images between the various camera-based art forms—cinema, video, photography and television. Chapter 4, 'Framing Australian video art', is an exploratory investigation of the complex cultural, historiographical and technical questions facing anyone who is interested in looking at Australian video art, a subject that is ignorantly taken for granted, in the popular imagination, as a medium without a highly visible history or cultural memory. Given its 'stop-start' history of cross-disciplinary activity since the 1970s, with artists like Mick Glasheen, Jill Scott, David Perry and Stephen Jones, etc., and the constant institutional refusal to archivally engage with its history, contexts and practitioners, one is obliged to contextualise video on a broad historical and political stage. Today, as I argue across the essays in this collection, video is an essential feature of the contemporary art world. Nevertheless, there remains a substantial propensity amongst the younger generation of visual artists working in installation, photomedia and mixed media, to reinvent the wheel as far as video is concerned.

Chapter 5, 'Collage, site, video, projection', examines the importance of collage as a key facet of video installation art and projections in the last three decades or so of the last century. This essay constructs an archaeology of sorts that addresses the complexities of video installation art as a postmodern art form par excellence. Now, since the 1990s, time-based projections have become a commonplace genre of the international art world. Why are artists turning to the 'cinema' as a social experience and film as an art medium for their gallery video, film and interactive installations and projections? And how did installation art evolve from its early historical avant-garde contexts, and subsequently, in terms of postwar Euro-American avant-garde art—in particular, the Fluxus movement? What role did experimental cinema play in the genre's overall development? Again, in this context, video (both as tape and as installation) has been a substantial agent in crossing film over into the contemporary gallery.

Chapter 6, 'Border-crossing: Jean-Luc Godard as video essayist', strives to locate Godard's immensely influential oeuvre—especially, for our immediate purposes, his video and TV work as an essayist—in the context of today's highly volatile audiovisual landscape. Godard is one of the greatest image-makers and thinkers about cinema and its futures. Godard's cinema is pivotal to any rudimentary exploration of the image-sound-space transformation that is taking place today in our art, culture and society. He remains one of the supreme cinematic artists, whose profound 'in between' cinema addresses the complexities of cinema as a medium and as a collective experience. As an essayist, Godard's art is intricately connected to the Montaigne–Mallarmé tradition of literature. While Godard linked Daney's film criticism, which he described as 'the end of criticism', with a tradition that began with Diderot, one could also arguably locate Godard's cinema and writings as belonging to this great 'border-crossing' tradition of criticism.[50] Thus Godard, who harnessed painting and literature to the cinema, remains one of cinema's original explorers apropos of its fertile interaction with other media.

In Section 3, 'Liquid screens: art, culture, new media', chapter 7, 'Australian new media arts: new directions since the 1990s', delineates some of the more critical issues concerning the development of new media arts in Australia. It also looks at some young artists, both established and emerging, who have been exploring art and digital technology in their practice for the last decade or so. Australia, because of its unique geopolitical position, and its legacy of receiving ideas from Europe, Asia and America in a markedly sceptical and inventive fashion, has been one of the countries (like Canada) that is more receptive to experimenting with media art. Historically, Australian artists working in this area of contemporary artistic and cultural production have been, to date, far more numerically visible than their traditional national counterparts in media and techno-arts festivals around the world.

Chapter 8, 'Entering the digital image: Jeffrey Shaw and the quest for interactive cinema', discusses the work of Australian artist Jeffrey Shaw in the context of his pioneering project to create interactive cinema.

Shaw's diverse expertise in media art since the 1960s underlines the shifting complexities of the artist's life-long ambition to critique the illusionism of classical cinema by locating aesthetic, cultural and technical correspondences between old and new media in his multifaceted practice. Shaw's art is a testament to his sophisticated understanding of how art, entertainment and technology have been interconnected since the Renaissance, in many intricate ways.

Chapter 9, 'The spiral of time: Chris Marker and new media', discusses the elusive French filmmaker Chris Marker and his negotiation of new media in his work since the 1980s. Marker's use of digital and video technology—installations, videotapes, CD-ROMs— is emblematic of his optimistic attitude towards 'the death of cinema' discourse of the last three decades or so—in radical contrast to Godard's more pessimistic views on this important subject—and suggests that his editing and polemical work with André Bazin in the 1950s was an invaluable basis for his creative approach to new media. One of the major themes informing Marker's recent media works is the cultural memory of technology.

Finally, in the conclusion, 'Media in transition, or, from montage to immersion', I endeavour to succinctly sum up some of the more critical ideas informing the essays collected here and propose that to understand how we are today encountering a pervasive complex transformation of the media—cinematic, televisual, photographic and videographic—that is always shaping art, mass culture and society, we need to remind ourselves that the media are always in a state of unpredictable transition. To take this further, if cinema is—as some are saying—'verging on obsolescence', what are the implications for our image culture? In what significant ways is the material complexity of cinema being affected by the new electronic and digital technologies, and what does this signify in terms of our more traditional academic analysis of film as an aesthetic form and the emerging desire to look at images in a broader discursive context?

We need to find new ways of looking at the moving image as it impacts across media. We also need to understand why film and art have been connecting to each other, over the last 20-odd years, in the performative space of the art gallery. Why are so many visual artists today raiding our archival memories of cinema—particularly

Hollywood and, to a lesser degree, art cinema and avant-garde/experimental cinema—to create their installations and projections in our museographic spaces of the art world? It is essential, therefore, for artists, educators, curators and spectators to see one media form through another, to practise an essayistic mobile form of image-making that hinges on a point of view that is highly elastic, always on the move, contesting the fixities of art, culture, society and technology. We need to insert ourselves into the intersections between media which initially seem to be antagonistic— through this we can explore multiple anti-binary meanings that cut across contexts, genres and forms that speak (as in Chris Marker's *La Jetée*) of both the cinema and photography. It is this intertextual hybrid freedom of investigating the variety of possible rich relational figures and intersections that link old and new media, and their 'zigzag' flights of highly mediated cultural expression that are embedded in Western representation, that remains such an untapped realm of critical enquiry and media experimentation.

NOTES

1 Raymond Bellour's critical work remains (despite the bulk of it as yet not having been translated into English) of crucial importance to anyone concerned with the fate of the image and its transformations in our recent audiovisual culture. Bellour's profoundly prescient criticism stands next to Serge Daney's criticism—they are in a class of their own. Needless to say, Jean-Luc Godard's commentaries, both written and filmed, are also of profound importance on this subject. For a recent overview of Daney's newly translated critical writings see Jonathan Rosenbaum, 'The missing image', *New Left Review* 34, July–August 2005, pp. 145–51.
2 See Jean-Louis Schefer, *The Enigmatic Body*, Cambridge University Press, Cambridge, 1995, p. xviii.
3 Cited in Chris Darke, *Light Readings*, Wallflower, London, 2000, p. 4.
4 British filmmaker/writer Chris Petit, in his recent work, particularly his collaborations with novelist/poet Iain Sinclair, is notable as a film/video essayist who is concerned with his own past as a cinephile engaged in working

with new technologies. Petit's aptly named *Negative Space* has the same title as Farber's monumental collection of film criticism, *Negative Space*, Da Capo Press, New York, 1998.
5 Darke, p. 7.
6 Jonathan Rosenbaum, *Movie Wars*, Wallflower, London, 2002.
7 Roland Barthes, 'Upon leaving a movie theatre', in Barthes *The Rustle of Language*, (trans. Richard Howard), Basil Blackwell, London, 1986, pp. 345–49. Barthes's essay is cited in Jonathan Rosenbaum, *Placing Movies*, University of California Press, Berkeley, 1995, p. 53. For a recent valuable analysis of Barthes' essay see Victor Burgin, *The Remembered Film*, Reaktion Books, London, 2004, pp. 7–28 and, especially, pp. 29–43. Burgin's book is an important study of how we encounter in everyday life isolated fragments of films, iconic images or scenes that pervade our media.
8 Barthes.
9 ibid.
10 See Raymond Bellour, 'Battle of the

images', *Art Press* 262, November 2000, pp. 48–52. Chris Marker's comments are cited on p. 49. Many thanks to John Gillies for introducing Bellour's article to me.

11 ibid., p. 48. On Daney's influential career as a post-New Wave critic, whose own critical trajectory existed parallel to the recent passage of the movie image itself in contemporary culture, see Darke, pp. 69–75.

12 See Alex Horwath's letter in 'Movie mutations', *Film Quarterly*, September 1998, p. 47. Also see Jonathan Rosenbaum & Adrian Martin (eds), *Movie Mutations*, British Film Institute (BFI), London, 2003. This is a timely and invaluable account of contemporary cinephilia and 'the death of cinema' debate (viz. Gilbert Adair, David Denby, Susan Sontag, David Thomson, etc.) in the context of a changing world film culture. On the latter issue, see also Rosenbaum, pp. 19–33.

13 Burgin, pp. 7–14.

14 ibid., p. 10.

15 ibid.

16 ibid., pp. 8–9.

17 ibid., p. 9.

18 Cited in Burgin.

19 See Raymond Bellour's essay 'Saving the image', in Tanya Leighton & Pavel Bucher (eds), *Saving the Image: Art after Film*, Centre for Contemporary Arts, Glasgow/ Metropolitan University, Manchester, 2003, pp. 52–77.

20 Burgin, p. 8.

21 ibid.

22 Leighton & Bucher, p. 28.

23 ibid.

24 Laura Mulvey, 'Stillness in the moving image: ways of visualising time and its passing', in Leighton & Bucher, pp. 78–89.

25 ibid., p. 87.

26 See Leighton & Bucher, p. 30.

27 Mulvey, p. 81.

28 Bellour, 2000, p. 52.

29 ibid., p. 50.

30 See Raymond Bellour, 'The power of words, the power of images', *Camera Obscura* 24, September 1990, pp. 7–9; Philippe Dubois, 'Photography mise-en-film', in Patrice Petro (ed.), *Fugitive Images*, Indiana University Press, Bloomington, 1995, pp. 152–71; Heinrich Klotz is quoted in Thomas Elsaesser & Kay Hoffman (eds), *Cinema Futures*, Amsterdam University Press, Amsterdam, 1998, p. 9.

31 See Peter Wollen, 'An interview with Steve Fagin', *October* 41, summer 1987, p. 99. And see Michel Serres, 'Northwest Passage', *Semiotext(e)*, vol. 4, no. 3, 1984, p. 67.

32 Serres (with Bruno Latour), *Conversations on Science, Culture, and Time*, University of Michigan Press, Ann Arbor, 1995, pp. 65–70.

33 John Rajchman, 'The lightness of theory', *Artforum*, vol. 32, no.1, 1993, pp. 165–66, 206, 211.

34 ibid., p. 211.

35 Darke, p. 161.

36 Quoted in Darke, p. 162. Original text is Bellour 1990, p. 7.

37 Christopher Phillips, 'Between pictures', *Art in America*, November 1991, pp. 104–16.

38 For Klotz's quote, see Elsaesser & Hoffman, p. 9.

39 Dubois, p. 152.

40 Michael Witt, 'The death(s) of cinema according to Godard', *Screen*, vol. 40, no. 3, 1999, pp. 331–46.

41 Nicole Brenez, 'Movie mutations', *Film Quarterly*, September 1998, p. 48.

42 Timothy Murray, 'Debased projection and cyberspatial ping: Chris Marker's digital screen', *Parachute* 113, 2004, p. 92.

43 ibid.

44 Pavel Bucher, 'Some notes on art as film as art', in Leighton & Bucher, p. 47.

45 ibid.

46 See Chrissie Iles's observations on film as a medium for socialising and communication in 'Round table: the projected image in contemporary art', *October* 104, spring 2003, p. 73. Organised by Malcolm Turvey & George Baker, this discussion group featured Hal Foster, Anthony McCall & Matthew Buckingham as well as Chrissie Iles.

47 ibid.

48 ibid., quoting McCall, p. 74.

49 Cited in Jean-Luc Godard & Youssef Ishaghpour, *Cinema*, (trans. John Howe), Berg, Oxford/New York, 2005, p. vii.

50 ibid., pp. 9–10.

Section 1

Then and now: cinema's passing shadow

One of the critical concerns informing the essays in *Mutant Media* is how today's audiovisual culture is rapidly transforming, because of—amongst many other significant factors—the complex mobile connections between cinema and the new digital and electronic technologies. As a collection of individual essays with their own particular points of genesis and concern this book is not a comprehensive or definitive look at this highly elaborate aesthetic, cultural, historical and technological phenomenon that defines our everyday life. Nevertheless, *Mutant Media* is a 'road map' of sorts, incomplete, speculative, and 'rhizomatic' in its overall conceptual architecture. In many ways, the book should be seen as a conversation about the continuities and discontinuities between art, cinema, video and new media.

In this way this collection is also a plea for a more open-ended, pluralistic way of speaking about the ongoing hybridisation of contemporary audiovisual media, of appreciating the complexities of how today's 'digital cinema' is emerging in our daily lives and talking about it all without resorting to values based on aesthetic and cultural short-sightedness. I hope that *Mutant Media*, in its own modest way, has something to offer in terms of how our present film culture is splintering, and how my own cinephilia is also being affected by a changing global film culture and new modes of viewing cinema (the Internet and all-region DVD players). Of course nowadays, film criticism and reviewing themselves have a new and expanding horizon, including online film writing and publishing. In short, we are encountering a rethinking of academic film theory and journalistic criticism and writing.[1]

Living in a 'post-postmodern age', anyone who is dealing with the shifting definition of the filmic image—including its presence in the international and local art worlds—is wise to take notice of all modes of film and media writing/criticism in order to evaluate and analyse the intricate complexities of how classical and contemporary cinema is being affected by the new technologies, global media corporate interests; amidst all this, we need to ask ourselves, can cinephilia exist? And if it can, in what contexts do we see it existing? And also, with all the current emphasis on 'the death of cinema', with the doomsayers making their pronouncements about the end of classical cinema—as we have known it for the last century—what are we to make of the future of the art form? In brief, the answer is that both the art form and cinephilia are alive and well, but living in new and uncharted contexts.

The cultural effect of the electronic screen on the moving image is immense and complex. To someone like Jean-Luc Godard, it is cause for lament, as he sees the magic of the big screen and its attendant historical memory mutating into the white noise of our proliferating TV monitors and the new media technologies.[2] Yet to others, such as Chris Marker, it is a welcome but challenging scenario of creative possibilities: of working with old and new media in new modes of hybrid image-making, of connecting high culture with popular culture, history with the personal.

Of course when we are discussing cinema's changing contexts and definitions in the last 20-odd years, it would be useful to remember that cinema has always been influenced by the other arts—painting, sculpture, literature, performance, photography and music are just a few of the more prominent art forms that have, over the years, substantially contributed to cinema as an art form.

Therefore, arguably, film, video art and new media have been significantly shaped by the rich allusive recombinatory poetics of such important modernist authors as T.S. Eliot, James Joyce, Samuel Beckett and Ezra Pound, who have in their respective ways been influenced by the 'new media' of their times, which would include the cinema, the typewriter, the gramophone and television. Of course, as the late Hugh Kenner points out in his informative look at literary modernism and the evolution of 20th century media technology, all of us—as visual artists, filmmakers, writers and video and new media artists—are, in one way or another, indebted to the ideas of appropriation, irony, intertextuality, parody and pastiche evident in the great fecund works of the first half of the last century.[3]

Art and cinema have always been inextricably linked, especially since the first two decades of the last century. As Chrissie Iles and Peter Wollen, amongst others, have clearly pointed out, avant-garde or experimental cinema 'did not develop in an artistic vacuum'; it had many connections to the other traditional arts—particularly painting, music and even poetry.[4] In fact, in the 1920s, the artist Marcel Duchamp was interested in the photographic experiments of Marey and Muybridge; his film and rotating discs, along with the films of Man Ray and Ferdinand Leger, represent a specific brief moment in France when artists experimented with film and motion.[5] Painting and music had a major role in creating abstraction in experimental cinema, seen in the striking works of Richter, Eggeling and Rutmann. Abstract painting and abstract cinema emerged at the same time, as they were both reactions to pictorial conventions.

Eggeling, for instance, was a visionary maker of abstract film who was committed to a synthesis of the arts—music, dance, poetry and painting. For this, film, according to Wollen, provided a dynamic, technological medium, much as today's experimental artists are attracted towards the new digital media.[6]

In the 1930s and 1940s in America, significant filmmakers, such as Feininger, Fischinger, the Whitney brothers and MacLaren, amongst many others, were searching for, as Iles puts it, 'a Kandinsky-like fusion between art, film and music, trying to create a synthesis between image, sound, and color'.[7]

After World War II, experimental film entered a new stage, with filmmakers such as Maya Deren, Ken Jacobs, Jonas Mekas and Stan Brakhage, who used the newly available 16mm camera for their films. These filmmakers had a background in the novel and poetry, and their films were notable for their interest in language and creative and personal expression. The Beat films of the 1950s such as *Pull My Daisy* (1958), Shirley Clarke's films, including *The Cool World* (1963), and not forgetting the cut-up films of William Burroughs, were all notable for their common focus on literature and language.

By the 1960s, Andy Warhol was a seminal figure in the interface between film and painting. Warhol's shift from painting to film was influenced by filmmaker Jack Smith and the painter/filmmaker Marie Menken. As the 1960s unfolded, artists, mainly sculptors, used film for a variety of different reasons. Some used film to document happenings and performances; others incorporated film into their conceptual practices.

Briefly, at the same time, structural film became a major genre of experimental film. Filmmakers such as Anthony McCall, Ernie Gehr, Hollis Frampton, Paul Sharits and Michael Snow explored questions of the film apparatus itself. As Frampton once said, 'the art of film consists in devising things to put into our projector'.[8]

By the late 1970s and 1980s, as Iles observes, narrative became foregrounded in the works of experimental filmmakers and artists.[9] There was a major shift away from structural ideas and process-focused explorations of space to complex narratives, both in experimental film and video.

How useful is it to articulate a basic genealogy of the long entanglement of art and mechanical reproduction for a basic understanding of the current developments around the projected image and artists who use film in their works? This is the question that George Baker asks of his *October* round table colleagues.[10] For Baker, what matters is not so much the shared dialogue between painting and film, but rather the moments or ruptures of 'intense technological transformation that have the effect of revivifying work on film'.[11] Thus for Baker, the 1960s and 1970s saw the rise of new media such as TV and video which stimulated experimentation with film; in a similar vein, since the 1990s the new digital media has had a similar effect. Paradoxically then, over the last two decades, as Iles notes, the emergence of new media technology has generated much new activity in film.[12]

With the current emphasis on film—Hollywood mainstream cinema, European art cinema, silent cinema and avant-garde/experimental film—in today's art world, what is intriguing to observe is how certain artists use film to create rich contrasts with the new media in order to critique it, whilst other artists are more interested in working with new media in order to articulate its futuristic horizons.

Historically speaking, experimental film spanned virtually the entire 20th century: from the beginning of the century, every film was 'experimental' in a certain sense, and it was not until the feature film was fully developed that the concept of 'experimental film' began to take on a specific definition of its own. Consequently, the relationship between a feature film and an experimental film is a highly complex one in terms of conceptual concerns, historical contexts, generic tropes and audiences. One of the more important things to note about experimental films and their marginalised avant-garde makers, as Wollen reminds us, was their interest in avant-garde art, their wish to synthesise technology with aesthetics and their innovative insistence that filmmaking should be highly personal and creative, just like music and poetry.[13] From the very beginning, experimental film had one foot in the art world and the other in the entertainment world. Ironically, today's artists working with film manifest similar aesthetic and cultural values.

However, certain questions arise when we examine the presence of film in contemporary art: does film belong to contemporary art? Is art the ultimate fate of film? Does contemporary art question cinema? And, as Mark Nash asks, are artists working with film and video today really artists or are they 'a different breed of filmmaker'?[14]

These questions are salient to any analysis of artists' fascination with all kinds of film—this has been at the forefront of many art installations, projections, and photomedia works, particularly since the 1980s. This conjunction between art and film has been acknowledged and embraced by galleries and museums and international art exhibitions and biennales, but what is plainly evident, is that—generally speaking—filmmakers are not as attracted to the art world as artists are to film. Film is an industrial craft-based art form, and artists love film, but filmmakers are often indifferent to the contemporary art world and its emphasis on concept, performance, randomness and process.

Thus, despite the art world embracing film and video, there remains a palpable tension between representatives of mainstream cinema and those of multi-screen film/video installations and projections in a gallery. Nevertheless, cinema has redefined the way we understand contemporary art.

A number of American artists who had star status in the 1980s then ventured into mainstream filmmaking, including Julian Schnabel (*Basquiat*), Robert Longo (*Johnny Mnemonic*), Cindy Sherman (*Office Killer*), David Salle (*Search and Destroy*) and Larry Clark (*Kids*), creating works that had (charitably put) mixed critical success. Critics such as Douglas Fogle and Michael O'Pray agree that these crossover endeavours by noted artists into narrative film stumbled by creating static art, art that was devoid of the essential dramaturgical and stylistic dynamism evident in classical auteur cinema.[15] Most of these visual artists failed in their feature narrative films to convincingly articulate, in O'Pray's words 'figures, objects and space itself through form and narrative as fantasy in the widest sense'.[16] These visual artists, like most of their peers, became intimate with mainstream cinema via its stars, genres, icons and mythologies. But despite their overall familiarity with cinema, these artists' crossover feature films do not, on the whole, succeed as works which are eloquently persuasive, in sharp contrast to cinema that is art and popular entertainment at the same time, such as the works of John Ford, Howard Hawks, Alfred Hitchcock and Orson Welles.

Cinema is a highly seductive cultural medium, which was critically foregrounded in exhibitions in the 1990s, such as the Los Angeles Museum of Contemporary Art's centenary celebration of cinema, *Hall of Mirrors: Art and Film since 1945*, London's Hayward Gallery's *Spellbound* and *100 Jahre Kino* at the Kunsthaus Zurich. This suggests an incestuous and troubling relationship between cinema and the visual arts. These exhibitions posed questions about the potential death of cinema as an art form and, as Fogle reminds us, the relatively new phenomenon of the museological desire to situate films as *objets d'art*.[17]

The abovementioned artists who ventured into the mainstream narrative film world created problematic crossover works because their creative efforts are primarily based around the single static image, be it the photographic print or the canvas.[18] Their aesthetic and cultural baggage did not include the basic narrative grammar of feature filmmaking. However, there are successful crossover projects, from 'single-channel' filmmakers such as Chris Marker and Chantal Akerman, who have contributed significantly to the art and film debate of the 1990s. Marker, with *Silent Movie*, which was commissioned by the Wexner Center for the Arts, and Akerman with her film and video installation of her feature film *D'Est*, succeed, as Fogle observed, in focusing on the cinematic (mise en scène, montage, movement in time, etc.) by using new technologies, and not bending to the usual constraints of the gallery world.[19] Both film artists questioned the overlapping worlds of art and film in terms of their respective advantages and limitations. And Marker and his contemporary, Godard, both speculative time-travellers of the cinematic medium, have both used the new technologies to eloquently pose essential questions relating to the history and memory of cinema itself.[20]

With the plethora of artists' film and video in the contemporary art world, we need to situate these works in the context of 20th century cinema to see how they may be part of an ongoing narrative, in Nash's words, 'of a history of a plurality of cinemas'.[21] Thus these new moving image practices in the museum and gallery circuit have several fundamental implications: (a) they challenge our relationship to the museum itself and our general understanding and perception of moving images and (b) they question our relationship to dominant prevailing regimes of film and television.

Nash's thesis that to value these new works of art it would be productive to advocate a tripartite view of cinema—narrative, avant-garde and the documentary—merits our attention.[22] It gives us a welcome conceptual flexibility by liberating the experimental avant-garde from its customary opposition to mainstream 'narrative' and enables us to appreciate mainstream cinema's role in the history of contemporary art.

On the latter point, it is useful to also remember that from the very beginning of the 20th century—before World War I—avant-gardists such as Apollinaire and Picasso embraced popular cinema (particularly silent comedies) for its humour, urbanity and sheer energy—in fact, popular cinema to them represented the essence of modernity.[23] For the surrealists, the B movie was valued for its oneiric features, which they sought to define in their own art. For complex reasons, the surrealists, with the exception of Luis Buñuel, only turned out (relatively speaking) minor film figures.[24]

Today, new artists are reconfiguring avant-garde and experimental movie image practices for new contexts of spectatorship, and familiar Hollywood narrative films are being redefined as critical pastiche (Douglas Gordon, Pierre Huyghe). And the documentary form itself has became a major source of deconstructive image-making, as the 20th century archive of photographic, film and video images is reworked and presented in a wide selection of artists' oeuvres (Anthony Buckingham, Yervant Gianikian, Pere Portabella, Trinh T. Minh-ha).

Consequently, early experimental cinema (Buñuel/Dali, Clair, Duchamp, Leger, Ray) and, as Nash correctly claims, pre-World War II documentary filmmaking (Buñuel, Cavalcanti, Vigo) responded to the challenges of Modernism in the 1930s. Narrative cinema, in the guise of European art cinema (Antonioni, Bergman, Dreyer, Fellini), responded much later.

What exactly is this new developing gallery-based cinema that is impacting on contemporary art practice? It is neither classical nor experimental, but is, according to Chris Dercon, 'a cinema of fragments', a cinema that is, in Dercon's perceptive words, 'responding to existing forms of mimesis in cinema itself. So we can now speak of a secondary mimesis, which is becoming recognisable in films made by visual artists.'[25] Interestingly enough, Nash speculates that this 'cinema of fragments' that is ubiquitously evident in the gallery and museum world is a delayed 'modernisation' of moving image practice that was for so long dominated by realist narrative and was first implicit in the Cubist and Duchampian project. However, Nash believes that this new fragmentation is 'also bound up with a resistance to and redefinition of narrative temporality as duration (Andy Warhol, Michael Snow) in the development of what Gilles Deleuze in *Cinema 2: The Time Image* has defined as the time-image—essentially a post-World War II phenomenon'.[26]

A case can be made that a fair amount of contemporary moving image art in the gallery and museum world evokes the Deren-Brakhage-Snow avant-garde film tradition in the United States, as suggested by Annette Michelson and P. Adams Sitney, in the critical sense that film is a metaphor for the mind.[27] This time, however, there is an emphasis with artists such as Gordon, on examining psychological processes such as identity fracture, psychological splitting, hysteria, etc., rather than exploring the psychoanalytical categories common in 1980s film and photographic practices. There is now a strong desire to use film as an immersive medium from the spectatorial point of view. This means there is an emphasis now on creating—to use Baker's apt expression— 'an aesthetic of emotional and psychic intensities'.[28]

Of course there are also recent works that espouse the speculative anti-aesthetic tradition of signification, as advanced by Wollen in his famous 1977 essay 'The two avant-gardes'.[29] The first tradition is the structural/reflexive approach to the material of film itself, as taken in the 1960s and 1970s by artists such as Frampton, Snow, and Sharits, etc.; the other approach that concerns us here is the probing of the ideological effects of cinematic codes, language and literary narrative, as done in the films of Godard, Marie Straub and Danièle Huillet, Harun Farocki, and Trinh T. Minh-ha.

The exhibition space of the gallery/museum world is a utopian space in the sense that cinema or projection will become sculptural, and will become—in all its multimedia formats—an object of interaction. Nevertheless, there is an urgent need at the moment for a more informed critique of film and its pervasive connection with contemporary art.

There is no denying that the moving image has altered the gallery-going experience. For Boris Groys, this has taken place in two different ways: (a) for the first time, artists can now control the light by which their exhibits are seen, as they emit their own light source, and (b) moving images have begun to dictate to us—the gallery visitor—how much time we should spend on contemplation.[30] Groys contends that whatever amount of time we spend interacting with a moving image installation or projection, 'we will inevitably be filled with that same feeling of having been in the wrong place at the wrong time', and 'whatever the individual's decision, either stay put or keep moving, his choice will always amount to a poor compromise'.[31]

This new emphasis on interacting with moving-image art in a gallery or a museum graphically contrasts with the traditional cinematic experience of being immobile in a darkened film theatre where the audience will see the entire film—from its beginning to its end—in order to understand it.

Nash makes some telling observations about how recent writing on film and video in the gallery world can too easily confuse '"sitting in a cinema" with "passivity", or "mobility" with "freedom".'[32]

To conclude, cinema's representational and cultural itineraries are expanding in different contexts outside the film theatre, especially in places like the art gallery and the museum, where art and film are interacting in complex ways. Not least, as Giuliana Bruno points out in her striking essay on the changing geography of museum culture and the critical interaction between art and film shaping contemporary exhibition practice, film in such a context is 'returning spectatorship to "exhibition"', echoing Peter Greenaway's observation, 'Isn't cinema an exhibition ...? Perhaps we can imagine a cinema where both audience and exhibits move.'[33] For Bruno, these new crossovers between art and film in today's museographic space have profound mnemonic implications for the gallery-goer and for our cultural landscape in general.

Cinema has been a vital and integral part of 20th century subjectivity. Though art and film theory have yet to adequately come to terms with the cross-pollination that is taking place between art, film and contemporary art practice, there is an emerging discourse in various academic, art and film contexts that is underscoring this important aesthetic, cultural and technological phenomenon. Cinema still exists, despite what the Jeremiahs amongst us are saying. Cinema has always been a history of pluralities, and what we are witnessing today with film in the art world is just one more expression of the medium in its ongoing fertile evolution.

NOTES

1   On academic film study and its future and the changing contexts of film criticism, see the exchange between Adrian Martin and James Naremore (2001–02), 'The future of academic film study', in Jonathan Rosenbaum & Adrian Martin (eds), *Movie Mutations*, BFI, London, 2003, pp. 119–32.

2   See Timothy Murray, 'Debased projection and cyberspatial ping: Chris Marker's digital screen', *Parachute* 113, 2004, pp. 92–93.

3   Hugh Kenner, *The Mechanic Muse*, Oxford University Press, New York/Oxford, 1987.

4   See Chrissie Iles's succinct summary of experimental cinema and its links to other art forms, such as painting and photography, in George Baker & Malcolm Turvey et al., 'Round table: the projected image in contemporary art', *October* 104, spring 2003, pp. 71–72. See also Peter Wollen, 'Knight's moves', in Richard Allen & Malcolm Turvey (eds), *Camera Obscura, Camera Lucida*, Amsterdam University Press, Amsterdam, 2003, p. 147.

5   Iles, in Baker & Turvey et al.

6   Peter Wollen, *Paris Hollywood: Writings on Film*, Verso, London, 2002, p. 54.

7   Iles, in Baker & Turvey et al., p. 72.

8   Cited in Pavel Bucher, 'Some notes on art as film as art', in Tanya Leighton & Pavel Bucher (eds), *Saving the Image*, Centre for Contemporary Arts, Glasgow/Manchester Metropolitan University, Manchester, 2003, p. 48.

9   Iles, in Baker & Turvey et al., p. 72.

10 See Baker, in Baker & Turvey et al., p. 73.

11 ibid.

12 Iles, in Baker & Turvey et al..

13 Wollen 2002, p. 148.

14 Mark Nash, 'Wait until dark', Tate International Arts and Culture, London, 2002, p. 55. Nash's article is a brief summary of his more extensive essay, 'Art and cinema: some critical reflections', *Documenta 11—Platform 5: Catalogue* [from exhibition], Kassel, 8 June—15 September, 2002.

15 Douglas Fogle, 'Cinema is dead, long live cinema', *Frieze* 29, 1996, pp. 31–32; Michael O'Pray, 'Movie wannabes', *Art Monthly (London)* 210, 1997, pp. 1–6.

16 O'Pray, p. 4.

17 Fogle, p. 32.

18 See O'Pray, p. 4.

19 Fogle, p. 32.

20 See Chris Darke, *Alphaville*, I.B. Tauris, London, 2005, pp. 86–89. Darke's study of Godard's 1965 hybrid sci-fi and film noir classic contains an entire chapter dedicated to the film's legacy in the art world and for other filmmakers. Darke's remarks on Godard and Marker as time-travellers are quite suggestive apropos of their different approaches to the use of video and new media in their oeuvres and their innovations in film form.

21 Nash, p. 56.

22 ibid.

23 O'Pray, p. 4.

24 ibid.

25 Chris Dercon, 'Gleaning the future from the gallery floor', *Senses of Cinema*, issue 28, Sept–Oct 2003, at http://www.sensesofcinema.com/contents/03/28/gleaning_the_future.html

26 ibid., see note 5.

27 See Turvey's remarks on Michelson and Sitney and the experimental film tradition of the United States of the 1960s and 1970s in Baker & Turvey et al., p. 84.

28 ibid., p. 85.

29 Peter Wollen's important essay is cited by Anthony McCall in Baker & Turvey et al., p. 80. Wollen's overall role as a film theorist and filmmaker (with Laura Mulvey) is summarised by Wollen himself in 'Knight's moves', pp. 150–59.

30 See Nash, p. 56.

31 Quoted ibid., p. 56.

32 ibid.

33 Giuliana Bruno, 'Collection and recollection on film itineraries and museum walks', in Allen & Turvey, pp. 231–60. Greenaway is quoted ibid., p. 235.

Cultural difference in contemporary Australian cinema

What was it like being an Italian migrant in Australia in the 1950s?
Very bad; very bad. I remember that 'dago' and things like that were written
in graffiti style in the condensation on the window of my studio.

Giorgio Mangiamele

Anyone who wishes to examine contemporary Australian cinema in
terms of cultural difference, ethnicity and migrants faces a plethora of
intricate aesthetic, hermeneutic and historiographical issues that have
not, as yet, been adequately made visible in the appropriate critical
literature.

There is also a temptation to shift (in an unproblematic fashion)
some of the more recognisable ideas of postmodernism and post-
colonial theory to the study of the relevant Australian films in the hope
that post-structuralist agendas and theoretical frameworks will prove
sensitive to a supple treatment of cultural 'otherness'.

One is obliged to discuss Australian cinematic representations of
non-Anglo-Celtic migrant groups, their cultures and languages, in a
hesitant, speculative manner, realising the extremely conditional nature
of such a relatively uncharted theoretical enterprise. This is particularly
so when dealing with 'European' and 'Asian' minority groups, and their
settlements in Australia since the arrival of the First Fleet.

However, 'European' and 'Asian' are categories which are too loosely
used and too simplistic. They are in need of deconstruction, as they
conceal elaborate behavioural and cultural differences of minority
individuals who are conveniently lumped together in monocultural
generic positions.

Thus, when we are looking at 'multicultural' cinema, to what
films, textual practices and problematics are we actually referring?[1]
Films made by filmmakers of a non-Anglo-Celtic background? Films
made by filmmakers who were born overseas? Do we also include films
made by filmmakers who do come from an Anglo-Celtic background?

And what kinds of films do we select here: institutional, educational and documentary films? Narrative features and shorts? Avant-garde /experimental films?

Let us, for the moment, analyse the (in)visible spaces of articulations representing biculturalism, migrants and xenophobia in all the above-cited categories of Australian cinema; I believe this constitutes the appropriate topography of cinematic concern for our enquiry. What we are required to do is to read the relevant films via cultural difference. This means looking at cultural difference in terms of class, gender, race and post-coloniality. It also means reading cultural difference in terms of identity, migration, pleasure and landscape (a vital dimension, and germane to any fundamental examination of postwar migration experience in Australian cinema).

Thus, in a post-colonial society such as ours, we need to analyse the relevant films so that we can render visible the cultural and ethnic antecedents, ideas, feelings, habits, memories and values of Australians who have long been unrepresented. The question we are obliged to negotiate is: How do we re-read the familiar canonic and the lesser-celebrated films in relation to these complex issues? The list of films we could examine includes not only the many films which are defined by their pervasive Anglo-American monoculturalism (the list is endless), but also films which are noted for their progressive themes and for styles that are sensitive towards the depiction of migrants.

The latter group includes such works as Harry Watts's groundbreaking *Eureka Stockade* (1949), a film that embodies many insightful observations about the migrant experience in 19th century colonial Australia in the context of a Republic discourse, the dramatised documentary short *Double Trouble* (1953), representing the insensitive hostility shown by Australians to non-English migrants, and the lyrical heroic images and sound configurations of *The Cane Cutters* (1948), where migrant cane cutters are illustrated as hardworking people crucial to Australia's postwar 'nation-building' drive.[2] All three films provide a stark contrast to the xenophobic rhetoric evidenced in the 'voice-of-God' commentary of the 1947 documentary *Land Short of People*, a film typical of the many made during that epoch that argued for closer 'purist' cultural and colonial links between England and Australia.

One should not overlook Ron Maslyn Williams's neo-realist influenced dramatised documentary *Mike and Stefani* (1952), which focuses on two displaced Ukrainian refugees who are taken to separate German labour camps and then reunited at a refugee camp in Australia. Both experience despair and loneliness, Kafkaesque interrogations by immigration officers and exhaustive examinations by medical officers.

The harshness of the couple's world is aptly incarnated in two extraordinary photographs (in Catherine Panich's 1988 book *Sanctuary?*), taken by a concealed camera at Amberg in Germany in 1948. The photos show a young couple (just like Mike and Stefani) being interviewed by officers of the Australian Department of Immigration and a middle-aged lady being inoculated as part of her medical examination.[3]

The panopticon morality of these basic situations in the 1940s and 1950s, where people are being assessed as possible immigrants to Australia, is foregrounded in the contemporary Film Australia documentary on the White Australia Policy, *Admission Impossible* (1992), where we are shown how Australian immigration doctors were trained to look out for any 'Asian' symptoms, such as skin colour and 'Oriental' eyes.

Before we proceed to discussing some of the earlier, almost forgotten, figures who substantially contributed to our multicultural cinema—Giorgio Mangiamele and Ayten Kuyululu, amongst others— it is important to note how in the 1970s and 1980s, the time of the '10BA' renaissance in the Australian film industry, films depicting multicultural themes were (relatively speaking) quite popular (one of the main conceptual focuses of this essay). Since then, however, there has been a new generation of films which are specifically (as Felicity Collins and Therese Davis suggest) 'coming of age' teen 'wog' narratives exemplifying questions of abjection, belonging and cultural identity.[4]

These films are vividly represented by such notable examples as Kate Woods's *Looking for Alibrandi* (2000), Ana Kokkinos's *Head On* (1998) and Ivan Sen's *Beneath Clouds* (2002). These distinctly non-nostalgia films—and these three are quite different in subject and style from each other—deal with the cultural, emotional and sexual conflicts and complexities of youth experience in the context of a country divided by its colonial past, race relations and national security in a globalised world of American-led neo-liberalism and post-McLuhanite transculturalism.

The teen subjects of these three films live in a highly divided 'post-Mabo' nation—thanks to John Howard's reprehensible retro-conservative wish to take Australia back to an idealised Anglo-Celtic colonial past, a past well rendered by satirist Barry Humphries's archetypal dressing gown-clad Sandy Stone and his monotonal soliloquies.[5] Their questioning sociocultural mobility suggests a fundamental distrust of their 'baby boomer' parents' values and symbols. In fact, as Collins and Davis indicate, these teen subjects are fuelled by a compelling drive to 'escape history' as they deal with their tumultuous surroundings across class, gender, ethnicity, sexuality, race and location.[6]

I shall return to especially Kokkinos's film later, as I am particularly interested in examining it as a more recent instance of the Greek-Australian diaspora in recent Australian cinema, but for now I wish to say a few words about the importance of our national cinema being, as Tom O'Regan once pointed out, simultaneously 'an aesthetic and production movement, a critical technology, a civic project of state, an industrial strategy and an international project formed in response to the dominant international cinemas (particularly but not exclusively Hollywood cinema) Australian cinema is formed as a relation to Hollywood and other national cinemas.'[7] Our multicultural cinema has (in its respective ways) all these critical attributes: it is a cinema concerned with displaced immigrant groups and their subcultural lifestyles—the Greek-Australians in *Heartbreak Kid* (Michael Jenkins, 1993), the refugee immigrants in *Silver City* (Sophia Turkiewicz, 1984) and the Italian Australians in *Rabbit on the Moon* (Monica Pellizzari, 1988).

As O'Regan reminds us, our local cinema, like many other national cinemas, functions within a multi-ethnic context.[8] Due to our large postwar migration program, and a steady inflow of refugees since the 1970s (with the Vietnam boat refugees and others coming into Australia)—and despite the obscene developments of privatised detention centres for asylum seekers in the last decade—the characteristic Australian cinema audience has been shaped by a multifaceted cluster of cultural influences. This is clearly and increasingly illustrated in our cinema: the Spanish family in *Strictly Ballroom* (Baz Luhrmann, 1992), the Greek family in *Death in Brunswick* (John Ruane, 1991), the young Chinese boy in *My Tiger's Eyes* (Tan Teck, 1992) and the Italian uncle in *The Artist, the Peasant* (Franco di Chiera, 1991).

At this juncture it would be appropriate, before we continue with our analysis of our multicultural cinema and its elaborate representations of the diverse diasporic/migrant communities that make up our polycultural society, to speak, on a more personal level, of my own childhood experiences of Greek cinema in Sydney 40 odd years ago. It should be remembered that a multitude of various 'ethnic' cinemas representing other national cinemas are experienced through various film festivals, exhibition and distribution contexts. These 'ethnic' films were and are seen as the (historically speaking) margins of our national film culture, even though during the last few decades certain national film festivals (French, Italian and Jewish) have been successful in art cinemas in our larger cities. Consequently, these diverse 'ethnic' films have contributed overall (to some considerable degree) to our local film culture.

Excursus: adolescence, Greek melodramas and the 1950s

My earliest memories of seeing Greek films was at a local Greek cinema in the late 1950s and early 1960s. I saw them at Redfern, in a rather large dilapidated building with a series of shopfronts—the building was where the TNT twin towers next to Redfern railway station are now.

Back then Redfern was a working-class suburb (the gentrification of Redfern took place later, in the 1970s and 1980s) noted for its concentration of European migrants—particularly Greek immigrants. However, the migrant concentration was not as high there as it was in the neighbouring suburbs of Newtown and Marrickville.

The postwar era was one of enormous migration; with the second generation of Greek-Australians, the Greek immigrants of these three suburbs moved southwards to Earlwood, Rockdale, Brighton-le-Sands, Kogarah and Hurstville, amongst other suburbs south of Cooks River.

But it was a time when Australia's shameful White Australia policy of immigration was still functioning and the *Bulletin* magazine's masthead still reflected the country's racist past; it was well before the implementation of 'multicultural' policy by the federal government in the 1970s and the subsequent creation in 1980 of SBS Television and its charter of 'multiethnic' programming. It was an era of unyielding Anglo-Celtic monoculturalism, as expatriate scholar Peter Conrad remembered in his recent 2004 ABC Boyer Lectures: 'The Australia I grew up in during the 1950s was as white as starch, and about as stiff. Everyone adhered to Anglo-Saxdom. Even if their lineage was doubtful.'[9]

At Redfern I would watch countless black and white (and the occasional colour) imported Greek melodramas, comedies, and costume historical films with my mother. Inside the rather cavernous and nondescript movie theatre—a theatre devoid of the elegant art deco character of Kings Theatre at Marrickville, where I would spend many a Saturday with either my father or mother during my cine-childhood days—I would watch these dramatic moral tales of mistaken identity, overreaching ambition, revenge and innocence lost, all of which posited the city as an inferno of damnation and seduction.

The melodramas of the wayward village girl seduced and lost in an urban hell were heavily marked by a stifling didactic patriarchal morality shaped by Greece's time-honoured church–state dialectic. Feuding village families, star-crossed 'Romeo and Juliet' lovers, avenging brothers seeking to restore the lost honour of their families because their sister had been bewitched by an unwelcome suitor, plus urban farcical comedies of rolling drunks, femme fatales, malicious gossips and a unflattering satirical worm's eye-view of Athenian upper-class society painted a weird Brueghelesque cinematic fresco of melodramatic 'country vs city' moralism and surreal possibilities.

Inside the Redfern cinema the movie spectators, including my mother and myself, would have a kind of a gestural and symbolic cultural conversation with the stereotypical characters, their emotions, and the predictable generic narrative events that was a running performative deconstructive reading of the films themselves. The spectators would constantly talk amongst themselves about what they were watching, smoke cigarettes, eat pistachio nuts, and drink their soft drinks; this would provide, for me, a telling contrast to the more sedate 'non-verbal' form of spectatorship I would find in non-Greek movie theatres. (It was not until 1979 that I witnessed a similar cinephilic experience: I watched a David Cronenberg horror movie in a 'fleamarket' movie theatre in San Francisco with Afro-American spectators who enjoyed themselves 'unpacking' aloud the cultural stereotypes of the movie.)

(Other than the Redfern movie theatre, Greek movies were also run during that time at the Hub Cinema near Newtown railway station—before it started showing exploitation and pornographic movies later in the 1970s.)

At Redfern, a Greek movie was often billed with, of all things, an Indian movie. Not because of some 'transcultural' programming philosophy, but because, historically speaking, Athens was the first port of call (in an exhibition and geographical sense) for Indian movies on their way to being exhibited in Europe.

These Indian movies, with their rich, saturated colours and symbolic emotional states of being—particularly the 'Mother Indian' genre—echoed, for me, the intense melodramatic feelings of fatalism and pathos that I would also find in the Greek movies (especially those featuring village feudal vendettas and lost innocent females in Athens and other Greek cities).

The Greek 'village' movies, located in a lyrical landscape of olive groves, high rugged mountains, shady ravines, valleys with silent sites of antiquity, gurgling brooks and rivers and the ubiquitous presence of sheep and their attentive shepherds, would often feature the haunting plaintive clarinet sounds of demotic Greek music. This genre of music, whose roots go back to the Ancient Greeks and their oral tradition of storytelling, provided a telling symmetrical counterpoint to the sub-proletariat 'blues' sounds of the *rembetiko* music found in the hashish dives, nightclubs and brothels of Piraeus, the busy port of Athens, Athens itself, and Thessalonika, amongst other Greek cities.

These early 'ethnic' movies, experiences of which formed a significant part of my overall cinephilia, are of cultural and historical importance in any adequate negotiation of the 'multicultural' complexities of Australian films that treat ethnicity, minority groups, migrants and cultural and racial displacement. However, it was not until the 1980s and more recently, partly because of the available secondary literature, that there was any systematic reading of these important 'ethnic' cinemas; until about two decades ago, only scant references could be found in the literature concerning this fairly critical issue.

Like Christos Tsiolkas with his mother and her vivid form of interacting with characters on the screen, my cinephilia was significantly nurtured by my mother's love for the cinema—she loved Tyrone Power and adored the Nelson Eddy and Jeanette MacDonald musicals. Unlike Tsiolkas's experience of his mother's cultural difference (read 'wogginess') in a 'non-ethnic' movie theatre, though, I experienced my own 'wogginess' inside the Redfern movie theatre, at school—and especially when I went (very reluctantly and with great resistance) to 'Greek' school—and of course, at the family milk bar, where the private and the public coalesced into a deep-seated form of bicultural surrealism.[10]

The forgotten directors of multicultural cinema: Giorgio Mangiamele and Ayten Kuyululu

Anyone who is engaged in reading Australian cinema in terms of its multiple representations of the non-Anglo-Celtic migrant since the 1920s will be confronted by a glaring absence: How have we come to terms with the works of two filmmakers who are foundational to such an enquiry? I refer to the invaluable (but relatively unknown and underrated) films of Giorgio Mangiamele in the 1950s and 1960s and Ayten Kuyululu in the 1970s. Both filmmakers in their respective oeuvres have created films which bristle with insights into the Anglo-Celtic, hegemonic culture which has shaped (and still shapes) the critical and textual agendas of mainstream Australian cinema. Both filmmakers are figures who must be negotiated in any theoretical examination of our films and their manifold representations of bicultural conflict, (multi)cultural difference, migrants and racism.

Traditional histories of Australian cinema have so far, generally speaking, erased the conceptual and textual merit of Mangiamele's and Kuyululu's films because they pose many unsettling questions about Anglo-Australian colonialism and the cultural, pedagogic and theoretical frameworks we use to represent cultural otherness.

Their films, and their low-budget production values, are characterised by a marked degree of hybridisation in their thematic interests, performative registers and stylistic visuals. They are transgeneric in their outlook, full of bicultural displacement, black humour, irony (usually a privileged aspect of the coloniser's discourse of containing, labelling and homogenising the marginal, the plural, in order to assert cultural authority) and heterogeneity. They are also critical of Australian liberal humanism with its emphases on centre, closure, homogeneity, totality and unity.

The critical treatment—or, rather, lack of treatment—of Mangiamele's and Kuyululu's films illustrates the fact that film history constitutes, on the most basic level of representation, in the words of Salman Rushdie, 'an interview with winners'.[11] Further, the tokenistic treatment they have received so far—insofar as they have been acknowledged at all—suggests what contemporary post-structuralist thought has to say about the fictionality involved in constructing (film) history.

Indeed, etymologically speaking, the Ancient Greeks regarded history as storytelling, and in the films of Mangiamele, such as his 1962 work, *Ninety Nine Per Cent*—a film significant on many conceptual, cultural and stylistic levels—we already see the articulation of the filmmaker's desire (first begun in 1953 with *The Contract*) to create a counter-cinema, a 'story' full of post-colonial themes and heterogenous textual stratagems.

Ninety Nine Per Cent poses many interesting questions about dislocation, identity and migration. Its witty black humour and sharp observations about a migrant widower searching for a wife to look after his young son show us the protagonist's decentred subjectivity situated in his urban cultural setting. We witness many of the misadventures and tensions he experiences as he encounters (time and again) Anglo-Celtic colonialism.

Specifically, the critical value of a film like *Ninety Nine Per Cent* lies in its healthy, sceptical response to orthodoxy and dogma; it represents (as do other salient examples of multicultural cinema) an incisive critique of the narrow-mindedness of monoculturalism, articulated from the site of marginality or contrapuntal existence.

What has been said about Mangiamele's work also holds (in the broadest sense of the term) for Kuyululu's harrowing examinations of Turkish migrants living in Sydney in *A Handful of Dust* (1973) and *The Golden Cage* (1975). Kuyululu's primary aesthetic and stylistic configurations centre on the alienation and marginal conflict her subjects experience because of their bicultural identity in post-colonial

Australia. The director's bold and tragic thematic outlook signifies a radical questioning of the centrist and homogenous assumptions and values that underlie representations of cultural difference in Australian cinema till then.

Common to both filmmakers' work is their key focus on the cross-cultural tensions incarnated in the postwar migration experience, and on the related idea that the stereotypical beliefs of Anglo-Celtic monoculturalism are structured on the idea (to quote Trinh Minh-ha) that the coloniser 'discovers with much reluctance, [that] he is just another among others'.[12]

What needs to be understood is that this essay is being written with the objective of, ideally speaking, opening up new spaces of critical possibilities in looking at some of the conceptual and textual problematics and texts that are arguably critical of the most elementary analysis of this topic. It is a tricky terrain of cultural, cinematic and theoretical considerations, considerations that are elaborately intertwined with each other, and one that requires the enquirer to problematise his own theoretical activity—the enquirer cannot, after all, stand outside his own culture, space and society. One is constantly faced, when discussing multicultural cinema, with the realisation that postmodern theory itself, with its globalising abstractions (emerging initially from Eurocentric sources), can be insensitive to the cultural, historical and textual characteristics of bicultural marginality and migration. In its own way, postmodern theory has its own master narratives—and they too are written and imported from the centre, thereby again colonising the marginal.

How does one theorise the cinematic representations of non Anglo-Celtic minority groups in general without resorting to schematic, reductive simplicities? Without, for instance, seeing all postwar migrants as 'cannon fodder' for Australia's industrialisation push in the 1950s or ignoring the enormous cultural differences between minority groups themselves?

Another urgent question that needs attention is: How can we speak of the multicultural plural without being critically aware of the many class, psychological and social tensions that exist within minority groups—migrants from the same ethnic category competing amongst themselves, etc.? Gayatri Spivak cautions us that not everything can be conveniently classified as 'Black against White, as there is Black against Black, Brown against Brown, and so on'.[13]

Then there is the major problematic of constructing a critical vocabulary supple enough to convey the elaborate cultural, historical and sociological features of what it means to be a migrant settler in a country which has over the years shifted its immigration policy from one of assimilation, where the new arrival is defined rather narrowly and homogenised within the cultural and institutional discourses of monoculturalism (the migrant is constructed as 'the same' as his or her Anglo-Australian contemporaries), to multiculturalism, where Australia is seen as being a culturally diverse country.

Seldom have our films in the past (both narrative and documentary) paid much critical attention to representing the ontological traumas of migrating to this country and the related necessity for many migrants to reinvent themselves in a strange country in terms that suggest the post-colonial contradictions and nomadic marginality inherent in the migration experience.

There are films which endeavour (with varying success) to portray the contrapuntal violence of migration, but the majority of films— especially those of the 1970s and early 1980s, particularly the many examples of the previously cited AFC and socialist-realist genres, and the countless educational 'trigger' shorts and documentaries of the same period—represent migrants and their problems in liberal humanistic terms.[14] What we find is a cinema that aspires to construct a cultural anthropological language which glosses over the many ambivalences and ruptures of migration. Rarely do we have films which focus in a non-binary, non-linear manner on the ongoing multifaceted process of migrant identity and bicultural dislocation.

And what aesthetic and cultural criteria can we use when we speak of our past cinematic representations of postwar migration, films that underline the migrant's negotiation of the Australian landscape, its Anglo-Celtic colonisers and their customs, rituals and values? On arrival, the European immigrant immediately encountered the taxonomic homogeneity of 'Australianness' inscribed in the actions of immigration officers who would convert an immigrant's surname as it was too long to pronounce. This was a common situation in our migration history, which is graphically rendered in *Silver City* (1984).

In the 1950 dramatised documentary *No Strangers Here*, in a sequence which has been quoted in several past compilation documentaries, we see an Anglo-Celtic doctor reassure his Baltic nurse companion (as he gestures with his hand the wide open landscape of rolling hills and plains) that Australia is his and her country. When she speaks enthusiastically of how she likes his country, he corrects her with the reply, 'Our country, Christina'. It is a sequence that neatly encapsulates the film's assimilationist position on migrants.

Though *No Strangers Here* is one of the more 'progressive' texts of its time, what are we to make of Christina's future settlement in this country? Are identity and migration easily absorbed into Australian mainstream culture or will she later encounter delayed intense reactions from being severed from her original home? And what of her own responses to the sights, smells and sounds of the landscape itself: is this another possible source of cultural dislocation?

As a post-colonial subject, how did Christina respond to seeing the Australian landscape for the first time? Was it similar to the way Jim Sakkas's protagonist, Ilias, from the novel *Ilias* of 1988, saw it? Standing on the deck of a sea liner, Ilias sees Australian landscape in the following terms (as described by the novel's anonymous narrator): 'So, the land was flat. That meant nothing. This country, on the other side of the world—the little he knew of it—held a fascination, almost mythical. At its centre, he was told, there was a desert, and blacks were here before the Europeans came. He'd seen pictures of kangaroos and emus and other curious animals. People spoke English, but what it was really like, was anyone's guess. What a person like he would make of it—or what this land would make of him—only the gods knew.'[15]

A sense of place is critical (as Paul Carter cogently argued a decade ago) to the way we attribute meaning and significance to our lives.[16] What we need to grasp here is how our migrants made sense of their experiences in a foreign country—not only through visual perception, speech (this would include your own fractured language as N.O.'s brilliant performance poetry illustrates), the many searching and suspicious gazes and silences that would (and do) take place between the coloniser and the colonised, but also, and most significantly, through touching the habitat with your body.

This is something valued by a filmmaker such as Laleen Jayamanne in her remarkable avant-garde film *A Song of Ceylon* (1985). This is one of the few seminal Australian works that contains engaging formal and theoretical ideas about the body, gesture and post-coloniality. It is critically aware of the problematical complexities in creating a cinema that is concerned with questions of colonialism, dislocation and racism.

Another compelling film which has much to offer on this theme by way of its conceptual architecture, as well as its stylised anti-naturalistic mise en scène and rich visuals, is Tracey Moffatt's *Night Cries: A Rural Tragedy* (1989).

Both films are appreciative of the necessity to construct non-didactic arguments, and to use visual and sonic stylistics which can persuade the spectator to start coming to terms with a complicated and changing subject such as post-colonial subjectivity in a country like Australia.

The filmmaker is obliged to create a cinema which both contests the ethnic stereotypes of past Australian cinema and is, at the same time, cinematically self-reflexive. Too often films that espouse multicultural themes are stiff with the sloganeering zeal of soapbox oratory. This was much the case for the 1970s and early 1980s. Thus, films which are concerned with the challenging task of finding new ways, new languages, to say complex things about migration are required to bear in mind this rule, here expressed by Salman Rushdie: to 'give voice to the voiceless, you've got to find a language ... Use the wrong language and you're dumb and blind.'[17]

In past films, such as the last two just cited or the astonishing collaborative effort of *The Occupant* (Michael Karris, Peter Lyssiotis & Ettore Siracusa, 1984) with its powerfully written voiceover, we perceive a foregrounded attempt to find new textual strategies with which to say difficult things about the silent untold stories of the (in)visible marginal subject.

Therefore, when we map out the cinematic topography depicting representations of migrants, identity and oppression, we have to examine such representations in films (as I have indicated earlier on) made by filmmakers from an Anglo-Celtic background as well as in those made from a European or Asian perspective. The former films may have very worthwhile assumptions, subtexts and values which speak of the migration experience and demand a close textual analysis. No one has a mortgage on multicultural cinema.

So we need to be conscious of a film like *Devrim* (1984) as much as *They 're a Weird Mob* (Michael Powell, 1966), of Paul Cox's sympathetic *Kostas* (1979) as much as the notorious silent *Birth of White Australia* (Phil K. Walsh, 1928), of Angelo Gigliotti and Brian McKenzie's noteworthy *Winter's Harvest* (1979) as much as *March to Nationhood* (1939). There are many examples one can draw upon from the past eight decades of Australian cinema, particularly from more recent filmmakers who, because of their own ethnic status in postwar Australia, are able to articulate compelling image and sound configurations which try to portray cultural minority groups and their ongoing difficulties in terms of adaptation, alienation and settlement. These filmmakers include Ettore Siracusa, Kay Pavlou, Michael Karris, Lex Marinos, Teck Tan, Monica Pellizzari, Aleksi Vellis, Luigi Acquisto, Anna Kannava, Franco di Chiera and Fabbio Cavadini.

These are only a few names that come readily to mind when discussing the more recent generations of filmmakers who are conscious of shaping multicultural cinema in Australia. In more recent times, certain other filmmakers should also be named in this context: they include Ana Kokkinos and Iven Sen, amongst others.

Of course, historically speaking, many other cultural institutions, such as SBS-TV, Film Australia, ABC-TV, the Office of Multicultural Affairs, the Australia Council for the Arts, the Australian Film Commission and other related federal and state funding agencies, have been instrumental in recognising the aesthetic and cultural significance of helping to forge such a cinema.[18] Historians such as Leonard Janiszewski, scriptwriters such as Petro Alexiou and Anna Maria Dell'oso, and photographers such as Effy Alexakis, are contributing in their own particular way to this kind of emerging cinema.

Ana Kokkinnos's *Head On* and beyond the Greek-Australian hyphen

Based on Christos Tsiolkas's 1995 novel *Loaded*, which depicts 24 hours of Ari's postmodern life of intense drug taking and sex, a life grounded in the multifaceted adventure of questioning his sexuality and ethnic identity, Ana Kokkinnos's adaptation of Tsiolkas's novel is the seminal coming-of-age gay and ethnic teen movie of the last decade. Kokkinos's honest and brutal movie effectively explores many different aspects of cinema narrative—hand-held camera, slow motion, graphic juxtaposing of fantasy with nitty gritty reality, and expressionist visual distortion—to engender a dynamic kinetic mise en scène that records a poetic, musical, squalid beauty of the abject, dislocation and the Greek-Australian diaspora.

Head On, with its Baudelairian lyricism of emotional and sexual anguish, urban alienation and anonymous sexual encounters, elicited few academic reviews and articles and polarised many film critics and reviewers. Chris Berry's main proposition that the movie was too easily categorised as either a teen or a gay movie and that it is much more than both of these things, because on numerous different levels it questions the either/or binarism of its complex identity politics, should be noted.[19] Clearly, as *Head On* unfolds in its inexorable speed, showing the far-ranging complexities of Ari's alienation and relationship with his parents, what is clearly discernible is that a huge cultural and behavioural gap exists between him and his parents (whose arrival to Australia is registered in iconic black-and-white footage of Greek migrants arriving in Australia in its 'nation-building' epoch of the 1950s in the movie's astonishingly powerful concluding scenes).

Ari's uncompromising status as an outsider who does not belong to his parents' new home of 'milk and honey', an Australia promising the newly arrived immigrant success and prosperity, suggests someone who characteristically lives a 'double life' (he simultaneously belongs to and is rejected by his patriarchal Greek community): in other words, Ari is arguably, in classical American sociology terms (Robert Park), a double-binded 'marginal' character. Someone whose self-destructive behaviour and hedonistic immediacy abundantly denote the extreme antagonistic forces that are tearing him apart. He lashes out at people he likes and people he loathes. Self-hate and disgust and a scorching refusal to live by the hypocrisies, limitations and contradictions of the Greek-Australian diaspora—this is Ari's world of the outlaw outcast. He does not know where he belongs. Consequently, Ari is engaged in a highly visceral existential roller coaster lifestyle, and his body is in a perpetual state of *in extremis*. His lifestyle immediately evokes deep-seated teen angst: he cannot find any kind of lasting solace in his endless drug and sex binge world.

Ari's hate of 'dumbfuck wogs' is vividly represented by the sequence where we see him in a car hurling abuse at numerous wog passers-by

('This isn't Europe any more; we're in Asia'). We also see his intense ambivalence towards his working-class Marxist homophobic father, who harangues Ari with bombastic lectures on work, responsibility and the right to earn one's freedom. The black-and-white scenes early in the movie depicting Ari's parents demonstrating under Marxist banners and placards against the military dictatorship of Greece in the 1970s echo the political beliefs of many of the postwar Greek immigrants who came to this country under the shadow of the civil war in Greece in the 1940s and 1950s.

The numerous scenes between Ari and his father and his browbeaten sacrificing mother (Ari's younger sister begs her not to live her life through her children, but to live her own life) accurately depict the complexities, tensions and problems that afflict many Greek-Australian homes. These scenes show Ari's loathing of the patriarchal and sexist values represented by his father—who we first see attending to his garden (a central motif in multicultural cinema and literature that warrants critical scrutiny). These and the scenes where his Aunt reads the coffee cup (she exclaims: 'The cups don't lie. I saw the face. My God. I don't believe it!') add up to a world that is governed by superstition as much as by familial moral rigidity, a world of conflict between freedom, gender and identity.

Despite many requests to compromise, Ari's refusal to yield to his father's insults only (in a Nietzschean sense) make him stronger in his interaction with his family, relatives and friends. Further, Ari's self-disgust, restlessness and overall rebellion against social conformity and ethnic and sexual identity lead to (at times) a recognition that he sometimes embodies the problematical values of his own familial background and even his father's patriarchal attitudes—as when he is over-protective towards his sister ('You're worse than Dad,' she informs him).

The reasons for Ari's rebellion against the world, including his angst and self-hate, elude him: as he tells us, he is no scholar or poet when it comes to analysing his own ambivalence, rage and rebellion—in other words, his own emotions. All Ari knows is that he must do what his emotions tell him to do. He can't accept the values of his 'baby boomer' parents—they lack any viable solutions to a world of global capitalism, ethnic and identity confusion and unemployment. Ari's self-destructive behaviour needs to be seen, as Berry, Collins and Davis and Nikos Papastergiadis indicate, in the context of the local and the global.[20] In a telling scene, Ari is confronted by his mother about his desire to leave home and go to Europe—to Greece, in fact—in the hope of finding employment. She begs him not to go, but to stay put, much to Ari's ambivalent displeasure.

Ari's world is Virilian in its contours: he is constantly transgressing many different zones, spaces and borders. His hyper-kinetic and negative interaction with Melbourne's working class ethnic minorities (Greeks, Lebanese, Turks, Vietnamese, etc) and their various spaces of urban gentrification, destitution, loss and encroachment attest to the way in which Ari's intense mobile lifestyle is an expression of the centrality of globalisation's focus on the 'time/space compression' as, in Zygmunt Bauman's words, 'the ongoing transformation of the parameters of the human condition'.[21]

Ari vehemently disowns the hyphen of equality in the category 'Greek-Australian' as much as he does the traditions, rituals and values of all the ethnic minorities that inhabit his domestic space. Ari's outlaw values hinge on his burning rage against the folkloric, the formulaic and the comforts of respectable multicultural society. He sees, feels and interacts with the spaces, textures and inhabitants of Melbourne as a roaming 'wired for sound' Genet-like fugitive seeking instant gratification in a hurly-burly nocturnal world of dazzling neon lights, dance music, and transitory gay sex. Ari rebels against the idea of the patriarchical and the matriarchical home and the ideal of a multicultural Utopia. Ari is as Tsiolkas describes him: 'a wogboy as nightmare', who wants 'to scream, "There isn't a home anymore. This is the big city, the bright lights of the west, this is wannabe-America and all the prayers to God or Allah or the Buddha can't save your children now. I put [on] a scowl and roam the North in my dirtiest clothes, looking and feeling unwashed."'[22]

He loathes the boredom, fakery and loyalty of the conventional mainstream world, a world run by one-dimensional conformists—for William Burroughs, the 'Johnsons' of the world. And yet Ari as a subject of the diaspora is tormented by conflicting feelings for family, friends and country. He is constantly dreaming of new worlds, new possibilities, but he is angry, dislocated and vulnerable because of his love/hate for his cultural and ethnic identity. He loathes the constraints and hypocrisies of his home, but a part of him still wants to be rooted there—yet he also yearns to be in other spaces, far away from home. This has dire cultural and emotional consequences for Ari, best summed up by Papastergiadis: 'At home he may not wish to disappoint, but to stay within the allotted space is also frustration. To leave home is to risk being a stranger, an abomination, a whore/*poutana*. Outside the home desire runs wild. It has no fixed shape. Ari knows that the satisfaction of being domestic, virtuous, obedient is not enough. He wants more. He doesn't know what is his ideal form. He does not know how to measure his future. The image of his place in the world is as husky as the contours of desire.'[23]

The pragmatic and wiser transvestite friend Johnny (Paul Capsis) likens Ari to the Greek myth character Persephone, who spends half the year in Hades and the other half in the world above with her mother. Ari's turbulent self-defining adventure in Melbourne as a rebellious, non-conciliatory Greek-Australian subject takes place in an expressionist, energetic mise en scène of two distinct stylistic configurations: Kokkinos employs a finely textured, hyper-realistic look to depict when Ari escapes from home to vibrant, exciting places, and for home and related domestic spaces, where his relatives and friends reside, Kokkinos uses stark and cold colours to suggest the radical contrasts in Ari's ambivalent, hallucinatory world.

Ari's world is not only deftly constructed by the movie's graphically dynamic, gestural and fast-paced visuals, which render his uncompromising hybrid world of confusion, rage and tenderness with remarkable directorial assurance; its ubiquitous pulsating soundtrack of popular music and Greek *rembetiko* music (including the great soulful Sotiria Bellou) also markedly suggests the underlying alienation, schisms, tensions—and the hedonism—of Ari's abject behaviour. The various trance-like dancing sequences clearly indicate how well Kokkinos is able to use and at the same time critique visual stereotypes; and also, as Sneja Gunew reminds us, to use dance as a register for the nuances of character of Ari and his family and their various emotional investments.[24]

Alex Dimitriades, as Ari, has given us one of the tour de force performances of the Australian cinema in the last 20 odd years.

The extraordinarily nuanced performance is notable for Dimitriades's elastic capacity to give complexity, strength and cohesiveness to the characterisation of Ari as a man out of control. It is truly a superb performance: unforgettable for its compelling emotional subtlety and power. The supporting performers also provide a great foil for Dimitriades: Paul Capsis as Johnny, someone who refuses to surrender to the reactionary forces in our society, particularly comes to mind. Johnny's impassioned plea to Ari not to give in, and to keep on asking questions of mainstream culture, is reminiscent of Cornelius Castoriadis's observation that the trouble with the contemporary condition of our modern society is that it has stopped questioning itself.[25]

Finally, the movie's concluding scenes—the black-and-white footage of European migrants arriving in Australia by boat and Ari dancing out his homosexual abjection—resonate with far-reaching poetic insight and power. Ari dancing his circular solitary testament of self-assertion, refusal and shame—'I am a whore, a dog, and a cunt …'— is an incandescent moment in recent Australian cinema. Ari's refusal to live out the conciliatory rhetoric of official multiculturalism, on a much deeper level of human conduct, represents the cultural, existential and sexual turbulence that propels his rebellious, high-velocity behaviour.

Conclusion

In conclusion, as we can see, there are many critical, historical and textual issues that are raised when one is examining the way Australian cinema has represented non-Anglo migrants for the past 70 years. It seems quite clear that these issues are still in need of theoretical ventilation. More to the point, there appears to be a substantial gap between modern film theory, post-colonial theory and current representations in mainstream Australian cinema of postwar migration, identity, cultural difference, etc. More work is needed in the sphere of reflexive filmmaking that knows the value of not being 'dumb and blind' as defined by Rushdie.

I have focused in my analysis of multicultural cinema on a broad contextualisation of some of the more significant filmmakers and movies germane to its evolution. In my mapping out some of these critical directorial voices and texts—particularly, the works of two of our most neglected contemporary Australian filmmakers, Giorgio Mangiamele and Ayten Kuyululu—I have tried to colour in also some of the more pressing aesthetic, cultural and historical concerns of these films and what they have to say about the Australian national identity in terms of ethnicity, gender, memory, space and time.

Further, I have also focused on the Greek-Australian diaspora—a subject salient to my own autobiography as a second-generation Greek Australian—where possible, and especially in my close reading of Ana Kokkinnos's brave and controversial *Head On*. Time will tell if it will become (as I suspect it may do) an unsentimental, multilayered coming-of-age classic of recent Australian cinema.

Finally, there is a moment in *The Occupant* where Lyssiotis's father is seen pruning a tree. (The garden motif once again.) He is frozen for a fleeting second as he looks directly at the camera. The accompanying voiceover informs the spectator that he knows he is dying from cancer. Without sentimentalising the situation, Lyssiotis and his collaborators have given us one of the most haunting images in contemporary Australian cinema. The gaze of Lyssiotis's father embodies the aspirations, hurt and poignancy of the migrant's lot in this country, as in any other. It is an image that will search you out in your quieter moments.

NOTES

1   The term 'multicultural cinema' is a problematic one in that it can incorporate films which exhibit migrants in dubious assimilationist, folkloric and humanistic terms. Nevertheless, given this main qualification and until a more satisfactory term is invented, I shall use it.

2   The term 'nation-building' belongs to Albert Moran. See his essay, 'Nation building: the post-war documentary in Australia (1945–1950)', *Continuum*, vol. 1, no. 1, 1987, pp. 57–79.

3   Compare this with Catherine Panich's valuable oral history of postwar immigration, *Sanctuary?*, Allen & Unwin, Sydney, 1988.

4   Felicity Collins & Therese Davis, *Australian Cinema After Mabo*, Cambridge: Cambridge University Press, Cambridge, 2004 (see especially Chapter 9).

5   Compare this with Colin O'Brien (ed.), *The Life and Death of Sandy Stone*, Pan Macmillan, Sydney, 1990.

6   Collins & Davis.

7   Tom O'Regan, 'A national cinema', in Graeme Turner (ed.), *The Film Cultures Reader*, Routledge, London and New York, 2002, p. 139.

8   ibid., p. 169.

9   Peter Conrad, *Tales of Two Hemispheres*, ABC Books, Sydney, 2004, p. 35.

10   Christos Tsiolkas, *The Devil's Playground*, and for my own illustrated essay describing my Greek-Australian milk bar background and its surrealist configurations, see John Conomos, 'Greek-Australian milk bar culture', *Object*, no. 3, 1998, pp. 35–37.

11   Salman Rushdie, quoted in Sneja Gunew & Kateryna O. Longley (eds), *Striking Chords*,

Allen & Unwin, 1992, Sydney, p. xv. I am indebted to this book for many arguments—on multiculturalism, etc—put forward by a number of different authors.

12 Tinh Minh-ha's quote is cited in Longley, 'Fifth world', in Gunew & Longley, p. 22.

13 ibid., p. 21.

14 For a detailed characterisation of the AFC and social-realist genres, consult Elizabeth Jacka, 'The aesthetic force field 1: The AFC genre and the socialist realist film in the '80s', in Susan Dermody & Elizabeth Jacka (eds), *The Imaginary Industry*, Sydney: AFTRS Publications, Sydney, 1988, pp. 88–97.

15 Jim Sakkas, *Ilias*, Allen & Unwin, Sydney, 1988, p. 2.

16 Paul Carter, 'Lines of communication: meaning in the migrant environment', in Gunew &Longley, pp. 9–18.

17 Salman Rushdie, 'Songs doesn't know the score', in Kobena Mercer (ed.), *Black Film Black Cinema*, ICA Documents 7, London, 1988, p. 16. See also Stuart Hall's reply to Rushdie, on p. 17.

18 The funding of the cultural landscape of the last three decades in this country—in relative global terms—despite its past limitations has been (in comparison with other national funding systems) a source of envy. Lamentably, it appears that (in very recent times) the Howard administration has questionable art policy objectives. This particularly applies with the new proposed changes in the Australian Council for the Arts. See Robyn Archer's well-aimed scorching critique of the increasing dogma and loss of dialectic in our recent (federal) arts policies and in our society at large: 'The myth of the mainstream', *Platform Papers No. 4*, Currency House, Sydney, April 2005. And relatedly, Martin Harrison has written a sharp, informative and perceptive analysis of our national radio and TV broadcaster, the ABC, in terms of its declining creative contribution to the Australian arts because of poor policy decisions, recent federal government interference, etc.: '"Our ABC"–a dying culture?', *Platform Papers No. 1*, Currency House, Sydney, July 2004.

19 Chris Berry, 'The importance of being Ari', *Metro Magazine*, 118, 1999, pp. 34–37. Also, in the context of analysing Kokkinos's transgressive treatment of the ethnic and gender stereotypes of *Head On* and, in a larger invaluable overview, the prevailing binary representations of femininity, masculinity and sexuality of Greek identity in postwar Australian cinema, see the highly recommended Freda Freiberg & Joy Damousi, 'Engendering the Greek', in Lisa French (ed.), *Women Vision*, Damned Publishing, Melbourne, 2003, pp. 211–22.

20 See Berry, passim; Collins & Davis, pp. 160–61; Nikos Papastergiadis, 'Cultural identity and its boredom', in N Papastergiadis (ed.), *Complex Entanglements*, Rivers Oram Press, London, 2003, pp. 171–77.

21 Zygmunt Bauman, *Globalization*, Polity Press, Cambridge, 1998, p. 2. Ari's complex frenetic and destructive behaviour, in terms of globalisation, can be seen as an expression of Paul Virilio's ideas of 'the end of geography' and speed culture.

22 Tsiolkas's description of Ari as 'a wogboy as nightmare' in *Loaded* is cited in Papastergiadis, p. 171.

23 Papastergiadis, p. 172.

24 Sneja Gunew, 'Multicultural sites', in Papastergiadis , p. 197.

25 For Cornelius Castoriadis's observation on the necessity to ask the right questions of ourselves and our institutions, see Bauman, p. 5.

Documentary surrealism: on Luis Buñuel's *Land without Bread* (1933)

Buñuel's surrealism is nothing more than his concern to get to the bottom of reality; what matters if we lose our breath as the diver loses his head when, in his cumbersome suit, he cannot feel the ocean floor under his foot.

André Bazin

Nothing is gratuitous in *Las Hurdes*. It is perhaps the least gratuitous work I have made.

Luis Buñuel

Luis Buñuel's *Land without Bread* (*Las Hurdes*,1933) is arguably, as Mercè Ibarz has recently pointed out, one of the most essential experiments of the filmmaker's entire oeuvre, and a key work in documentary cinema during its early sound era, as well as in the subsequent development of the genre itself.[1] What follows is a discussion of Buñuel's influential documentary as a seminal example of surrealist documentary, in terms of its radical image–sound configurations, juxtaposed narrative forms based on existing written press, travelogues, new pedagogy techniques and photographed and filmed propaganda material and, most significantly, its powerful subversive use of sound. Further, because of the documentary's innovative experiment in documentary mise en scène and sound, and not forgetting its reflexive treatment of the death of a goat (more of this later), it is unequivocally one of the key (but much undervalued) texts in terms of film and television history.

One significant aspect of my analysis of *Land without Bread* will be its recent representation in Ramón Gieling's documentary *Buñuel's Prisoners* (2000). This new documentary examines *Land without Bread*, which is set in one of Spain's most isolated impoverished region —Las Hurdes—through the eyes of contemporary Hurdanos, including some of the remaining actual characters seen in Buñuel's scorching social documentary. My approach to Buñuel's documentary will be not only to examine its ironic stance to the travelogue genre and ethnology in general, but also to show, as James F. Lastra has persuasively argued, that *Land without Bread* is equally notable for its complex conceptual and formal strategies of equivocation regarding its treatment of the Hurdanos themselves.[2]

Land without Bread followed directly after Buñuel's two most famous avant-garde surreal films—*Un Chien Andalou* (1928) and *L'Age d'Or* (1930), both made in collaboration with Salvador Dali. Funded by a lottery, *Land without Bread* is a devastating social critique of the poverty, superstitions and disease that afflicted Las Hurdes.[3] For Buñuel, although *Land without Bread* is based on social concrete reality and is thus a documentary, it should also be seen as an uncompromising poetic illumination of the social concerns of the Surrealist movement. In this sense, *Land without Bread*—which is one of the most harrowing documentaries ever made—should also be contextualised within a certain avant-garde documentary tradition of the 1920s and 1930s (Joris Ivens, Walter Ruttmann, Henri Storck, Jean Vigo).

Land without Bread, according to Buñuel, was not elaborately scripted, but was instead based on a series of notes the filmmaker made—concerning the harsh landscape, its inhabitants, its flora and fauna—during a visit to the region ten days before the shoot. It was a low-budget production which was edited (without a Moviola) on a kitchen table, with the aid of a magnifying glass.

The documentary itself, through its introductory written text, declares its experimental status as a 'cinematic essay in human history' at the beginning of the 1930s. And in the context of the tremendous political and social upheaval of the Spanish Republic, and the rise of fascism in Europe at the time, Buñuel's choice of film crew reflected the revolutionary times the documentary was made in (and the course of future events). Buñuel selected Acin as the film's producer, and Rafael Sánchez Ventura as assistant director. Both Acin and Sanchez Ventura were part of the surrealist Group of Zaragoza. Buñuel selected two crewmembers who belonged to the Paris movement: camera operator Eli Lotar and photographer Pierre Unik. Despite their different political views—both Acin and Sanchez Ventura were libertarians, whilst Unik and Lotar were communists—the four co-operated quite well amongst themselves for the filming of the documentary, but their attitudes and values would inevitably divide them during the war and subsequent dictatorship. Therefore *Land without Bread* is also a touching and vivid testimony to the possibilities of collective filmmaking: Jean-Luc Godard, who refers to the documentary in several of his works, speaks of it as 'a moving experience in the interior of history'.[4]

Buñuel had complete control over the documentary, a work which, according to Ibarz's detailed research on its production history and critical reception, he always distanced himself from throughout his life. Towards the end of his life, though, he made his most personal statement about it, saying that he regarded it as his most controlled film. (Hence Buñuel's quote that prefaces this essay.)[5] Buñuel had total control of its script and editing, and although Unik wrote a fair part of the commentary (with ideas submitted by Acin), Buñuel substantially contributed to it as well. The inventive distancing use of Brahms's Fourth Symphony, according to Buñuel, who ordinarily used music very sparingly in his films, came to him while he was editing the film. It should also be noted that *Land without Bread*, according to the filmmaker, 'shares the same outlook' as his earlier two groundbreaking surreal classics, *Un Chien Andalou* and *L'Age d'Or*.[6] The documentary was adapted, time and again, for very complex censorship, historic, distribution and exhibition reasons, but over the years it retained its disturbing ironic and radical surreal concerns. Buñuel, as Ibarz correctly reminds us, went into exile with a copy of it; it later helped him access the Museum of Modern Art, and inspired Robert Flaherty to shoot *The Land* (1942), which was banned, as Buñuel's film had been.[7]

Land without Bread is a documentary whose form is at odds with its content: it is a seminal surreal documentary that—as Gilberto Perez, James F. Lastra and Ibarz, amongst others, have suggested—'calls itself into question' (Perez's phrase). In many different and telling ways, it asks us to not to trust it, to question the fictions of the traditional documentary genre; it frequently, as Perez puts it, 'declares the contrivance of its representation'.[8] Like Dziga Vertov's documentaries, which radically acknowledge their own artifice, *Land without Bread* significantly underlines its own fictionality in that it presents itself as parody of the traditional travelogue and the ethnographic documentary. Further, the film's highly distinctive 'neutral' commentary—Buñuel said it was 'very dry, very documentary-like, without literary effects'—

often radically contradicts the images that we see, as in the situation of the sick girl in the street and the baby in the house.[9] Neither the girl nor the baby is dead, although the narrator informs us that they are; the images contradict him. Fundamentally, the documentary's ambiguous stance towards the spectator presages similar concerns in publicity, propaganda and television. Further, Buñuel's radical use of sound (including Brahms's music) can be traced back to the surrealists' deployment of imagery and text with the end objective of producing shock—as, for example, in Ernst's or Magritte's paintings.

One of the documentary's most important incidents, one that acts as a metaphor for the film's overall reflexive project of critiquing the travelogue and ethnographic representation, is the death of a goat. This takes place around the middle of the film. After we learn that the Hurdanos' diet is almost entirely potatoes, consumed in May or June, and unripe cherries which cause dysentery, we see two goats scaling a precipice. We are then told by the narrator, as if to magnify the misery the Hurdanos experience, that goat meat is only eaten when a hapless goat falls off a cliff to its death. This seems a very unlikely and surreal event—but it immediately takes place. However, what we also notice is a puff of smoke emanating from the right edge of the frame, suggesting that the goat has actually been shot. Buñuel shot the goat and staged the event, which reflects his radical documentary mise en scène composition. In fact, as Ibarz clearly demonstrates via uncut footage of the film discovered in the early 1960s, the crew pursued the goat in order for its death to be staged thereby underlining the ambiguity of the documentary.[10]

However, according to Lastra, this notorious scene is characteristic of *Land without Bread* as a whole: it exemplifies the dehumanisation of the Hurdanos and questions the film's claims to objectivity.[11] But most importantly, as Lastra also observes, the goat's death has connotations of ritual death and exile, symbolising the Hurdanos as scapegoats in terms of their problematic relationship to Spanish culture and history.[12] But what needs to be emphasised here is the fact that the documentary's uniqueness resides in its overall strategy of equivocation: Buñuel, as Lastra suggests, engages in a complex 'double movement of embracing and repelling the Hurdanos at the same time', thereby destabilising the film's overall position.[13] *Land without Bread* arouses both—and simultaneously—empathy and antipathy for its subjects; eschewing the stifling binarisms of aesthetic, social and political discourse, Buñuel characteristically neither demonises nor appropriates them; he locates them on the border—neither inside or outside—as the radically other.

For what Buñuel did not do in this film, as Ibarz reminds us, was look for the Other/Different as they had been evident in the travelogues or documentaries in the tradition of *Nanook* (1922); instead, he sought the other/same.[14] But a kind of other/same that was prevalent in the two distinct themes of documentaries of that era: (a) European cities (Vertov, Ruttmann & Vigo) and (b) working-class labour (Grierson, Ivens & Strand). Therefore, Buñuel, to complete the famous triptych that begins his oeuvre, decided to search for an other/same that was already familiar to his spectators, thanks to photography and other related mass media (and King Alfonso XIII's visit to Las Hurdes in 1922).

Land without Bread, in its drive to create a post-Griersonian documentary, thanks to its sympathy with Georges Bataille's Nietzsche-inspired heterology and its basic engagement with fundamental sources like Maurice Legendre's 1926 anthropological study and Miguel de Unamuno's 1922 travel essay, did endeavour to create an accurate image of Hurdanos life. This meant, most significantly, in keeping with the film's characteristic strategies of equivocation, a refusal to treat the Hurdanos as either noble (as Unamuno did in his essay) or ignoble.

Although Las Hurdes consisted of over 52 communities, *Land without Bread* was primarily filmed in Las Hurdes Altas, which is noted for its wild mountains, mineral landscape and arid gulches. Around thirty of these communities, Buñuel once claimed, did not have chimneys, songs or bread.[15] In short, Buñuel paints Las Hurdes as a living hell on earth: a very remote region cut off from civilisation and characterised by cretins, mass starvation, prematurely aged women and disease, including malaria. Not surprisingly, despite Buñuel's statements about the documentary, most of today's Hurdanos in Gieling's already cited *Buñuel's Prisoners* are still angry about what they feel is a biased portrait of their region and lives in Buñuel's documentary.

This equivocation is characteristic of the Buñuelian vision: his investigations into human behaviour are no less detached or objective than his interest in insects (which can be traced back to his childhood in Calanda). Buñuel's relentless and poetic feelings about human suffering are not indicative of a quasi-scientific liberal view; as E. Rubinstein suggests, for Buñuel 'it is [rather] a condition of existence, a given, common to all mortals and merely exemplified to a bizarre degree and in a spirit of exemplary acquiescence by the Hurdanos'.[16] Critically, then, *Land without Bread*'s scathing critique of church and capital is emblematic of the filmmaker's constant probing in his surreal cinema to expose the injustices of human society, to explore 'the problem of man' and the complex issues of representing otherness.[17] In this context, Bazin's famous description of Buñuel's probing cinema of X-raying human reality as a cinema of 'cruelty', and his assertion that Buñuel does nothing less than 'probe the cruelty of creation itself', merits our attention.[18] The Bazinian perspective on Buñuel's 'cruel' methods as a filmmaker suggests that Buñuel uses the camera as a scalpel, utilising 'surgical obscenity to make an incision in the corpus of reality'.[19]

It can be argued, as Buñuel's Spanish biographer Francisco Aranda did, that Buñuel's triptych represents a clearly progressive approach to documentary, and Buñuel never abandoned the use of documentary elements in his subsequent films.[20] *Land without Bread* became a propaganda film for the Spanish Republic, which in fact censored the film even though the film also deconstructed the mechanisms of propaganda. Further, it is a work that unsettles all conventional forms of documentary cinema, as it time and again tells us that its main subject is the crew itself. Its radical use of sound engenders unease in the spectator—as Adonis Kyrou pointed out in 1962, words are denser than images and dangerous when launched onto the masses.[21] Thus the aesthetics and the politics of the film's voice-over indicate a deep-seated critique of 'the imperialism and colonialism of documentary' (Pascal Bonitzer); in keeping with the disembodied voice of a permanently off-screen narrator, 'two kinds of voices without bodies immediately suggest themselves—one theological and the other scientific (two poles which, it might be added, are not ideologically unrelated: 1. the voice of God incarnated in the Word, and 2. the artificial voice of a computer' (Mary Ann Doane).[22] Thus we have here Buñuel's distinguishing ironic play with the dissonance between image and off-screen word—and its overall generic legacy, which is in newsreels, travelogues, scientific films and the problematic ethnographic ideas of the Parisian surrealists.

Land without Bread has, historically speaking, been seen as a controversial perverse travelogue film. It was inspired, as suggested earlier, by Buñuel's discovery of Maurice Legendre's book (based on his PhD), which is a comprehensive look at the region's social, botanical, climatological and zoological features. For 20 consecutive years Legendre visited the region. What attracted Buñuel to the region was, in his words, 'its intense drama, its terrible poetry'.[23]

Gieling's documentary focuses on how, 60 years later, Buñuel's film has became a major curse on the present-day Hurdanos. Time and again, we encounter the local inhabitants being angry and puzzled by the negative reputation that *Land without Bread* has created for them. Buñuel is seen as an outsider, someone who has misled the world regarding the region, its people and their beliefs. Armed with a copy of Buñuel's documentary plus a bust of Buñuel himself, Gieling and his crew try to follow Buñuel's original tracks in *Land without Bread*. *Buñuel's Prisoners*'s investigative art documentary mise en scène centres on Gieling's efforts to create a form of media archaeology concerning Buñuel's visit to Las Hurdes and his filming of the region. Often, we see Gieling gently trying to coax Hurdanos into telling him whether or not there are any existing survivors of Buñuel's film—there are—and trying to find certain locales that Buñuel used.

The bust of Buñuel's head is presented as a gift from Gieling to the mayor of the town. The mayor is visibly embarrassed when Buñuel's face is revealed to him by Gieling, such is the hurt that Buñuel's documentary caused to Las Hurdes and its people. The bust is uncannily similar to the one at Zaragoza that adorns the last page of Paul Hammond's brilliant 1997 book on *L'Age d'Or*.

Throughout *Buñuel's Prisoners*, Gieling's enquiry about Buñuel's documentary and its impact on Las Hurdes is aided by the presence of an elderly male who was a youngster in Buñuel's film. He takes Gieling and his crew around the various locales that were used *Bread*, including the hillside where Buñuel shot the goat. We also enter the school building featured in *Land without Bread*, where one of the film's survivors speaks about her teacher and her classmates, who are in Buñuel's documentary.

One of the more engaging aspects of *Buñuel's Prisoners* is its subtext about a contemporary Spanish town whose various pro- and anti-Franco citizens reminisce about their childhood hardships. We also meet a young man who raises pigeons and talks of Las Hurdes as a provincial town with positive and negative features. Among the former is the fact that it has a more subdued way of life than the large cities of Madrid and Barcelona, and amongst the latter is the drift of his peers to these vast labyrinthine metropolises.

Stylistically, Gieling's documentary is quite simple. To illustrate its points, *Buñuel's Prisoners* uses numerous clips from Buñuel's rarely seen documentary. Occasionally, however, Gieling sets up a particular viewpoint about Buñuel's approach to documentary making and then leaves it suspended midair. This meandering unresolved form of filmmaking is an irritating limitation of *Buñuel's Prisoners*.

Nevertheless, Gieling's documentary is a welcome contribution to our understanding of Buñuel's surreal cinematic art, which is noted for its mocking anti-clerical humour, discontinuous narrative structures, social melancholy and preoccupation with sexuality and repression. *Buñuel's Prisoners*, in this context, sheds some appreciable light on Buñuel's preferred style of documentary: psychological rather than descriptive.[24] *Land without Bread* is clearly an example of the psychological form—which, according to Buñuel, was the less common form. For Buñuel, the psychological documentary is both descriptive and objective in its approach to interpreting reality. It appeals to the spectator's artistic emotions and can 'express love, sorrow and humour'.[25] And, decisively, it is more complete than the descriptive model, Buñuel argued, 'because besides illustrating, it is moving'.[26]

On one level, *Buñuel's Prisoners* gradually builds to a fairly spectacular penultimate sequence displaying an evening screening of *Land without Bread* in the village square. Gathered for this open air screening we see the various Hurdanos who testified to Gieling's camera about Buñuel's anti-documentary and its undesirable affect on their lives, as well as other (much younger) villagers.

Central to *Land without Bread* is, as the late Raymond Durgnat once stated, Buñuel's distinctive use of contradiction in shaping his film's cinematic and semantic elements.[27] As Vivian Sobchack has recently persuasively argued, it is this unsynthetic contradictory mode of the documentary that forces the spectator to question the very core foundations of perception itself.[28] Buñuel refuses, as Sobchack puts it, to synthesise for us the documentary's markedly 'systematically unsynthetic presentation of thesis and antithesis, sound and image'[29] We are forced to question the documentary's conceptual architecture by (as earlier noted) the use of Brahms's Fourth Symphony, the dry tone of the narrator's commentary, the narrator himself, and the manipulation of reality itself, including the representation of the Hurdanos as 'objects' for Buñuel's camera. All these important and controversial aesthetic and cultural issues relating to *Land without Bread*'s dialectical structure and method become abundantly clear in Gieling's film as we see Gieling encounter these unsettling issues as mediated by the Hurdanos of today. In summary, *Buñuel's Prisoners* is an interesting (but flawed) attempt to contextualise Buñuel's only documentary in terms of how it was received by the Hurdanos of the 1930s, and by those same people, and the younger generations in the town, today.

Land without Bread was never commercially released in Spain; given its complicated exhibition and critical reception history, it is usually only seen in repertory cinemas, museums and on television. And although it is, undoubtedly, one of the least appreciated and discussed works in Buñuel's entire corpus, it still continues to problematise classical film spectatorship. The revolutionary Goyaesque character of this work reflects one of Buñuel's most intense political crises, and as Bill Nichols recently indicated, its location within the modernist avant-garde of Alberto Cavalcanti, René Clair, Louis Delluc, Sergei Eisenstein and Man Ray, among others, suggests that it drew upon ideas about photographic realism, narrative structure, and modernist fragmentation.[30] Buñuel's *Land without Bread* also echoes Adrian Brunel's earlier precursive mock travelogue about a journey across the Sahara Desert: *Crossing the Great Sagrada* (1924).[31]

There are also notable similarities between Buñuel and Cavalcanti, a filmmaker the Spaniard filmmaker liked, especially in terms of his approach to experimenting with sound. In 1933, as Ibarz observes, when Buñuel shot and edited his film using a preconceived soundtrack as a base, Cavalcanti was doing the same in London.[32] And, like Cavalcanti, who worked later with Grierson, Buñuel worked towards the articulation of the voices of the ordinary citizen, plus music and poetry, thereby defining sound as a multifaceted link between reality and its documentary representation. This is something that the late Jean

Rouch, the groundbreaking cinema vérité filmmaker, would pursue later in his ethnographic surrealism.

Land without Bread, as an (anti)travelogue, is a unique and complex work, notable for its political and aesthetic tensions: it is the only documentary that Buñuel produced, but he did so at a critical juncture, in terms of the modernist avant-garde and documentary film traditions of the 1920s and 1930s. The film embodies Buñuel's questioning approach to traditional ethnographic documentaries and the Griersonian documentary genre, and in so doing it also acts a poetic testimony to why people in a certain region of Spain in a time of European political turmoil lived the way they did. And as Lastra argues, the interest the film shows in cultural scapegoating and equivocation resonates profoundly, in terms of exile and the search for redemption, with the new title that Buñuel gave his film when (as mentioned before) he gave a copy of it in 1940 to the Museum of Modern Art: *Unpromised Land*.[33] In a word, the film is a cult avant-garde documentary that pushes us to question our personal biases about the world and vision itself, and about the documentary form itself.

NOTES

1   See Mercè Ibarz, 'A serious experiment: *Land without Bread*, 1933', in Peter William Evans & Isabel Santaolalla (eds), *Luis Buñuel: New Readings*, British Film Institute, London 2004.

2   James F. Lastra, 'Why is this absurd picture here? Ethnology/equivocation/Buñuel', *October*, 89, summer 1999, pp. 51–68.

3   Compare Buñuel's remarks concerning Ramón Ancin's lottery funding of the documentary, in Jose de la Colina and Thomas Perez Turrent (eds), *Objects of Desire: Conversations with Luis Buñuel*, Paul Leni (trans. 1986), Marsilio, New York, 1992, p. 31.

4   See Ibarz, p. 36.

5   ibid., passim.

6   ibid., p. 35.

7   ibid., p. 39.

8   Gilberto Perez, *The Material Ghost*, Johns Hopkins University Press, Baltimore and London, 1998, pp. 43, 44.

9   Colina & Turrent, p. 34.

10   Ibarz, pp. 36–37.

11   Lastra, pp. 51–52.

12   ibid.

13   ibid., p. 53.

14   Ibarz, p.31.

15   Colina & Turrent, p. 35.

16   E Rubinstein, 'Visit to a familiar planet: Buñuel among the Hurdanos', *Cinema Journal*, vol. 22, no. 4, summer 1983, pp. 5–6.

17   Lastra, pp. 54–56.

18   Bazin's words are quoted in Rubinstein, p. 6.

19   ibid., p. 5.

20   Francisco Aranda, *Luis Buñuel: A Critical Biography*, D Robinson (ed., trans.), Secker & Warburg, London, 1975, p. 116. See also Ibarz, p. 38.

21   Ibarz, p. 34.

22   Rubinstein, pp. 12–13.

23   See Buñuel's essay '*Land without Bread*',

in *Luis Buñuel, an Unspeakable Betrayal*,
University of California Press, Berkeley, 2000,
p. 217.
24   ibid., 'From Buñuel's *autobiography*',
p. 256. (This unfinished essay was written in
1938.)
25   ibid.
26   ibid.
27   Cited in Vivian Sobchack, 'Synthetic
vision: The dialectical imperative of Luis
Buñuel's *Las Hurdes*', in Barry Grant &
Jeannette Sloniowski (eds), *Documenting the
Documentary*, Wayne State University Press,
Detroit, 1998, p. 71.
28   ibid., p. 73.
29   ibid.
30   Bill Nichols, 'Documentary film and the
modernist avant-garde', *Critical Inquiry*, 27,
summer 2001, pp. 580–610.
31   ibid., p. 588.
32   Ibarz, p. 38.
33   Lastra, p. 68.

Art, cinema, Hitchcock

Do you think of yourself as an artist?
No, not particularly.

Interviewer and Alfred Hitchcock, 1972

Perhaps there are ten thousand people who haven't forgotten Cézanne's apple, but there must be ten billion spectators who will remember the lighter of the stranger on the train, and the reason why Alfred Hitchcock became the only *poète maudit* to meet the success was that he was the greatest creator of forms of the 20th century, and it's forms that tell us finally what lies at the bottom of things; what is art if not that through which forms became style.

Jean-Luc Godard, *Histoire(s) du Cinema*, 1998

Cinema and art have always had a complex problematic relationship. During the last decade, this has became abundantly clear through the various curatorial, theoretical and cultural interests in the uneasy dialectic between cinema and the visual arts, especially as represented by painting and sculpture. For example, the current interest in this crucially important (but often) overlooked question as evinced by contemporary French filmmakers and artists is, according to Thomas Elsaesser, vividly foregrounded in Jacques Rivette's 1991 film *The Beautiful Troublemaker*.[1] Elsaesser's argument that this film is preoccupied with cinema's attempt to align itself with an 'authentic' art form—such as painting—in its present cultural debate with the digital image makes a lot of empirical sense in the light of the rapid hybrid developments that are taking place between cinema, photography, video, TV and the new media arts. Today many established and young artists are seriously engaged in film and video installations, single-channel works and multimedia projects. Everyone, it seems, has fallen under the spell of cinema. The century that has just passed us is, as Gore Vidal and Cabrera Infante, amongst others, have testified, 'the cinema century'.

To remind us of this, Sydney's Museum of Contemporary Art in 1999 had two fine and thoughtful exhibitions concerned with Alfred Hitchcock and contemporary art, under the generic title of *Hitchcock: Art, Cinema and … Suspense*. The first exhibition, *Notorious*, curated by Kerry Brougher, Michael Tarantino and Astrid Bowron for Oxford's Museum of Modern Art in 1996, is an enticing and informative exhibition marking the centenary of Hitchcock's birth. The second exhibition, *Moral Hallucination*, curated by Edward Colless, operates like an atmospheric seance or a dream, where selected Australian exhibits act like a medium to channel, in the words of the curator, 'a force I call Hitchcock'.[2] The two exhibitions, in their different critical and curatorial ways, ricochet off each other, giving the gallery spectator a highly expressionist (and surreal) collage of aesthetic, cultural and historical possibilities centred around Hitchcock, modernism and postmodernist art. Hitchcock's complex popular figure—the exiled British auteur director in postwar America, casting a huge shadow over contemporary artists, filmmakers, writers and the public alike—looms over these two exhibitions.

Hitchcock's interest in modernist painting, and ways in which his oeuvre manifests a wide array of influences from literature and the visual arts, was the primary curatorial concern of the 2001 exhibition *Hitchcock and Art* at the Centre Pompidou in Paris.[3] The exhibition focused on the intuitive constellations of images, objects and situations that unforgettably define Hitchcock's films. It was designed so that the gallery visitor could establish a familiar metonymic system of the many different moments and motifs that are inventively repeated throughout Hitchcock's exhilarating and vivid oeuvre. Therefore *Hitchcock and Art* amounts to a form of film criticism, but as Geoffrey O'Brien states, that criticism is based not so much on verbal analysis as on images and objects, in the way Godard discussed in *Histoire(s) du Cinema*.[4] All of us are familiar with the glass of milk from *Suspicion*, the rope from *Rope*, the set of keys from *Notorious*, the necklace from *Vertigo*, the broken eyeglasses from *The Birds* and so forth. The exhibition, in fact, allows the visitor to construct links between the objects themselves, rather than to interpret the narrative machinery of death, disquiet and suspense that characterise Hitchcock's cinema. Overall, *Hitchcock and Art* is an open-ended immersive exercise in construction rather than interpretation.

What is interesting to observe is how the exhibition itself illuminates the pictorial importance of Hitchcock's earlier films—*The Ring*, *The Skin Game* and *Number Seventeen*, and others—in shaping the iconographic look of the filmmaker's later works. More important, however, is the legacy of the double in Hitchcock's cinema: the visitor is aware of watching and being caught up in the visual and narrative sophistication of his cinema and its marked story logic of inexorability, and also aware that there is another film embedded in the more outward and conscious one—a film of enduring strange and hypnotic images of power. In this context, *Hitchcock and Art* becomes (as O'Brien suggests) an intriguing comment on the hidden powers of Hitchcock's art, which reside in its equal concern with concealing and with showing.[5]

Further, the exhibition vividly underlines how Hitchcock's scenographic art is indebted to influences, legacies and inspirations from the visual arts from the past two centuries. And in Hitchcock's work, high art is not separated from fashion design nor magazine illustration.

Hitchcock was an admirer of painters such as Georges Rouault, Paul Klee, Raoul Dufy, Walter Sickert and Maurice de Vlaminck, amongst others. He and his wife Alma started to collect paintings around 1944, the year he collaborated with Salvador Dali to produce *Spellbound*: they collected paintings by Fauvists and Cubists, including Dufy, Klee, Rouault and Maurice Utrillo. They also collected graphic artworks by Claude Guaraches, nudes by Henri Gaudier-Brzeska and drawings by Marie Laurencin.

Hitchcock saw himself as a master artisan or craftsman rather than as an artist. He firmly believed that cinema was the 20th century's most innovative art form, but he regarded himself as a commercial filmmaker of highly polished mass entertainments. Craft before art was Hitchcock's cardinal belief as a filmmaker. Despite the unbridled enthusiasm of the *Cahiers du cinéma* group of critics (Jean-Luc Godard, François Truffaut, Jacques Rivette, Claude Chabrol & Eric Rohmer) for Hitchcock—which was in radical contrast to the qualified respect Andre Bazin had for the director—Hitchcock found the comparison with artists flattering, but preferred to see himself as a craftsman of technical virtuosity.

One of the persistent myths of Hitchcock's screen art is the one dealing with his obsessive concern to have his films completely storyboarded, so that the direction of them could be achieved even if he was asleep. Hitchcock's pre-production approach to his films did rely significantly on storyboards, but there was (when needed) always room for chance and improvisation in his filmmaking. This view of Hitchcock's creative and work methods has been recently persuasively argued by Bill Krohn's absorbing book on the director at work.[6] Importantly, Hitchcock always had pencil and paper at hand to visually present his ideas to his collaborators, composing his films, characters, emotions and settings as a painter would. In fact, the modernist notion of Hitchcock in control of his universe was ironically criticised by Godard when he dubbed him, in Chapter 4A of his *Histoire(s) du Cinema*, 'THE ARTIST'.[7]

From the beginning, Hitchcock's cinema consisted of a complex amalgam of American and English elements; this mixture continued throughout the filmmaker's career. So the prevailing characterisation of Hitchcock's oeuvre into two distinct periods—his 'English' and later his 'American' films—is, at best, simplistic and problematic. Although Hitchcock's worldview was quintessentially English and lower middle-class, his actual experience of the art form, in terms of working in the industry and as a spectator, was with American films. Hitchcock wanted, as Peter Wollen has recently stated, to combine his English values with a professionalism that belonged to the American cinema.[8] For him, the three main significant requisites for the cinema—finance, technology and professionalism—were abundantly evident in Los Angeles. In essence, then, Hitchcock Americanised himself professionally in London, and then took his Englishness with him to America.

But it was in England that Hitchcock acquired his interest in modern art, his willingness to experiment and his enthusiasm for new techniques. Ironically, it was through his social superiors, such as Adrian Brunel and Ivor Montague at the London Film Society, that Hitchcock found this enthusiasm for experimentation. This, in Wollen's words:

> led him towards the dream sequences in *Spellbound* and *Vertigo*, the rolling camera in *Rope*, the virtuoso montage in *Psycho*, the use of the Kuleshov Effect in *Rear Window*, the electronic soundtrack in *The Birds*, and the unachieved collaboration with Len Lye on *The Secret Agent*.[9]

Given the vast and ever-expanding literature on Hitchcock, the many different constructed Hitchcocks—Hitchcock, the moralist; Hitchcock, the modernist-formalist; Hitchcock, the aesthete; Hitchcock, the postmodernist, etc.—how do we locate him, to echo Slavoj Žižek, with reference to Fredric Jameson's triadic formulation (realism–modernism–postmodernism) of cinema history?[10] If cinema is the 20th century's paradigmatic art form, is Hitchcock one of its greatest artists? For Žižek, Hitchcock paradoxically incarnates all three categories of the Jameson triad, and for Gilles Deleuze, Hitchcock, through framing, camera movement and montage, represents, in the tradition of English empiricism, 'the filmmaker of relations' par excellence, the last of the classic movement—image directors (paraphrasing Deleuze) and 'the first of the moderns'.[11]

In any attempt to assess Hitchcock's achievement as a filmmaker, the intricate relationship between both the artist and the meticulously self-staged persona (the droll, dead-pan English observer of human foibles), and his oeuvre and its legacy to contemporary visual arts, we need to contextualise Hitchcock's art within the larger cultural, economic and political forces that shaped it. Hitchcock's American films not only testify to the filmmaker's own ironic encounter with American cultural life and its diverse public spaces, popular cultural and literary narratives, and its cultural and ideological tensions and textures, as Jonathan Freedman and Richard Millington have recently argued; his films clearly suggest that the filmmaker had a supple and adroït understanding of cinema as a major modernist cultural form of visual representation, and of its key role in reconfiguring the cultural, social and emotional life in the American public sphere.[12] Hitchcock's playful and self-reflexive awareness of cinema's mutating imbrication in the entertainment industry (à la Horkheimer and Adorno) suggests that he instinctively understood Leo Charney and Vanessa Schwartz's following observation:

> Cinema ... must not be conceived as simply an outgrowth of such forms as melodramatic theater, social narrative, and the nineteenth-century realistic novel ... Nor can technological histories sufficiently explain the emergence of cinema. Rather, cinema must be understood as a vital component of a broader culture of modern life which encompasses political, social, economic, and cultural transformations.[13]

Like Luis Buñuel and Fritz Lang, Hitchcock's career was closely tied up with the history of the cinema. Hitchcock's birth coincided with the birth of cinema as a mass medium of audiovisual entertainment. Hitchcock and his canon fascinated generations of film spectators because they came to signify the innovative aesthetic and technical possibilities of the cinema medium itself. No one else had such a profound reputation for high-art filmmaking coupled with huge mass media popularity. To be sure, Hitchcock became a household celebrity, his name transformed into an adjective—we speak of a 'Hitchcockian' cinema, or of life itself having its absurd and suspenseful 'Hitchcockian' moments, etc. His witty cameo appearances in his own films ('Hitchcock's signature system', as Raymond Bellour once called it), the reflexive ironic commentaries that he used in their advertising campaigns, and the waggish introductions to his own television programs all contributed to Hitchcock's own commodification as one of cinema's most recognisable popular figures.[14] The François Truffaut interview book (in collaboration with Helen G. Scott) with Hitchcock in 1966 also played a vital role in promoting the director's public authorial identity.[15] Hitchcock was seen as the canny insider/outsider, the chameleon trickster, the man who knew how to cultivate himself as the exiled Englishman serving tea in Hollywood amongst the many displaced émigré European filmmakers, writers and intellectuals, playing the detached dandy aesthete observer of American mass culture with calculated precision and delight.

Elsaesser's persuasive view should be mentioned in this context. He saw Hitchcock as a conservative dandy surrealist, whose own little-known private life and exceptional highly visible public persona, concerned with form for form's sake and ritualistically making no concessions to nature or to chance, created a paradoxical form of 'dandyism of sobriety' that sought complete professional perfection and effortless ease at the same time.[16] Hitchcock's inordinately controlled art of surface, irony, wit and metonymy is predicated on the filmmaker's post-symbolist desire to make life imitate art. Hitchcock as the roguish aesthete–dandy whose films and persona are preoccupied with dizzying formal structure, repetition and rhymes (the Magritte-looking suited Hitchcock always booked the same hotel room whenever travelling, year in, year out) shaped character identity and relationships as an expression of effect and surface. Hitchcock's cult of artifice, surface and unseriousness, and its attendant clever self-definition of the filmmaker as a unique combination of the dandy, the rogue and the mountebank, Elsaesser eloquently argues, emanates from a deep-seated working-class English Catholic moral stance and an intimate familiarity with the writings of Charles Baudelaire, Gustave Flaubert, Edgar Allen Poe and Oscar Wilde.[17] Moreover, Hitchcock's realisation that the profundity of cinema resides in its surface means that, as Bellour's insightful analyses of Hitchcock's cinema attests, in the way Hitchcock looked at segmentation, the subtle interplay that arises from the musical precision with which Hitchcock obsessively controlled the direction of the gaze, the camera's mobility and the size of the shot, he saw himself as a composer of cinema.[18]

Hitchcock acts as an indispensable totemic figure in the popular imagination, someone who straddled both art and film in many dynamic and interesting ways. Notwithstanding Hitchcock's dramaturgical and sophisticated visual understanding of cinema as an art form of popular storytelling, an understanding that embraces avant-garde cinema (including expressionist and surreal cinema), painting, photography, literature and theatre, he also had an innovative grasp of the film apparatus as an interactive dream machine that has shaped the seminal contours of our lives. Hitchcock's profound expressionist visual and absurdist verbal wit originate in his early training as a graphic artist and his masterly self-conscious exploration of narrative structure as a source of meaning. The director's path-breaking experimentation with the form of narrative is evident in his influence over filmmakers such as Michelangelo Antonioni, Brian De Palma, Francois Truffaut, Claude Chabrol, David Cronenberg, Stanley Kubrick and Alain Resnais. Hitchcock is one of the artists of the 20th century: he showed us that mainstream films could also be highly individual works of art. In a word, Hitchcock's deftly crafted parables about love, death, loss and obsession are predicated on Eisensteinian montage as much as they are on surrealism, expressionism and existential black humour (Kafka/Sartre).

The filmmaker's quest for 'pure cinema' (René Clair/Jean Epstein), in radical contrast to what is possible in drama and literature, meant for him the painstaking creative adventure of constructing the architecture of a movie—frame by frame—as a means of producing the desired emotional response from an audience. In other words, he aimed to produce cinematic meaning through the purely visual rather than the literary. Hitchcock, in collaboration with his screenwriters, always 'wrote' his movies with the camera in mind. Not that Hitchcock actually wrote his scripts, as Larry Gross reminds us; it is rather that through intervention, dialogue, instruction and invention, Hitchcock knew exactly where to place his 'self-conscious, self-mocking' (Freedman & Millington) camera.[19] In this sense, in the context of Alexandre Astruc's idea of a highly personal '*camera-stylo*' cinema, Hitchcock was one of the seminal auteurs of modern cinema. Hitchcock claimed that screenwriting was the most significant part of filmmaking, for him. He had an organic notion of filmmaking which relied on the visual and the literary elements of a movie being designed as a total, dynamic, interactive system.

Some commentators—Camille Paglia, Chris Marker and Peter Wollen, among others—have described Hitchcock as a surrealist, and it this important (but not sufficiently examined) facet of his cinema which I look now at in terms of *Vertigo* and its characteristic 'vertigo of time' aesthetic of self-referentiality.[20] *Vertigo*, as a detective/ghost story of the fantastic and the uncanny, epitomises Hitchcock's 'closet' surrealism. It is based on Boileau-Narcejac's *amour fou* novella, aptly named *The Living and the Dead*, which was written with Hitchcock in mind, and features the author's interests in Edgar Allen Poe and the surrealists. As an enigmatic 'text of limits' of delirium, psychosis and perversion, the film incorporates Hitchcock's similar interests in Poe, surrealism and tales of the uncanny.[21] *Vertigo* is arguably Hitchcock's most personal film, and is, as Wollen reminds us, not only the director's own visual encyclopaedia of psychopathology, but transcends its detective/suspense configurations to become a haunting mystery tale of the fantastic. Hitchcock, despite his household reputation as a 'master of suspense', was more accurately a master of the fantastic. Hitchcock's cinema is therefore close (temperamentally speaking) to Luis Buñuel's, in that both oeuvres share, as Robert Stam once pointed out, similar 'subterranean analogies'—located in their interest in authority and revolt, desire and the law, the rational and the irrational.[22]

Before we proceed to discuss these two exhibitions, it is apt at this point to say a few words about the relatively unexamined rich terrain between art and cinema. The recent proliferation of moving analog and digital images in the museum is a phenomenon whose genealogy goes back over 100 years or so. To think that art's embrace of cinema is a very new thing is to be mistaken. The two forms of cultural reproduction have been highly intertwined with each other since the 1920s, when Max Reinhardt's expressionist theatre influenced the films of Fritz Lang, F.W. Murnau and other prominent Weimar filmmakers. And we should not overlook the important German abstract filmmakers such as Viktor Eggeling, Oskar Fischinger, Hans Richter and Walter Ruttmann, whose abstract films drew upon painting, graphics, drawing, music and the synaesthetic ideas manifested in Kandinsky's *On the Spiritual in Art*.

Since the historical avant-garde and the Bauhaus, art and cinema have been interacting in many different historical contexts (Hollywood cinema, Joseph Cornell, Weegee, Black Mountain College, Fluxus, French New Wave, Warhol, 1960s experimental cinema, Richard Hamilton), and with different blurring crossover concerns and effects for filmmakers and artists. This meandering and complex history of the fusion taking place between art and cinema is comprehensively documented in the Los Angeles Museum of Contemporary Art's aptly named 1996 show *Hall of Mirrors: Art and Film*. This important thematic benchmark exhibition, like other similar-minded exhibitions staged in England in the same year, including *Spellbound* and *Scream and Scream Again*, attests to the diverse interactions of art and cinema and how artists and filmmakers are concerned with the critical question: What is—or was—cinema? This is particularly evident in the *Hall of Mirrors* exhibition (with its accompanying impressive catalogue), where diverse artists, including Andy Warhol, Cindy Sherman (who features in the *Notorious* show), Weegee and Salvador Dali, mingle with filmmakers such as Godard, Orson Welles, Hitchcock and Antonioni in today's expanding enterprise of colliding the cinema's dynamic images and sounds with the meditative character of traditional visual art's static imagery.[23] All these figures, who are rapidly becoming canonised in these art/cinema exhibitions and related symposia, are fundamentally posing questions concerning cinema's colossal hold on 20th century culture and cinema's 'death' and its subsequent fragmentation.

Further, these exhibitions persuasively indicate how the explosion of new media in the last 20 years is compelling artists not only to use installations, video projection and multimedia art to go beyond film, video and electronic media as an expansion of painting and sculpture (echoing one of the more essential objectives of avant-garde cinema), but also to explore these media in their own right and thereby encounter the many fascinating complexities of the uncharted intersections between art and cinema.

Let us now return to our two MCA exhibitions and examine their aesthetic, cultural and thematic merits. Both exhibitions focus on how Hitchcock's art has resulted in many of us seeing the world through his camera. Hitchcock's ability to generate landscape as real and unreal at the same time has dramatically altered our basic perception of reality. This is vividly registered in Chris Marker's extraordinary 1982 essay film *Sunless*, which is on show in *Notorious*, and includes sequences of San Francisco through Hitchcock's eyes. It is a city, according to Marker's fictional narrator, defined according to Hitchcock's *Vertigo* (1958); a city converted into an unsettling dreamscape and then recouped by Marker as fact. This excavation of Hitchcock's surreal poetry of transforming cityscapes into dreamscapes and use of cinema to delve deep into the film/gallery spectator's own voyeurism and obsessions is markedly evident in a number of works in the *Notorious* exhibition.

Cindy Bernard's luminous installation, *Location Proposal No. 2* (1997–99), has digitised the redwood forest sequence in *Vertigo*. This moving moment in Hitchcock's film, which looks at an ancient redwood tree stump and its rings as an index of time, memory and measurement, evokes Cabrera Infante's description of *Vertigo* as 'the first great surrealist film'.[24] As we circumnavigate Bernard's three suspended digitised screens, on which are shown carefully recreated shots from this specific sequence in the film, we are gaining a new 'walk-through' perspective on Hitchcock's forest. The artificial aura of Bernard's digitised forest images allude to the highly artificial other-worldly spaces and travels of Hitchcock's cinema, and its multifaceted representation of the disturbed vertiginous state of mind of his obsessive characters.

Walking through the *Notorious* exhibition is a fairly enthralling experience if you are especially concerned with art, cinema, *flânerie*, neurosis and spectatorship and their relevance to Hitchcock's incandescent modernist cinema. This has a double significance when you enter David Reed's eerie installation, *Scottie's Bedroom* (1994), and discover Jimmy Stewart's *Vertigo* character in Scottie's bedroom, with its rumpled bed sheets, bathrobe, lamp and a TV set playing *Vertigo*. Reed has carefully replaced the generic painting (in the film) that stood over the bed Judy (Kim Novak) slept in after she was rescued by Scottie from the cold waters of San Francisco Bay under the Golden Gate Bridge with one of his own paintings. Although bedroom installations by the 1980s became an international art phenomenon, Reed's installation is refreshingly evocative.

As is Victor Burgin's iconographic black and white photo installation *The Bridge* (1984), with its non-didactic Freudian reading of *Vertigo* as an expression of Hitchcock's characteristic treatment of objects, inhibitions, symbols and obsessions, and the open-ended way the film—with its swirling geometric cubist credit images designed by the late underrated Saul Bass and a dream sequence featuring a pulsating coloured light bathed over a severed head hurtling towards us by painter John Ferren—is constructed as narrative. Burgin's work, which neatly shares certain pictorial elements with John Baldessari's 1999 deconstructive narrative-based works *Telrad Series: To Be A* and *Telrad Series: What Was Seen*, shadows the San Francisco of the ghostly roaming figure of Madeline (Kim Novak), with its allusions to Dante and Pre-Raphaelite art, and is a gentle surprise when encountered in the flesh (so to speak) in the wake of our 'textbook' familiarity with it.

Several exhibits were specifically commissioned for the show (a growing curatorial trend abroad, but lamentably absent locally) and displayed one of the prevailing tropes of the hybrid experimentation that is occurring today between art and cinema and can be traced back to structural cinema: the idea of art looped for exhibition thanks to film and computer/video technology. Christoph Girardet and Matthias Müller's *The Phoenix Tapes Nos 1–6* (1999) is a subtle series of videotapes that meticulously examine Hitchcock's art and life by locating certain echoes and contrasts in particular shots and sequences from his movies. Hitchcock's problematic characterisation of women—the mother is an evil villain alarmingly often—the fragmentary depiction of the body and objects and architecture and space related to paranoia are all looked at in these videotapes. In their arresting *Necrologue* video, we encounter a strange, hybrid, slowed-down image of Ingrid Bergman's face from the film *Under Capricorn* (1949), following the barely visible journey of a tear rolling down her face. This image evokes a certain moment in Marker's sublime sci-fi meditation *La Jetée* (1964), where we encounter the only moving film part in a work made entirely of black and white photographs: the reflexive act of a female winking at the spectator.

Another notable loop work is Stan Douglas's immersive black and white film installation *Subject to a Film: Marnie* (1989), which atmospherically reconstructs a sequence featuring Marnie (Tippi Hedren) committing a robbery in an abandoned office building, and is installed in a dark cavernous room. Douglas has recreated the original Hitchcock sequence, but this time it is in silence, with different camera movements, and all we hear is the sound of the film being fed through the film projector.

Atom Egoyan's chilling video *Evidence* (1999) is an edited tape of scenes from his recent Hitchcockian thriller *Felicia's Journey* (1999) which show a serial killer filming his intended female victims in his car, talking about their lives. In a critical sense, it is a mobile homage to Michael Powell's *film maudit* classic *Peeping Tom* (1960). Pierre Huyghe's photo and film installation *Remake* (1995) is a low-budget reconstructed look at Hitchcock's *Rear Window* (1954), and deals with how we account for the past and try to visually describe it. Finally, Douglas Gordon's suspended video screen slow motion riff *24 Hour Psycho* (1993), a work which has visited our shores before, replays a video copy of Hitchcock's film at two frames per second. Its 'yBa' (Young British Art) aesthetic of focusing on image and event—here by obsessively caressing objects, glances, facial tics, and shadows in Norman Bates's disturbed world—provides a stark contrast to Gordon's two playful conceptual 'stamp art' pieces, *Airmail White Portrait* and *Surface Mail White Portrait*, both made in 1999, which feature US stamps of Hitchcock released in that year.

Notorious, like any other art/cinema exhibition, poses numerous questions about the difficulties of showing cinema (a kinetic light–time–space art form) in an art museum where static art is the curatorial norm. As Peter Wollen has observed, there is a substantial essentialising tendency to believe that if cinema (in all its forms) is exhibited in a museum as a sculptural object or as an installation then, *ipso facto*, cinema has become a serious art, because visual art is assumed to be 'the touchstone of aesthetic authenticity'.[25]

Colless's *Moral Hallucination*, mercifully, does not suggest any of the more familiar shortcomings of such recent museological endeavours. The eleven Australian artists involved, including Dale Frank, Bill Henson, Rosemary Laing and Robyn Stacey, are represented by works that—according to Colless—are susceptible, under the right circumstances, to being possessed by Hitchcock as hallucinatory after-images. In a critical sense, Colless's curatorial rationale was to select exhibits that allude to Hitchcockian evil as an aesthetics of psychosis. Hence, artists' perennial complicit interests in sadism, evil, voyeurism and necrophilia in Hitchcock's movies and their many references to art, photography, painting and theatre. If art (including cinema) is, as Colless cogently argues, a perfect crime, a hallucinatory lie, a fabulation, then Hitchcock seduces us into immersing ourselves in his evil art.

Colless has arranged the various exhibits in a seance setting in order to channel Hitchcock's phantasmic presence—much as the different time-capsule rooms in Fritz Lang's *Secret Beyond the Door* (1948) were designed to produce certain psychotic reactions in humans. There are three rooms that classify the exhibition: 'Jack Ruby', a surreal shadowy zone, 'Syrup', a garish neon-lit atmosphere, and finally 'Vogue', the *noir* flare of a camera flash. Hitchcock's presence, his evil, is therefore 'felt' everywhere in the world's banal materiality, seducing us in deep and ambiguous ways.

Anne Wallace's mesmerising *tableau vivant*-styled paintings, *The Next Room 1* (1999), *The Next Room 2* (1999) and *One Second* (1999), suggest the pervasive menacing atmosphere of sexual intrigue and domestic masochism embedded in the ordinary everyday spaces of our lives—which Hitchcock so cleverly represents in his dark comedic oeuvre. Louise Hearman's powerfully intense exhibits, especially *Untitled # 586* (1997), representing a white cat's head suspended in the void, clearly project a supernatural dread worthy of Poe's pen. Sean Bacon's cage-like interactive installation *CU-See-ME* (1998), with its ability to manipulate Scottie's scopic wheelchair from *Rear Window* and catapult it into the webcam aesthetics of the Internet, is one of the exhibition's more compelling works.

The low-budget sampled 'grudge' video installation of movie background noise and video footage by Matt Warren, *Residual Memory* (1999), conjures a 'conspiratorial' Pynchonian collage of John

F. Kennedy's and Lee Harvey Oswald's assassinations and Jack Ruby's role in this seemingly endless narrative of paranoia with its Hitchcockian undertones. Laing's Virilio-inspired enigmatic photograph greenwork *TL#8* (1995), with its hovering, flying saucer-like apparition above an empty aerodrome runway contrasts quite effectively with Henson's cinematic photo narrative of twilight desire and despair amongst fated young suburban youngsters in his series *Untitled* (1997–98). And Stacy's appealing spectral photograph *The Spot* (1996), with its abstract human figure looking like a crossover between an 18th century costumed fancy dress party participant and a stylised cyborg, suggests poetic mystery.

In conclusion, Colless's elliptical approach to curating a show around Hitchcock and contemporary Australian art has been successful in opening up new and stimulating non-categorical perspectives on a difficult curatorial theme. As we have seen, Hitchcock's cinema was, as the Pompidou exhibition *Hitchcock and Art* demonstrated, inflected by visual artists such as Edvard Munch, Paul Klee, Aubrey Beardsley, Giorgio de Chirico, Edward Hopper and René Magritte, and lesser figures such as Alberto Martini, Ralston Crawford, Carel Willink and many others. And it was also significantly connected to the work of writers such as John Buchan, Daphne du Maurier, Patricia Highsmith and Robert Bloch. Hitchcock was an artist in spite of himself—he preferred to be regarded as a master craftsman—and, in fact, embodied the cinema. Art and cinema and their complex interactions, concerns and effects have become a highly fecund area for curatorial and critical investigation. Despite the several exhibitions held to date, and their merits and limits, this area deserves substantial long-term and self-critical attention. The MCA's *Hitchcock: Art, Cinema and ... Suspense* exhibition is a rewarding starting point in this creative aesthetic and cultural adventure. The catalogue for the *Notorious* show has Hitchcock holding a torch in a movie theatre on its title page—he is presented to the reader side-on. It is a surreal image, signalling to us that art and cinema are best discussed in an oblique, off-centre manner.

NOTES

1   See Thomas Elsaesser, 'Rivette and the end of cinema', *Sight and Sound*, 1, 1992, pp. 20–23.

2   Edward Colless, 'Moral hallucination channelling Hitchcock', in *Hitchcock: Art, Cinema and ... Suspense Visitors Guide*, Museum of Contemporary Art, Sydney 1999.

3   See Dominique Païni & Guy Cogeval (eds), *Hitchcock and Art*, The Montreal Museum of Fine Arts Montreal, [Mazzotta, Milan], 2001.

4   Geoffrey O'Brien, 'Hitchcock: the hidden power', in O'Brien, *Castaways of the Image Planet*, Counterpoint, Washington DC, 2002, pp. 240–48.

5   ibid., p. 246.

6   Bill Krohn, *Hitchcock at Work*, Phaidon Press, London, 2000.

7   See Jacques Aumont, 'Paradoxical and innocent', in Païni & Cogeval, 2001, p. 79.

8   Peter Wollen, 'Hitch: A tale of two cities (London and Los Angeles)', in Richard Allen & Sam Ishii-Gonzales (eds), *Hitchcock*, Routledge, London, 2004, pp. 15–21.

9   ibid., p. 16.

10   Slavoj Žižek (ed.), *Everything You Always Wanted to Know about Lacan (But Were Afraid to Ask Hitchcock)*, Verso, London, 1992, p. 2.

11   Gilles Deleuze, 'On the movement-image', in *Gilles Deleuze, Negotiations*, Columbia University Press, New York, 1995, p. 55.

12   Jonathan Freedman & Richard Millington (eds), 'Introduction', in Freedman & Millington (eds), *Hitchcock's America*, Oxford University Press, New York, 1999, pp. 3–14.

13   Cited in Freedman & Millington, p. 8.

14   ibid., p. 7.

15   François Truffaut, (with the collaboration of Helen G. Scott), *Hitchcock* (revised edition), Simon & Schuster, New York, 1984.

16   Thomas Elsaesser, 'The dandy in Hitchcock', in Richard Allen & Sam Ishii-Gonzales (eds), *Alfred Hitchcock: Centenary Essays*, British Film Publishing, London, 1999, pp. 3–13.

17   Elsaesser, in Allen & Ishii-Gonzales 1999, passim.

18   For Raymond Bellour's influential work on Hitchcock, see 'Le blocage symbolique', *Communications*, 23, 1975, pp. 235–50. For his analysis of *Marnie*, see 'Hitchcock, the enunciator', *Camera Obscura*, 2, 1977, pp. 66–87. And for Bellour's analysis of *Psycho*, see 'Psychosis, neurosis, perversion', *Camera Obscura*, 3–4, 1979, pp. 66–103. On Hitchcock's personal analogy of the filmmaker as a musician, see Peter Wollen, '*Rope*: three hypotheses', in Allen & Ishii-Gonzales, 1999, pp. 80–81 and Nathalie Bondil-Poupard, 'Alfred Hitchcock: an artist in spite of himself', in Païni & Cogeval, pp. 188–89.

19   Larry Gross, 'Parallel lines', in *Hitchcock Sight and Sound* [booklet], British Film Institute, London, 1999, pp. 39–40. See also Freedman & Millington 1999, p. 3.

20   See Camille Paglia, *The Birds*, British Film Institute, London,1998 ; Chris Marker, 'A free replay (notes on *Vertigo*)', in John Boorman & Walter Donohue (eds), *Projections 4 1/2*, Faber & Faber (in association with Positif), London, 1995; Peter Wollen, 'Compulsion', *Sight and Sound*, New Series 7, April 1997, pp. 14–18.

21   See Katie Trumpener, '"Fragments of the mirror"', in Walter Raubicheck & Walter Srebnick (eds) *Hitchcock's Rereleased Films*, Wayne State University Press, Detroit, 1991, p. 187.

22   Robert Stam , 'Hitchcock and Buñuel', in Raubicheck & Srebnick, pp. 116–145.

23   Russell Ferguson (ed.), *Art and Film Since 1945: Hall of Mirrors*, The Museum of Contemporary Art, Los Angeles/ The Monacelli Press, New York, 1996.

24   Guillermo Cabrera Infante is quoted by Marker, in Boorman & Donohue, p. 125

25   Peter Wollen, 'Together', *Sight and Sound*, vol. 6, no. 1, 1996, pp. 30–34.

Section 2

Video art: from the margins to the mainstream

Video is not just a technique, it's a state of mind, a way of seeing images in the future perfect tense.

Serge Daney

Video was born in the utopian moment of the 1960s, that decade of artistic, cultural and socio-political turbulence in the first world. A decade that witnessed a sustained questioning of modernism in the form of conceptual art, minimalism, performance, experimental film, dance, earth art and music, etc. All these art forms concretised a common interest in the dematerialisation of the modernist art object—particularly painting and sculpture. Video art developed in this multifaceted context as a medium of techno-creativity, and expressed itself in a variety of different genres or forms, including documentary, essay video, feminist, installation, landscape, literary/new narrative, performance, and scratch, amongst other genres.

Back in the 1960s and 1970s, video was also known as 'experimental video' and, in some other contexts, as artists' videos or videotapes, suggesting that artists utilised the then-new Portapak video technology to create their artworks. Truth be told, it was not just visual artists who deployed the medium for their creative ends. Video emerged as a speculative, cross-disciplinary collage art form that reflected the wide background from which these video artists emerged: architecture, film, dance, literature, music, theatre, painting, etc.

Video, as a highly intertextual medium, is a paradoxical art form, because it manifests modernist and postmodernist features which can be traced back to the principal aesthetic, conceptual and visual concerns of the avant-garde movements of early 20th century art. Back in the 1960s, video's imagistic and temporal structures challenged our cultural expectations and perceptual habits in terms of spectatorship.[1] Back then, video questioned the ideological myths of television— which was daily broadcasting the horrors of the Vietnam

War to the households of middle America —and, in general, the 'one-dimensional' society (Herbert Marcuse) that was evident throughout the Western world.[2]

Video's image language of collage intertextuality characterises it, in Katherine Dieckmann's fitting phrase, as a 'medium in suspension', whose valorisation of art as a synthesised process of audiovisual information emanates from Duchamp's aesthetic of delay, response and stasis as much as it does from the Bauhaus experiments of the 1920s, Fluxus, machine art, kineticism, and the 'death of modernism' in the late 1960s and early 1970s.[3] Thus video's intertextual and stylistic elasticity as a medium of electronic image-making critiqued, over the years, the essential curatorial and theoretical parameters of high art discourse as defined by traditional art history and Greenbergian formalism. Video art's entry into 'the white cube' space of the gallery (Brian O'Doherty) and museum world took over three decades to achieve, and it was primarily through its installation and sculptural forms that it received international and local curatorial recognition.

In the last decade, video's ubiquitous presence in the art gallery has taken expression in the form of moving image installations and projections that are concerned with the increasing convergence between art and film.[4] Very rarely were videotapes welcome as part of its overall legitimisation process in the gallery/museum world. In the 1970s and 1980s video had already, in its relatively short but complex history, been a troubling presence in the high art gallery and museum world.

Video emerged as a ubiquitous medium due to a variety of intricate aesthetic, cultural, historical and technological factors. One of the main reasons video became more accepted within the broader parameters of new art history and theory, and as a gallery/museum object, is that it was first curated and presented in the numerous film, video and media festivals that were established in the 1980s and 1990s throughout Europe, Canada, the United States and Latin America. One cannot ignore how influential these festivals proved to be for the wider acceptance of video as an art form.[5]

It was only in these festival sites, certain art galleries and artist-run spaces that video as an art form found critical and curatorial acceptance: catalogue essays, manifestos, certain visual art journals and a few anthologies were all that existed back then in terms of critical/theoretical writing on the subject. This changed in the 1990s, when there was an encouraging increase in the number of books, journal/periodical articles and exhibition catalogue essays on video being published.[6]

Note I say 'video', because even by the 1990s the term 'video art' was not so readily used in the art world (except by the converted amongst us) or in everyday life. And indeed, with the proliferation of film, video and media festivals during that decade, in tandem with a similar explosion of international art biennales and art fairs, only a few artists, critics and viewers were aware of the medium's artistic heritage in terms of what it was called as an art form. The term 'video art' was and is still deployed by anyone who has witnessed its evolution since the 1960s and 1970s as a time-based medium.

In a significant way, the tendency amongst the older generation of video artists, curators and viewers to still use the term 'video art', bearing in mind the monumental aesthetic, cultural and historical shifts taking place with the moving image arts today, represents a critical contestation of the canonising impulses evident in the various emerging accounts of video and its dynamic elaborate contextualisation with film, TV, photography and computers.

Video art from the 1960s until the 1980s focused primarily on the monitor. The central significance of the monitor in video art can be traced back to 1959, when the late Nam June Paik and Wolf Vostell utilised modified and partly demolished television sets in their Fluxus-inspired 'happenings', signalling a radical shift of television from basically home entertainment to gallery artefact, as Catherine Elwes observes.[7] It was in the mid-1960s that the monitor was used as an adapted television set that could display an electronic signal from a camera or a video player, allowing the artist, as Elwes puts it, 'to use the flickering "fourth wall" as a sculptural object as well as a monitor to artistic activity and creative imagination'.[8]

Today, living in a 'post-medium world' (in which, according to Rosalind Krauss, neither art nor artist can any longer be defined in terms of media-specificity), video has made a fundamental flight from the monitor, from the traditional view of the medium as a sculptural object; the ubiquitous contemporary video projector is now the liberator of the video image. In other words, the video image is no longer restricted to the monitor; it can now be projected as film in new gallery/ museum contexts, onto any objects, into space, etc. Video has moved on, as Elwes correctly notes, towards the cinematic, and towards 1970s conceptualism's rejection of the physical object of art.[9]

The evolution of video art since the 1960s closely reflects the changing character of modern technology. In the beginning, to paraphrase Elwes, cameras and Portapaks were quite heavy and cumbersome, so fixed camera positions were favoured.[10] And before video editing became popular, videotapes tended to be long and 'durational'. As post-production technology became more affordable and sophisticated, colour, montage and image processing followed. Video projection became a popular reality in the 1990s, when it was cheap and the resolution was sharp enough for the video image to go beyond the monitor. By the 1970s and 1980s, many video artists were seeking new ways of extending the image beyond the sculptural confines of the monitor screen. Spreading the video image across several monitors became a popular solution to this problem. In due time the technology of the video wall became quite accessible for artists, who used it for their video installations and sculptures.

It is also significant to note that video replaced film for many artists towards the end of the 1960s, because it was less complicated technically and far easier to use. It fundamentally meant that artists could shoot works that were far longer in duration than film, without the complication of reel changes. Consequently, film and video, though both are time-based media, developed their own specific traditions, forms of distribution and presentation.

This leads us to the contemporary situation—for many artists, curators and spectators, the differences between the two are rapidly becoming of secondary importance, as Peter Wollen indicates, because of the development of digital technology as an editing tool.[11]

Clearly then, with the technological convergence that is occurring between video and film, and with the ubiquitous use of digital imaging techniques, the fundamental distinction between the two media has virtually disappeared. This has aesthetic, cultural and technological implications. It means that no matter what formats artists wish to deploy, their final creative work will invariably be digitally edited and displayed on a monitor or exhibited by a video projector. Nowadays, video projections and installations have become one of the dominant features of the contemporary art world.

Relatedly, in this context, one should also mention the popularity of plasma screens, on which video can be screened with the resolution of a hyperrealist painting. The Bill Viola exhibition at the National Gallery of Australia in 2005, *The Passions*, is a fitting and controversial example of how plasma screens have became central to Viola's acclaimed video art[12]

However, as we can all attest, with the huge technological improvements in the recording and projection of video, it is becoming progressively difficult to differentiate video from film. However, since the late 1980s in fact, artists started to describe their video works as film. Although there are artists who work only with film in their gallery practice, such as Tacita Dean, for example, there are many artists whose gallery and museum works exhibit what some have termed the 'cinematisation' of video.[13] Artists as varied as Mathew Barney, Robert Cahen, Isaac Julien, Michael Mazière and Shirin Neshat are exploring the moving image in terms of its cinematic heritage, while others are maintaining critical links to early video, televisual practices, video games, surveillance and the Internet, as Elwes puts it.[14]

So video artists working today are challenged by two outstanding questions: how does video art differentiate itself from cinema, and does where the artist exhibits his or her work (galleries, museums, art spaces versus movie theatres) mark the major distinction between cinema and video art? Never before, because of the intricate mutability and unpredictably of the moving image and its interconnections with visual art and video in particular, have we known less about these multifaceted aesthetic, cultural and technological issues.

Bellour's speculative commentary on the 1999 Venice Biennale's emphasis on the reconfiguration of classical cinema in video installations and projections suggests that through the eruption of television in the 1950s and the emergence of video art in the following two decades, and with the connection between television and computer, not only have our viewing experiences of the museum and the movie theatre became mixed with each other, but it is an extremely complex situation at the moment, and difficult to understand how video, television and computer installations are competing with cinema in various ways.[15] But as Bellour argues, celluloid cinema is being 'destroyed and redistributed' in a new installation/projection space, so that what is being exhibited is not exactly a film 'but the equivalent of a film', meaning that it 'is something relatively new'.[16]

Coming to terms with video art's evolving images, genres and sounds over the last three decades has always been a challenge— something that Bellour has constantly acknowledged in his critical writings—in terms of how relevant the traditional critical categories of modern art are in dealing with the transforming complexities of video and media art.

For Bellour, these new moving image and video installations and projections of the 1990s represent a new situation, one that can be best described as 'expanded cinema', which was championed by Gene Youngblood 30 years ago. Thanks to the rise of video and 'a new type of projection' through the medium in the 1970s, what we are presently witnessing is, according to Bellour, an extension of expanded cinema— and it is also now quite difficult, he says, for many reasons, 'to know what cinema exactly is'.[17]

Thus we are obliged, when encountering the kinetic, divergent mixes of media and presentation systems that make up today's installation and projection exhibitions, to be careful in how we theorise the multifaceted complexities and shifts of this emerging phenomenon. Rather than just repeating the familiar canonical names of art history in painting, sculpture, etc., it is far wiser to be attentive, as Bellour cautions us, to Michel Foucault's instructive clarion call to stick to 'the basic tasks of description'.[18] This reflects the realisation that it is more important now than ever before to value artworks in terms of their various mixes of different art forms. And to remember how video art history is always being rewritten and revised.

Further, we need to be mindful of how video, an electronic, digital medium, has become the essential medium for both the computer and television and, as Canadian artist Tom Sherman reminds us, the technical base of cinema.[19] However, for Sherman, it is crucial to distinguish film from video: video flows through all other media, and given its Fluxus background, it is no surprise that video connects new hybrid relationships between media and genres redefining the boundaries of artistic expression. Video is not inherently cinematic in nature, Sherman argues, despite its convergence with cinema, and he is therefore critical of artists, curators and writers who blithely regard video as film.

Video's complex cultural-historical and technological formations and its markedly elastic textual multiplicities oblige us to not subscribe to any distorted and dated concepts about the medium. Overall, video has had a tremendously fast-paced development since the 1960s, with the emergence of conceptual art, the counter-cultural revolution, minimalism and pop art.

Central to any elementary negotiation of video's historical trajectory is the prolific and innovative roles of Paik and Vostell in contributing to the medium's basic syntax and vocabulary. Yet we need to be doubly cautious, as Martha Rosler and Martha Geever, amongst others, have noted, especially when discussing Paik's videos, installations and performances, and certain historiographical accounts of Paikian video and video in general. Simply put, discussing Paik's oeuvre requires us to confront the enshrined mythic figure of Paik, which is often, to quote Rosler, 'at the head of virtually every history'.[20]

Thus to speak of video's past is to tackle one of its more urgent problems: how do we talk of the medium without a litany-like account of its historical 'facts' and canonic 'personalities'? We need to be aware of the numerous cultural, curatorial and historiographical issues relating to the problem of constructing (as Rosler argues) a *social* history of video and not use only the prevailing ideas of traditional art in order to legitimate the medium as an art form. In other words, we have to ask ourselves what exactly we do when we are constructing a history of video. Paul Ryan, in his Foucauldian account of the medium, has endeavoured to do such a thing from the point of view of a participant in video's evolving development, as it moves from a 'counter-cultural gesture to an art gesture'.[21] Ryan, like Rosler and others, speaks of the necessary task of defining a genealogical perspective on 'the fiction of video'.[22] Though Ryan's objective—to demonstrate video's failure to sustain its alternative TV/media ecology roots—is arguably somewhat one-sided, he does argue persuasively for the necessity to analyse video's emergence in the 1960s in terms of conflict, power and social change.

Video art as a counter-cultural practice was tamed by a number of significant factors, including the fact that television itself re-appropriated many of video's specific forms and effects, and the way the art gallery in the 1990s placed video art in the broader mainstream vocabulary of younger artists, who legitimised it as a medium within their larger portfolio of interests and talents. Indeed, as Elwes correctly observes, video indisputably played a large role in the expanding art of the 1990s, even though the majority of younger artists of the time did not specifically express a strong interest in video art's genres, practices and intrinsic properties as such.[23] Also, many of these artists showed scant interest in video's complex history by making passing reference only to certain male figures, such as Paik, Viola or Gary Hill.

In order to appreciate the continuities and discontinuities between video art, film and new media, it is important to ensure that video art does not become consigned to cultural nostalgia but is appreciated as an elaborate mutating art form that has contributed in many intricate and complex ways to the concepts, effects and direction of digital cinema. We need to remember that nowadays we speak of how cinema, the dominant art form of the last century, has become permeated by digital video. In other words, cinema has become a digital art form and its directors, from Jean-Luc Godard to Steven Spielberg and Mike Figgis, have become new media artists.

The centrality of video to contemporary art does not ipso facto indicate the success of the museum's film and video department, because it was inevitable that video and the new screen technologies would be absorbed into the mainstream. Hence the pervasive presence of artists such as Douglas Gordon, Matthew Barney, Doug Aitken and Pierre Huyghe, whose moving image projections and installations signify the critical aesthetic and technological success of digital video's intrinsic properties in relation to the more established art forms of drawing, sculpture and photography. These artists' cinematic installations represent an apotheosis of the multi-screen projections that have been with us since the 1960s.

Video art is an art form whose unique complex past needs to be understood in terms of its pluralistic generic contexts, history and effects. Further, and underlying the basic architecture and thematic sweep of this book, we need to value video art, alongside film and new media, as three art forms that have interacted and are continually interacting with each other in unpredictably complex and dynamic ways. One may argue, after Bellour, that these art forms—including photography and television—are contaminating each other, and thereby producing new anti-binary visual forms, visual forms that signify new nonalogical systems of representation, spatialisation and temporality that contest the logic of binarism that still characterises our expanding dynamic non-linear world.

We also need to appreciate that today it is more accurate to speak of the various camera-based art forms and technologies—16mm film, 35mm film, 70mm film, VHS tape, beta tape, digital beta tape, DV cam tape, etc.—representing the many different hybrid manifestations of the moving image. Therefore, studying 'film' means understanding that film itself has become part of the larger narrative of the moving image, and has become markedly heterogeneous in character. And in order to comprehend the mutant quality of film, it is critical that we negotiate, as artists, teachers and researchers, with the moving image in all its myriad manifestations, including video art. Noel Carroll's recent point that video and computer-generated imaging represent film media is quite apt in the current cultural landscape, and most significantly, his comment that 'film is not specifically a single distinctive physical medium, but an array or ensemble of media, some of recent invention, and some still not invented, whose stylistic potentials cannot be fixed by the film theorist now, since the film theorist has no crystal ball into the future' merits our immediate attention.[24] As Carroll goes on to argue, what we call film now is arguably a specific moment in the history of the moving image. Clearly, then, what matters is, to echo Carroll, 'the movement of history and the movement of the image'.[25] Video art is, and has been, a critical art form in the overall evolution of the movie image.

NOTES

1   It is hard to imagine how video art in the 1970s, 1980s and early 1990s was, generally speaking, regarded as a problematic art form and not worthy of critical scrutiny. For a succinct critical summary of past objections to video art being considered a legitimate art form, see Maureen Turim's early influential essay 'Video art: theory for a future', in E. Ann Kaplan (ed.), *Regarding Television*, University Publications of America, Los Angeles, 1983, pp. 130–37. Despite the popularity of video in the international contemporary art world, there is still a lingering scepticism in certain circles relating to video art's status as an art form.

2   Herbert Marcuse, *One-Dimensional Man*, Beacon, Boston, 1964.

3   Katherine Dieckmann, 'Electra myths: video, modernism, postmodernism,' *College Art Association Art Journal*, vol. 45 no. 3, fall 1985, pp. 195–203.

4   For a brief lucid discussion of the digital

cinematic installations and projections of the 1990s by noted artists such as Isaac Julien, Eija-Liisa Ahtila and Doug Aitken, amongst others, see Michael Rush, *New Media in Art*, [new edition], Thames & Hudson, London, 2005, pp. 196–201.

5   Video, film and media festivals have, on the whole, been very influential in giving aesthetic and cultural legitimacy to video art as an art form. Many video artists in the 1980s and 1990s exhibited their tapes and installations in such contexts despite their self-referential status as sites of exhibition. Many video festivals also, over the years, commissioned artists to create installations, tapes and performances. Certain artists made (and still make) a living on the international video festival circuit.

6   Prominent amongst these publications include Sean Cubitt, *Videography, Video Media as Art and Culture*, St. Martin's Press, New York, 1993; Doug Hall & Sally Jo Fifer (eds) , *Illuminating Video, an Essential Guide to Video Art,* Aperture/Bay Area Video Coalition, New York, 1990; Julia Knight (ed) *Diverse Practices,a Critical Reader on British Video Art*, John Libbey Media, Faculty of Humanities, University of Luton, Luton, 1996, among numerous others.

7   Catherine Elwes, *Video Art, a Guided Tour*, I.B. Tauris, London/New York, 2005, p. 141.

8   ibid.

9   Elwes is quoting Chrissie Iles's point, that the contemporary video projector liberated the video image from the standard monitor and this may be read as a move towards the cinematic and 1970s conceptualism. See Catherine Elwes, 'The big screen,' *Art Monthly*, no. 199, September 1996, p. 12.

10   ibid.

11   Peter Wollen, *Paris Hollywood: Writings on Film*, Verso, London/New York, 2002, p. 240.

12   Writing on Bill Viola's more recent plasma screen installations, Siegfried Zielinski wonders, 'Is an installation by Bill Viola media art or is it actually electronic painting, because it fits in the big museums so nicely?' See Zielinski, 'Time machines', in Annette W. Balkema & Henk Slager (eds), *Screen-Based Art*, Editions Rodopi B.V., Amsterdam/Atlanta GA, 2000, p. 173.

13   On the idea of the 'cinematisation' of video, see Rush 2005, p. 194.

14   Elwes 2005, p. 172.

15   See Raymond Bellour, 'Challenging cinema,' in Balkema & Slager, pp. 35–43.

16   ibid., p. 37.

17   ibid., p. 40.

18   Raymond Bellour, 'Battle of the images,' *Art Press*, no. 262, November 2000, p. 52.

19   See the following three texts by Tom Sherman: 'Video (intermedia)', 'Video just under forty' and 'Video not film' in *Canadian Art*, vol. 22, no. 1, 2005, pp. 56–58, pp. 58–60 and pp. 60–62 respectively. Thanks to Gary Pearson for drawing my attention to Sherman's essays.

20   See Martha Rosler's important essay, 'Video: shedding the utopian moment', in René Payant (ed.), *Video*, Artextes, Montreal, 1986, p. 248.

21   Paul Ryan, 'A genealogy of video', *Leonardo*, vol. 21, no. 1, 1988, pp. 39–44.

22   ibid., p. 44.

23   Elwes 2005, p. 160.

24   Noel Carroll, 'Forget the medium', in Balkema & Slager, p. 61.

25   ibid., p. 62.

Framing Australian video art

One of the objectives of this chapter is to examine in a speculative, non-anthropological manner the aesthetic, curatorial, historical and technological discourses that have been responsible for the shaping of video art in Australia since the 1970s.

It is important to say at the outset that this chapter is an endeavour to map out the more critical issues that confront anyone who wishes to engage in the writing of a historical account of the subject. In any given historiographical effort to delineate Australian video art over the last 30 odd years, it is critical to acknowledge the provisional nature of such a theoretical project because of the sheer pluralism that constitutes Australian video art.

From our vantage point today, we can see that (Australian) video art has shifted, over the last three decades, from being an avant-garde medium of representation-production located in the margins of our art world to now being at its centre. Indeed, video art's radical progression from its initial marginal status as a time-based art form to its present acceptance as one of the more established art forms in the local and international art worlds is a testament to the American artist John Baldessari's prediction that one day video would become as common as the pencil. That day is now. However, this shift in video art's status in the art world can be viewed from two diagonally opposed points of view that can be extrapolated from an interview that took place in 1993 between curator Regina Cornwell and artist Gary Hill, in which Hill took exception to an emerging belief—back then—among curators, critics and museum directors that video art had finally caught up with the art world.[1] For Hill, as a practitioner familiar with video art's complex histories, effects and genres, it was the reverse: the art world had caught up with the art form itself.

Nowadays, because of intricate aesthetic, cultural, funding and technological considerations, no one calls themselves 'video artists'. Twenty or 30 years ago, declaring yourself such a thing was an act of radical positioning in the art world. It spoke of being outside looking in, so to speak, creating video art as an articulation of utopian experimentation and a general 'counter-cultural' and anti-art historical gesture.[2] Again, for many reasons, video has now become the norm in the international art world of biennales, large-scale theme and survey shows and the like. However, lamentably, with this fundamental change in video art's status as a fine arts discourse in the international art world, certain problematic developments need to be addressed.

Although plenty of video work is shown in big international art shows, it is usually limited to an emerging international 'star' system of video artists that has formed an orthodoxy. This is a serious limiting factor in local and international curating: there are numerous innovative artists who fall outside of this star grouping but appear regularly in smaller and specific video and media festivals and whose work is overlooked for international biennale shows, including important artists who have a substantial history as video artists, such as Irit Batsry, David Larcher, Robert Cahen, Shigeko Kabuto and Daniel Reeves, to name a few. Instead, what we get, year in and year out, is a canon of more predictable video artists whose very busy schedules and packed oeuvres exactly reflect the concerns of the curators and dealers who show them. (Of course this situation does not just apply to video and new media artists—it works across the board.)

It behoves curators, critics and museum directors to look (in a self-questioning spirit) beyond the familiar and search widely in different exhibition and cultural contexts in order to short-circuit the relatively stale familiarity of the international biennales and related large-scale exhibitions.

Nevertheless, video art has 'come of age' as a major art form. It seems wherever you look you will find video, as one of numerous mixed media elements used in installations (the postmodern art form par excellence of the 1990s) or as a single channel work (videotape) or specifically as a video installation. Moreover, what we are witnessing now is, unquestionably, a proliferation of crossover forms of electronic art (film, television, video, new media art) spawning 'in-between' (Raymond Bellour) images, forms, sounds and textures that are reconfiguring today's mediascape.

Yet 30 years ago in Australia, video art was a 'minority' art form in search of its own aesthetic and cultural definition. It is crucial to understand that before we can write a history of its origins and genesis as an unfolding, highly multifaceted medium in the wake of the counterculture of the 1960s and commonly known back in the 1970s as 'experimental video' we need to acknowledge how little it has been adequately documented and historically known. Of course, as I and many others have written in the past, to begin a viable history of Australian video art we need also to recognise that the relevant catalogues, manifestos, documents and existing archives one could turn to begin such a history are very much scattered.[3]

Despite artists, curators, critics and polemicists advocating the necessity for our existing cultural institutions to create video art archives, collections and dedicated screening/exhibition venues, video art in this country has (relatively speaking) missed the proverbial bus. Further, established art museums and galleries have always been reluctant to engage in the archiving and exhibiting of video art because of the ephemeral nature of the medium in comparison with the more conventional art-object exhibitions and collections that are the norm of such institutions. This is not to detract from the critical importance of certain institutions that did make the occasional effort to exhibit video art in their 'white-cube' gallery spaces—such as the Art Gallery of New South Wales in the 1970s (more of this later)—or to exhibit video in the Biennales of Sydney since 1976.

Other than these specific issues, there is the perennial one: who will actually write such a history? And what kind of cultural familiarity has that person with the complexities—the contexts, practitioners, genres, movements, polemics and so on—of such a history? Who, except those who were participants in its emerging narrative in Australia, has a working, intimate knowledge of the subject? Because of these limitations, there is a temptation to engage in conveniently periodising your subject according to broad thematic or generic categories, or by decades. Such an undertaking would neatly erase the messy overlappings, contradictions and complexities that characterise Australian video art's 'stop-and-start' evolution from the 1970s to today.

We, therefore, if we wish to write such a history, are compelled to put into critical relief the considerable aesthetic, socio-cultural and stylistic changes that Australian video art experienced through the last three decades and see how its changing and rich identity evolved in the context of other relevant art forms, such as digital media, performance, earth art, sculpture, installations, filmmaking, photography, sound art and painting. Of course, as in video art elsewhere (particularly America), we need to include television, as a source of oppositional critique (especially after Paikian, feminist and 'scratch' video) that so markedly influenced Australian video in its first two decades.

As well as the specific issues germane to a critical and historical understanding of Australian video art there is the question of the cultural amnesia that increasingly characterises our moving image culture. What is challenging for anyone concerned with defining a cultural cartography of video art and its development (since the 1990s) into new media is the need to formulate a critical discourse that is supple enough to adequately acknowledge these aforementioned questions. We are, to put it simply, living (to quote Andreas Huyssen) in a culture that is 'terminally ill with amnesia'.[4] This applies especially when we are endeavouring to create a history of local video art. It is only since the early to mid-1990s that commentators like Sean Cubitt, Paul Virilio and Nicholas Zurbrugg, amongst others, agreed that—despite their own critical and theoretical efforts—there was a tremendous lack of critical or theoretical material pertaining to video and/or media theory.[5] Indeed, with the exception of a few anthologies and related monographs and specialist catalogues in the 1970s and 1980s, it has only been in the last decade or so that more substantial books have emerged on the subject.

Historically speaking, Australian video art first emerged—both as single channel tape form and as installation/performance—in the early 1970s in several Sydney art galleries: the Tin Sheds of Sydney University, Bush Video at Nimbin's Aquarius Festival, and the independent video access centres during Whitlam's era, seminal examplars being Mike Parr, Tim Johnson, Michael Glasheen (our 'first' video artist, with the 1970 Buckminster Fuller homage work *Teleological telecast from Spaceship Earth*), Jill Scott, Tim Burns, David Perry, John Kirk, Phillipa Cullen, Jeune Pritchard, Stephen Jones, Peter Callas, Leigh Hobba, to name a number. Since then there have been successive generations of video artists from diverse backgrounds—photography, writing, dance,

architecture, painting, filmmaking, sculpture—who have explored
the medium's distinctive collage aesthetic of hybridity, multilayering,
decentring and intertextuality in various pliable generic forms
(landscape, performance, documentary, dance, literary, for example).

This aesthetic has, during the last two decades, significantly
mutated into the discursive digital realms of images, graphics, sound,
text and music belonging to the new media arts. It is therefore worth
noting that artists who work in video may also work in other areas—
sound art, interactive media, digital photography, computer animation,
and Internet art, for instance.

Artists such as Carol Rudyard, Julie Rapp, Philip Brophy, Warren
Burt, 'Randali' (Robert Randall and Frank Bendinelli), David
Haines, Joyce Hinterding, Dennis Del Favero, Chris Caines, Eugenia
Raskopoulos and Lyndal Jones, amongst numerous others, have
contributed to the as yet unwritten diversified narrative of local
video art.

The majority of these artists have also worked in video installations,
which represent a complex interface of late 20th century art—art and
technology, high art and low culture, analog and digital media, and
private and public space—that can be traced back to specific works
and manifestos from the various movements of the historical avant-
garde (Surrealism, Futurism, Dadaism, Constructivism and numerous
Bauhaus experiments). Video installations, regardless of their varied
formal, spatial, temporal and theoretical attributes, evoke the concept
of the total artwork (*Gesamptkunstwerk*), and function as a spectacle of
mise en scène and staging by embracing all our senses and calling for a
highly kinetic form of spectatorial participation.

Before we discuss some of the more distinctive conceptual, formal
and technical configurations of Australian video art during the last 30
years and its emergence into new media art, it is important to note,
as Daniel Palmer correctly observes, that here in Australia there is no
mythic narrative to account for video's origins, as there is with Nam
June Paik's early experimentation with the Sony Portapak in New York
in 1965.[6] Aside from engaging in a problematic logocentric account of
video art's origins with Paik in America, it is more accurate to speak of
a complex cluster of different artistic personalities, art forms, energies
and discourses feeding into the early developments of (Australian)

video art. Thus, in the early 1970s, artists such as Jill Scott, David Perry, Peter Kennedy and Mike Parr, to mention four already cited seminal Australian video artists, emanated from performance, experimental cinema/painting, and conceptual art/performance.

Back then, it is fair to say that video art was commonly described as 'experimental video', signalling its emergence from the counterculture of the 1960s and its diverse anti-establishment art forms—underground cinema, street theatre, body art, earth art, sculpture and performance.

Anyone who writes on the history of video art in Australia is indebted to two essential documents and their authors. I refer to three texts edited together as a working document written by curator Bernice Murphy—'Towards a history of Australian video'—and another equally seminal essay by Stephen Jones.[7] Jones, who is one of the art form's pioneering figures and is actively engaged today as new media artist, video engineer and theorist, is Australian video art's unofficial archivist and polemicist. Jones's abiding drive to collect invaluable documents, essays, manifestos and other related ephemera is a testament to his passion for video art's unwritten history in Australia.

Our knowledge of early Australian video hinges on these two 'foundational' texts. In any historical negotiation of a subject one needs to acknowledge that such a challenging theoretical enterprise is a risky undertaking because of the obvious hermeneutic, historiographical and methodological problems relating to questions of canonic texts, evidence, representation, power and subjectivity. These questions directly concern the critical theoretical scaffolding of writing the history of video art in this country and its integration into the high-art world. Thus, to take up the task of writing a history of Australian video today would mean evaluating the medium's gradual process of 'museumisation'.

Australian video art in the 1970s emerged from such artistic and cultural concerns, and it was generally a substantial shift away from the more traditional media in the 1960s and the following decade. Hence the critical activities at the Inhibodress Gallery from 1970 to 1972 with Peter Kennedy and Mike Parr engaged in a variety of video recordings of performances that took place in the gallery or outside in the landscape. As Jones reminds us, these tapes were the first in the country to utilise a conceptual art context.[8] Also, at the same gallery, David Ahern and his AZ Music group used video documentation of their new and experimental music performances.

Sydney University's Tin Sheds, around the same time, was a site for the use of video in performance: namely, Tim Johnson's performance work in the *Disclosures* series. Johnson, along with filmmaker/performer Tim Burns, was included in a show entitled *Recent Australian Art* at the Art Gallery of New South Wales in 1973. Burns's installation *Forces to Climb* consisted of a room with a monitor outside; inside the room there was a camera and two naked actors smoking, lounging around, eating, and the video images relayed to outside spectators only became anchored in *their* everyday reality when one of the naked actors had to come out of the room to go to the toilet.[9]

Aside from the early video art dedicated to conceptual art and performance, a lot of video was also concerned with the idea of the medium as a countercultural agent for social change. This main notion of 'experimental video' principally emerged from America and, to a lesser extent, England and Europe. During Gough Whitlam's Labor Government in the 1970s, a series of video access centres was established; these were responsible for the production of socially informed videotapes. These centres conducted workshops in video production and thus allowed anyone to use video technology as a government-sponsored medium to engage in the overall social experimentation of the era.

The so-called Bush Video movement of Australian video was also a vital factor in its overall evolution: many diverse figures, such as John Kirk, Tom Barbour, Anne Kelly, Melinda Brown and Joe Kourri, to name a few, got involved with Mick Glasheen and explored issues of video ecology, cybernetics, architecture—what Jones termed 'the architectural and information-alchemy framework'.[10] In 1972 a group of them got together to apply for a grant (from the then Film, Radio and Television Board of the Australia Council for the Arts) to create an experimental cable network at the Aquarius Festival in Nimbin (NSW). According to Tom Zubrycki, a dedicated videomaker of the 1970s, this video access experiment was the first of its kind in Australia.[11]

After the festival, Bush Video moved back to Sydney, where a studio was established at Ultimo. There key video artists such as dancer Phillipa Cullen and computer graphics activists Doug Richardson and Jones himself were involved in critical video events. The 1970s, in general, witnessed many different activities, at Bush Video, City Video (Paddington) and the Paddington Video Access Centre at Paddington Town Hall, and different video events, festivals, exhibitions and experimental spaces, such as the Open Processes space at Watters Gallery. Amongst these events was the Sydney Filmmaker's Co-op Video Mayfair weekend event in 1977, and in the following year, a second Video Mayfair event, which took place over three successive weekends. Video artists and activists such as Jeune Pritchard, Carole Sklan, Dasha Ross and Kimble Rendall, amongst others, were involved.

The 1970s saw many different kinds of social documentary, image-processing and synthesising and community-based videotapes being produced, given the Zeitgeist of that particular era, but it was also a time of more gallery-based performance videos that dealt with issues of identity, duration, human consciousness, and so on. Broadly speaking, there were two groups of people involved with the medium: video artists concerned with contemporary post-object art and performance, and videomakers/activists concerned with social and political change and human consciousness. Of course, with the complexities of the medium's development over the last 30 years, these two categories of video artists and videomakers/activists were not mutually exclusive. Instead, as the medium of video was explored for a variety of different aesthetic, cultural, generic and technology reasons, there was a continuing state of fluidity and exchange between these two general groups.

The same decade witnessed American video artists visiting Australia; they included Nam June Paik and his then collaborator Charlotte Morman in 1976, Les Levine in the same year, and Bill Viola in the next. These video artists had a considerable impact on the local art world in terms of the introduction of video in an art gallery context. And as Jones documents in his essay, video was first used in the second Biennale of Sydney—it has (in varying degrees) been used in all of them since then.[12] By 1979, Jones and Murphy curated a collection *Videotapes in Australia*, which travelled in America, starting from New York's notable The Kitchen (which was founded by Woody and Steina Vasulka, pioneers of the medium, who visited Australia in the late 1980s) and ending up in Vancouver, Canada.[13] This collection came back to the Sydney Art

Gallery of New South Wales in 1980 as *Project 30: Some Recent Australian Videotapes*, and then it went to the Venice Biennale during the same year; finally, it toured through the regional galleries back home.

Australian video art, by the 1980s, became consolidated as an art form of rich diversity and elaborate technological experimentation in its vocabulary of colourisation, special effects and computer graphics.[14] Given the medium's increasing trajectory towards postmodern concerns of appropriation, deconstruction, pastiche and sampling, video art benefited from the expanding use of VCRs in our local image culture and the rapid changes that were taking place with video technology. In fact, it was influenced by the visual stylistics of the music video clip as much as it was by television, cinema, literature, performance, photography and painting. But what needs to be noted is that video art, in a self-reflexive manner, also became aware of its own generic heritage from the 1980s onwards. Too often, video art was not, in the popular imagination, adequately recognised for its breadth of experimentation: it included documentary, image-process, essay, feminist, landscape, literary, new narrative, performance and scratch, to name a few. (Lamentably, even today there is a tendency to think of video art as a monogeneric form.)

I agree with Palmer's claim that in the 1980s, Australian video art had a prominent stylistic concern with a deconstructive and playful reconfiguration of existing media imagery.[15] This was not unique to local video art: in America, France and England it was also evident; this is not surprising given the commonality of the cultural industries in these advanced industrial societies. Video artists such as Philip Brophy, Peter Callas, Ian Haig, Ross Harley and 'Randeli' (Robert Randall and Frank Bendinelli) come to mind as exemplars of this concern in video art.

Callas's oeuvre at that time embodied his inventive visual wit and montage style as he created works of distinctive deconstructive manga-inspired animated images.[16] His critical understanding of the Japanese televisual 'infoscape' of the 1980s, foregrounded in his videos, developed through living in that country for quite a while.

All in all, these video artists engaged in a playful interrogation of the media image as, to quote Gary Shapiro's words in the context of Michel Foucault's commentary on the French artist Gérard Fromanger, a form of nomadic wandering or 'deterritorialisation' (Deleuze and Guattari), where the artist is engaged in sending 'the equivalent of a computer virus into the image-machines of advertising, media, and state. The best video art has this character of deforming the omnipresent "channel" of the image, performing it otherwise, liberating and multiplying the contents of the screen.'[17] For Foucault, this kind of image-making constituted '"the autonomous transhumance" of the image'.[18]

It is also critical to observe that when we speak about Australian video art we need to see its development as an art form in the context of its inextricable connections to the local film culture. This is an essential concept to grasp if one is to understand video art's emergence in the 1970s in the wake of experimental film in the 1960s and subsequently. The film critic Adrian Martin, in a seminal 1990 essay, deftly articulates the role of collage and montage in experimental film and video, including the Super-8 film movement of the 1980s, which had a special resonance for video art in terms of their shared interest in deconstructing popular media icons, genres and narratives.[19] If one wishes to locate local video art (and new media) in the broader narrative of Australian film culture from the 1950s onwards, including the Super-8 scene, Barrett Hodsdon's invaluable book *Straight Roads and Crossed Lines* (2001) is also mandatory reading.[20]

One of the main factors in video art's consolidation as an art form was the development of certain organisations dedicated to the medium. These included the Australian Film Commission—especially its New Image Research section, which was established in 1988—and the Australia Council's New Image and the Visual, Arts and Craft Board.

Both organisations then and since have been instrumental in promoting video art. Also, one should also acknowledge here the NSW Government's Ministry for the Arts as a substantial funding agency for video art.

With the help of Murphy's inclusion of video in the first Australian Perspecta show in 1981, and Jones's equally important promotion of video in the 1970s, video emerged by the early 1980s as an art form in the art gallery context alongside other traditional art forms, such as painting and sculpture. In 1986, with seed funding from the Australian Film Commission, the Australian Video Festival was established. This festival, which changed its name in 1990 to the Australian International Video Festival, was instrumental in conducting seven festivals, all told.

The last one was held in 1992. And as the then video and new media curator Brian Langer notes in his two key articles of 1994, the festival played a considerable role in curating exhibitions, conducting seminars and workshops and, importantly, bringing American, European and Japanese video artists, curators and art historians to this country.[21] The festival's guests over the years included Woody and Steina Vasulka, Jeremy Welsh, Dominik Barbier, Hiro Sakurai, Alf Birnbaum, Nan Hoover, Jeffrey Shaw, Robert Cahen, Maria Vedder and Gene Youngblood. In 1988, as a special initiative of the festival, *Scan+*, a video art/new media journal, was co-founded by Langer, Eddy Jokovic and myself. The first issue acted also as the catalogue for the third Australian Video Festival.

In terms of exhibition and distribution, there have been several key stakeholders in this critical context, as well as the Australian International Video Festival: Electronic Media Arts, Matinaze, Experimenta and, more recently, the Australian Network for Art and Technology, Metro Screen and dLux Media Arts. All these organisations played a substantial role in fostering a receptive ethos for the creation, exhibition and promotion of video art and later new media.

A critical watershed event that took place in Sydney in 1992 clearly registered not only the complex shift from video art to new media art in this country in the last 20 odd years, but also the numerous curatorial and theoretical discourses that have helped define our evolving techno-culture—this was TISEA. Anyone familiar with the (in)visible histories, textual practices and multiple meanings of Australian video production since the early 1970s will agree that the aesthetic–technological differences that distinguish video as a fine arts practice from video as a media discourse were clearly evident in the proceedings and exhibitions of TISEA. The event was promoted by the Inter-Society for Electronic Arts (ISEA), a major new media/electronic arts organisation that stages global events every two years or so, and was specifically organised locally by the Adelaide-based Australian Network for Art and Technology. (The latter organisation is one of the critical organisations in terms of the promotion of the techno-arts in this country.)

With the ascendancy of the new media arts in the 1990s, video art became less prominent in the local contemporary audiovisual media scene. Although commentators such as Callas have stated that video art became virtually 'an anachronism', this is debatable: did it literally vanish, or did its concerns simply change in the context of the large-scale video installations and projections that became more curatorially centre-staged by the end of the 1990s?[22] Callas and others are correct, however, in saying that video art as defined in the preceding decade or so became quite a different, hybrid medium in the light of Raymond Bellour's thesis about the 'in between' art forms that have proliferated in the last 20 years as the computer has allowed cinema, video, television and photography to 'contaminate' each other.[23]

Bellour's 'in between' art forms of techno-creativity were evident at the TISEA proceedings and exhibitions to those who valued the increasing image–sound alchemy between camera-based art forms via the computer. Viewed in terms of its curatorial and rhetorical configurations, TISEA incarnated a very elaborate complex of different—and antagonistic—discourses mobilised around the expanding, dynamic world of new media arts. These ranged from the cautionary tenor of seminar participants such as Simon Penny, Robert Fischer, Shalom Gorewitz, Maria Fernandez and David Tafler, to the incisive anti-phallocentric and anti-techno-fascination critiques that emanated from work by artists such as VNS Matrix and Linda Dement and the sustained stream of unsettling questions from the floor that critiqued TISEA's overall curatorial and theoretical architecture. In retrospect, TISEA functioned like Adorno's metaphorical splinter of glass in one's eye in terms of its productive diacritical focus on the various contradictions and tensions that increasingly characterised the direction and shape of electronic arts in Australia.

Opening up new significant debates in our moving image culture, TISEA brought to the fore the hermeneutic necessity of looking more closely at the cultural, historical, gender and textual specificities of the various art forms (video art, digital media, holography, computer animation and graphics, etc) that together constitute what we call 'electronic media'. Clearly, these new media art forms, along with emerging new technologies, have altered and continue to alter the very cultural, social and political concerns and textures of everyday life. New electronic art forms, including video art, question the very cultural and ontological order of how we see and hear. I don't wish to exaggerate their importance in our cultural lives, in either utopian or dystopian terms; nor do I wish to speak of them in a smug self-congratulatory manner. For this is a tricky terrain to inhabit and comment upon, as will be clear to anyone who has in one way or another contributed to the production, exhibition and critical reception of new electronic art forms. It therefore behoves us to speak of them in a balanced, informed and self-critical fashion, avoiding both the grand neo-Marxist and metaphorical pronouncements about video art à la Fredric Jameson and today's digitised media culture as envisioned by Baudrillard's apocalyptic theory of simulation and the simulacrum.[24]

As curators Stuart Koop and Max Delany pointed out in 2002, Australian video art—like video art elsewhere—has ceased to engage our attention through its 'textures' and 'feedback', features that enthralled the 1970s video vanguard.[25] Video has became one of many available options for the younger generations of artists exhibiting installations, large-scale video projections, sculpture, etc. Video has become the common aesthetic and technological currency of our postmodern culture and its ubiquitous fluid digital media. No longer the countercultural gesture that it once was, critiquing fine arts and television art, video has moved from a marginal practice to what Catherine Elwes calls, 'the default medium of 21st century gallery art'.[26] Given the rapid convergence of video art, new media and artists' film, the video monitor has returned to the contemporary art gallery as a viable object in video installation practice alongside multiple screen projections and mixed media installations. Whether flat or cuboid, the video monitor still maintains its critical links with its domestic origins.

Plasma screens are becoming the norm in video installations and projections today: witness Bill Viola's recent 12-installation exhibition at the National Gallery of Australia—*The Passions*—where he has collapsed the video monitor and focused on the image as two-dimensional representation.[27] Viola's extremely slow-moving plasma screen portraits and crowd scenes are, as Elwes notes, less concerned with cinematic traditions than with traditions belonging to Italian Renaissance art.[28]

Here in the antipodes, we have always been strategically positioned—mostly because of our geography—to appreciate the fundamental aesthetic, cultural and historical relationships that exist between the development of video art and new media and the curatorial, institutional and theoretical meta-narratives that have been operating in the (post)modern metropolises of America and Europe and our peripheral shores.

To talk about video art in the context of contemporary Australian culture is difficult because of our island continent's particular inversed geographical position in relation to its relevant global cultural and media vector flows.

Australian video and media artists have in the past manifested, in their own peculiar conceptual and textual concerns, a common preoccupation with questioning either (a) the received cultural beliefs, icons and systems of representations of other cultures or (b) the more fashionable characteristics of the various postmodern theories of identity, gender, hybridity and power coming from abroad. In addition, many of their works share a certain critical commonality in enunciating a meta-commentary about the cultural politics of identity and techno-representation.

Because of Australia's distinctive geopolitical status in the world of nomadic media flows (defined by the ubiquitous tyranny of distance), local video artists have been highly sensitised to the aesthetic, formal and theoretical issues concerning their electronic techno-culture and its indebtedness to the major Anglo-American sites of cultural and media hegemony. This awareness of what represents postmodernity being an expression of Europe's and America's relations to their many antipodes (including Australia), rather than of what's happening inside these countries, is (as McKenzie Wark cogently maintains) what counts when examining more recent instances of Australian multimedia art.[29]

It is important to note that Australian artists, with their non-binary interdisciplinary art forms (through the computer with its rhizomatic possibilities of techno-creativity), are ideally trained to see and hear across the horizons of their discipline in a lateral and self-questioning spirit.

However, there is another salient concept that needs to be noted in relation to our general capacity to see things from afar, across our seas from our beaches: as Greg Dening suggests, our beaches represent (metaphorically speaking) 'spaces in between', 'spaces of defining rather than definition', and as such are appealing for our artists and social thinkers.[30] Although video and new media arts do not necessarily imply, ipso facto, new aesthetic paradigms, artists working with these cross-disciplinary art forms are in position to see—if they imaginatively question the various personal, creative and professional horizons that surround them—in Dening's apt phrase 'beyond the ordinary limits of our vision'.[31]

I will now discuss a few examples of recent Australian video works in the last five years or so and then conclude with a few general remarks on the present state of video art in this country.

Chris Caines's *Enemy of Fun* (1998) is a playful, evocative and open-ended view of a female character located in the vortex of melting post-Ballardian cityscapes, phantasmic fish and scrolling superimposed text. The video's first-person narration vividly encapsulates the protagonist's adventure in a fabulous, almost Borgesian, world of mystery, play and enchantment. *Enemy of Fun* is a fairly characteristic example of this artist's highly experimental approach to digital image creation.

Ian Andrews' Orwellian look at our emerging panopticon society, *Datapanik* (1998), displays a multifaceted view of a runaway surveillance culture of paranoia and control. We encounter a sinister 'Big Brother' world of automata, corporate alienation and burnout. Andrew's video is a subtly crafted work that conveys the 'white noise' and many other sociocultural myths of our increasingly technocratic society.

Datapanik is aptly named, as it successfully conveys Andrew's subtle image and sound skills with a biting satirical post-humanist approach to his main theme of 'one-dimensional' techno-culture.

The following two videos, both dance videos, are indicative of a renewed interest in this particular video genre that can be traced back—in terms of Australian video—to the pioneering work done by Cullen in the mid-1970s.

Samuel James's *Potsdamer (Reconstruction 1)* (2000) is a fairly intelligent choreographed representation of the human body *in extremis*, located in an urban space of social anonymity. James's economically sparse use of the camera— with its impressive display of an almost 180-degree turn of the camera in one particularly riveting scene—denotes the artist's understated mise en scène of human movement in an alienating urban world. The dancer's sharp, short, slow gestures are fittingly accompanied by a soundtrack of cacophonous industrial noise. The only moment when we witness any evidence of human society is in the video's unexpected concluding scene, where we see a lift open up to reveal a few individuals inside.

Rose Turtle's absurd fractured fairytale *Aaaaaaaaagh* (1999) is a highly watchable inventive dance piece that conveys a female dancer as a rag doll-like marionette figure undergoing a wide spectrum of burlesque adult/child human emotions and gestures. Turtle's creative pulsating camera style of representation ideally suits her almost bizarre David Lynchian mise en scène of the human body in extreme emotional states of expression. The expressionist style of editing also enhances Turtle's clever jagged form of dance choreography. *Aaaaaaaaagh* is a creatively stimulating dance video that expands the genre's possibilities.

Denis Beaubois's witty black and white performance video *In the Event of Amnesia the City Will Recall* (1996/7) exemplifies the artist's fertile capacity to create an absurdist resonant examination of the individual taking a Don Quixote-inspired stand against the claustrophobic and alienating configurations of Virilio's 'overexposed city'. Beaubois's sparse economy of expression is a hallmark of the artist's oeuvre, as is his underlying subtle comedic ironising of our individual and collective shortcomings and foibles. In another video, *Writing* (2000–03)—which consists of three different versions of one basic piece—Beaubois looks at the complexities of translation and writing. This interesting work evokes the malleable stylistics of Astruc's notion of *camera-stylo* filmmaking, as all we see is the artist's hand with a pen in it, engaged in the act of writing onto a pad. The event takes place in a busy urban environment, and as Beaubois writes down what he is observing around him, we can only appreciate his surroundings through the video's soundtrack, which records passers-by in their everyday activities. Theses sounds increase in a cumulative fashion as Beaubois writes. Beaubois, who is a member of Sydney's performance group Gravity Feed, is starting to create some intriguing videos, which have the ability to insert the viewer as performer.

Geoffrey Weary's recent videos *Scenes from a Shanghai Hotel* (2005) and *The Captive* (2005) signal his long-term interest in using video to explore the complexities of identity, cultural memory and history. Central to Weary's open-ended, poetic aesthetic is the interplay between the cinema, photography and painting. The former work deftly tells the story of a Russian woman living in China, who is expelled after the Communist Revolution in 1948. Her story begins in a Shanghai hotel room and ends on a suburban street in Sydney. The video's fragmentary manipulated tableaux images centre around her and another young woman—who is also seen in a hotel room in Shanghai and is presented in a series of photographic images, and also, ambiguously, resembles her. The video, which mixes up documentary, performative, fictional and digital media forms, centres around these two women—are they actually the same person? Do they just resemble each other? Is the second woman a fusion of both identities?

The latter video collides evocative grainy VHS footage of the Berlin Wall in the early months of 1990 with blurry scenes shot in a forest and fragments of Cold War archival footage. As we see the real Berlin Wall crumbling under the hammer blows of street hawkers and souvenir hunters, ghosts of the past appear then dissolve back into the scratchy surfaces of a long-forgotten newsreel. The imagery of the Berlin Wall and the forest scenes acquire actual and symbolic importance as psychological spaces of confinement and escape.

Both works deal with the Cold War, conflict and exilic displacement, but in terms of the textual materiality of the videos there is also an effort to evoke the tropes of the experimental film tradition—especially structural cinema's project with the cinematic apparatus itself—which is significantly linked to video art's history.

Let me now make a few concluding observations concerning the transformation of Australian video art over the last 30 years into today's digital media, and its vast impact on contemporary art practice. As suggested above, many artists are now using the medium of video in their installations, projection-based presentations, performances and single-channel videotapes. Artists as varied as Destiny Deacon, the Kingpins, Patricia Piccinini, Lyndal Jones, David Noonan, Debra Petrovich, Eugenia Raskopoulos, Chris Caines, Justine Cooper, Mari Velonaki, Lynne Sanderson, David Haines, Joyce Hinterding, TV Moore and Shaun Gladwell, to name a few, are using video in the their artworks in a variety of different contexts. Video art has morphed from its original 1960s/1970s 'countercultural' opposition to television, when video artists made their work generally outside the art world, to a position where it is an integral part of artists' spaces, galleries and museums.

Further, artists using video today are not, generally speaking, concerned with the technical aspects of the medium in the way they were back in the 1970s and 1980s, because video has become very accessible to anyone. And as video is now highly identifiable with the personal computer and DVD storage, artists from a more traditional visual representation tradition are also using video in many different and flexible ways. But it needs to be said here that in Australia, video art remains an art form without any theoretical or historical understanding specific to its complex history, genres and social formations. In 1994, Chris Darke, talking about Gary Hill's exhibition *In the Light of the Other*, made the telling remark that 'the British don't know how to talk about video art. We had better learn, and fast.'[32] That was over 10 years ago. One may say quite confidently that (regrettably) the same still applies in Australia. How many of us are familiar with the critical figures of Australian video art in the 1970s, 1980s or even the last decade? How many of us are aware of the rich diversity of the video art genres that have evolved over the last 30 years? How many of us are engaged in trying to articulate a critical language that is supple enough to accommodate the art form's rapid analog and digital transformations?

With the creation of Melbourne's Australian Centre for the Moving Image in 2002, a centre dedicated to the exhibition of film, video and interactive installations, a new critical and curatorial focus on digital media in the context of contemporary art, culture and technology was established.

Australian artists are using video for a range of aesthetic, cultural and generic reasons. Some do so to explore the embodied space of the interactive image, others do so to work with popular music video forms and styles, and others do so to work within the broader cinematic, conceptual and performance traditions of the visual arts. Most of them work in gallery spaces and, like everywhere else in the international art world, they are creating sculptural installations, mixed-media performances, and large-scale video projections. Of course with video installations we are encountering all kinds of single- and multiple-screen formats, and the return of monitor-based exhibitions. What is clear is that many artists are now working with video because of its immediacy and everyday familiarity. However, as we know, video is also unfortunately becoming (though it does not have to be) an international art world cliché because of its ubiquitous presence in advertising, fashion, television and our consumer culture in general. Some artists are happy to create moving image art that plunders many existing popular genres, and do not, as Elwes notes, feel any necessity to define a critical stance towards their content or 'the position they occupy in the marketing structures of a consumer culture'.[33] But other artists feel compelled to critique the shifting dialectic between art, culture, gender, spectatorship and technology.

In sum, Australian video art remains—in terms of its intricate history, figures, genres and contexts—relatively unknown today. Today's video art as a time-based art form has been transformed from its 1970s origins into what is commonly known today as 'video', in all its current installation, performative and theatrical contexts. Lamentably, and without wanting to sound nostalgic for video art's past, the majority of today's younger artists who are using video as a part of their toolkit are ignorant of its rich cultural, historical and generic diversity as an art form. It is still an art form in search of better-informed critical, curatorial and theoretical recognition.

NOTES

1   See Regina Cornwell, 'Gary Hill: an interview', Art Monthly (London), 170, October 1993, p. 11.

2   Although video artists in the 1960s and 1970s came from a diverse cross-disciplinary background—cinema, engineering, literature, music, painting, performance, sculpture, etc.—to call yourself a video artist was an act of cultural transgression in the context of the art establishment at that time.

3   Anyone who is engaged in writing a history of Australian video art will recognise (a) the scant nature of existing relevant historical documents, manifestos, catalogues, etc. (b) the lack of proper archival treatment of such documents and (c) the sheer ephemeral nature of such documents. It is hard to imagine, given the ubiquitous presence of video in today's art world, that as recently as the 1980s there were hardly any critiques and/ or histories of the video medium itself. One had to fossick amongst video exhibition and festival catalogues to find information about the early origins of video as broadcast, gallery and agitational/'countercultural' practice.

4   See Andreas Huyssen, Twilight Memories, Routledge, New York and London, 1995, p. 1. For Huyssen's ideas on how the new technologies are affecting our sense of temporality in an era of increasing cultural amnesia, see especially pp. 1–9.

5   See Sean Cubitt, 'What's wrong with video criticism', Variant, issue 14, summer 1993, pp. 31–34; Gregory Ulmer, 'One video theory (some assembly required)', in Simon Penny (ed.), Critical Issues in Electronic Media, State University of New York Press, New York, 1995, pp. 253–74; Paul Virilio (interview with Nicholas Zurbrugg), 'The publicity machine and critical theory', Eyeline, no. 29, autumn/ winter 1995, pp. 11–12; Nicholas Zurbrugg, Critical Voices, G+B Arts International, Amsterdam, 2000.

6   Daniel Palmer, 'Medium without a memory: Australian video art', Broadsheet, vol. 33, no. 3, 2004, p. 20.

7 Refer to Bernice Murphy, 'Towards a history of Australian video', in *The First Australian Video Festival Catalogue*, Australian Video Festival, Sydney, 1986, pp. 17–21; Stephen Jones, 'Some notes on the early history of the independent video scene', ibid., pp. 22–28.

8 Jones, p. 23.

9 ibid.

10 ibid.

11 Zubrycki is cited ibid.

12 ibid., p. 26.

13 ibid., p. 28.

14 Palmer, p. 21.

15 ibid.

16 On Peter Callas's video art practice in the 1980s and early 1990s, see John Conomos, 'Cascading mediascapes: on Peter Callas and reverse appropriation', in *Conomos, Video as Electronic Collage and as Writing*, [MA research thesis], University of Technology, Sydney, 1994, pp. 51–65.

17 Gary Shapiro, *Archaeologies of Vision*, University of Chicago Press, Chicago and London, 2003, p. 373.

18 ibid.

19 Adrian Martin, 'Collage and montage in contemporary Australian experimental film and video, and its origins', in Arthur McIntyre, *Contemporary Australian Collage and Its Origins*, Craftsman House, Sydney, 1990, pp. 49–61.

20 Barrett Hodsdon, *Straight Roads and Crossed Lines*, Bernt Porridge Group, Sheraton Park WA, 2001.

21 See Brian Langer, 'Video art and the Australian International Video Festival', in Nicholas Zurbrugg (ed.), *Electronic Arts in Australia*, special issue of *Continuum*, vol. 8, no. 1, 1994, pp. 259–66; Langer. 'Chronology of the Australian International Video Festival', ibid., pp. 267–79.

22 'Peter Callas, interviewed by Nicholas Zurbrugg', ibid., p. 112.

23 On Raymond Bellour's ideas on the 'in between' images that circulate between film, video and photography and, consequently, the increasing hybridisation of visual media, see Bellour, 'The double helix', in *Passage de l'image*, Centro Cultura de la Caixa de Pensiones, Barcelona, 1992, pp. 48–75; Bellour, 'The letter goes on ...', *Camera Obscura*, no. 24, 1990, pp. 207–14; Bellour, 'The power of words, the power of images', ibid., pp. 7–9; Bellour, 'The book, back and forth', in Yves Gevaert (ed.), *Qu'est-ce qu'une madeleine? Apropos du CD-ROM* In memory *de Chris Marker*, Centre Georges Pompidou, Paris, 1997, pp. 109–54, amongst other articles. Bellour, for me, is one of the most perceptive critics on the analog–digital frontier of the contemporary art and film/media scene.

24 For an incisive critique of Jameson's and Baudrillard's problematical responses to video art, see Nicholas Zurbrugg, 'Jameson, Baudrillard and video-art', in Brian Langer (ed.), *Video Forms: Passages in Identity*, Australian Video Festival, Sydney, 1989, pp. 5–8; 'Jameson's compliant: video art and the intertextual "time-wall"', *Screen*, vol. 32. no. 1, 1991, pp. 16–34 (reprinted in Zurbrugg, 2000, pp. 85–103).

25 Koop & Delaney are quoted in Palmer, p. 21.

26 Catherine Elwes, *Video Art: a guided tour*, I.B. Taurus, London/New York, 2005, p. 191.

27 See the lavish exhibition catalogue publication for the Bill Viola installation show: John Walsh (ed.), *Bill Viola: The Passions*, J. Paul Getty Museum, Los Angeles, (in association with the National Gallery, London), 2003.

28 Elwes, p. 157.

29 McKenzie Wark, 'Autonomy and antipodality in global village', in Alessio Cavallaro et al. (eds), *Cultural Diversity in the Global Village: The Third Symposium in Electronic Art*, Australian Network for Art and Technology, Sydney, 1992, p. 99.

30 Greg Denning, *Readings/Writings*, Melbourne University Press, Melbourne, 1998, pp. 85–86.

31 ibid., p. 7.

32 Chris Darke, *Light Readings*, Wallflower, London, 2000, p. 180.

33 Elwes, p. 191.

Collage, site, video, projection

Video installation is the conjunction of opposites (or, to put it another way, video installation is like having your cake and eating it, too).

Vito Acconci

(In memory of Joan Brassil)
The underlying aim of this chapter is to discuss video installations, in contrast to single-channel video, as a collage genre of electronic art-making. I will also examine some of the more critically singular features of this recently popular form of video in the light of its own particular aesthetic, cultural and technological formation over the last 45 years. I am not interested in chronicling the video installation's genesis, as such, but rather in forming a workable identikit profile of its conceptual, formal and spatial collage configurations and interdisciplinary background.

It is important to observe how video installations, as part of the larger narrative of postmodern installation art, typify such art's three-dimensional capacity to challenge our prevailing ideas about the conceptual, formal and material parameters of art in general. During the last three decades or so, the term 'installation' has become an integral part of the vocabulary of the visual arts. One of the key points often raised by recent commentators on installation art is how its meaning is, to quote Andrew Benjamin, 'in part, structured by its own negotiation with the question of art. With such a negotiation, art is present as a question.'[1] This is especially the situation with video installations and sculptures. Benjamin's perceptive analysis of installation art foregrounds the fact that one of its more striking characteristics is its capacity to question its own open-ended materiality and relationship to sculpture and the readymade. Installations, particularly video installations, because of their collaged sculptural configurations and three-dimensional space, constantly pose essential questions about their connections to the historical avant-garde and the meaning of art's material presence in late-capitalist culture.[2] With installation art, as Benjamin observes, there is an ongoing hermeneutic enterprise (regardless of the installation's materials and modes of expression) to create a textual architectonics which suggests a non-commodifiable art form that seeks to keep on problematising itself as art: 'Art's material presence, present here with the installation, founds and confounds sites of signification and in so doing allows for a practice that in the continuity of the creation of a topos and thereby in the resisting of restrictions, continues an opening of meaning. This continuity is the work of art.'[3]

Furthermore, installation art is, by its very definition, as Adam Geczy and Benjamin Genocchio indicate, 'an unstable and extremely fluid notion, ranging from the intangibilities of a critical attitude to large-scale work and architecture ... [it is] an activation of space which takes into account the subjective, temporal specificity of the beholder'.[4]

Thus video installations represent a complex interface of late 20th and early 21st century art—art and technology, high art and low culture, analog and digital media, and private and public space—that can be traced back to specific works and manifestos from the various movements of the historical avant-garde (surrealism, futurism, Dadaism, constructivism and numerous Bauhaus experiments). What this means is, as Nicholas Zurbrugg once rightly noted, that the many varied forms of (video) installations make critical sense (in a hindsightful way) in the context of their origins in the early 20th century avant-garde movements.[5] There is an evolutionary logic informing installation video that can be glimpsed in the different aesthetic, formal and artistic efforts of the numerous artists who constituted these various movements of the historical avant-garde. In the words of Zurbrugg, 'it seems evident that postmodern installation art derives from the modernist experimentation in terms of an *evolutionary* dynamics, elaborating, extending and making explicit the implicit potential of these artists' differing aspirations towards an art of installation'.[6]

Video installations are fundamentally different from single-channel tapes in terms of how they operate: the latter are transmitted, while the former *reveal* themselves in a specific space in clearly specific ways. All forms of video installation—irrespective of their critical and material diversity—display strong elements of mise en scène and staging, which are indispensable conceptual and textual elements contributing to the genre's overall collage ambience.

Because the field of video installation encompasses such a diversity of ideas, forms and media, it resists (as does installation art in general) a clear and precise definition.[7] This appears to be the consensus among scholars, curators and artists who have been involved in the ongoing 'museumisation' of the genre. Its collage elements take many different open-ended forms, which focus around the genre's sculptural, spatial and thematic configurations. Not only do video installations, through their elaborate contextuality and shifting temporality, reaffirm and 'problematise' their diversity of forms, materials and means of representation; they also demand an active bodily form of spectatorship. The gallery-goer, who is generally either circumnavigating a video installation or being surrounded by it, becomes a critically vital catalyst and receptor of the work. Thierry de Duve's definition of installations as a new Minimalist sculptural art form captures the active mode of spectatorship that video installations demand: installation is 'the construction of an ensemble of spatial relations between an object and an architectural space in which the viewer is made conscious that he/she is an integral component'.[8]

Today, as Dominique Païni notes, the viewer of these video (and film) installations has once again—after being held captive in the film theatres of the last century—become 'a flâneur, mobile and solitary'.[9] This form of nomadic spectatorship is, for Païni, inextricably connected to both Baudelaire's 19th century flâneur and the various pre-cinematic technologies of vision, such as the magic lantern and the 'stream praxinoscope', and our contemporary seated (but mobile) human interactor, with the personal computer and the Internet. As he puts it, 'The Baudelairian flâneur, thrilled by the toys in the Tuileries, makes an unexpected return to the epoch of the solitary internaut who, while chained to his chair—it is what there is in common with the spectator at the movies—is nonetheless mobile, or more exactly, interactive, among the metamorphoses of the text–image. But don't the long evenings of the Internet fanatics recall the family evenings around the 'stream praxinoscope' or the lantern? From the magic lantern to the console of the domestic computer at the end of the twentieth century, it is the spiralled return of the omnipresence of the machine as image.'[10]

So far I have spoken about how video installations, as complex art forms of contemporary image culture, generate 'sites of complexity' in which the gallery-goer is enclosed by collage images, textures and sounds.[11] Although video installations, regardless of their varied formal, spatial, temporal and theoretical attributes, evoke the idea of the total artwork (*Gesamptkunstwerke*), and operate as spectacle by embracing all our senses and calling for a highly kinetic form of spectatorial participation, it should be noted that certain commentators, such as Margaret Morse, have argued that video installations are representative of the so-called new arts of presentation rather than the more traditional proscenium arts (cinema and theatre) and painting and sculpture.[12] Morse contends that with a video installation, the artist vacates the site and the visitor (rather than the 'spectator') becomes the experiential subject 'not by identification, but in body'.[13] Morse's analysis of the genre (which can be interpreted as a fertile, speculative step towards a *poetics* of video installation art) includes a well-grounded emphasis on the way video installations stress a collage plane of expression, with many different levels within the plane and (equally critical) a temporal and experiential passage (the 'space in between') in which gallery participants move around.[14]

Video installations, like all forms of installation art, are ephemeral by nature in that, as Morse demonstrates, they are never entirely disconnected from the time, subject and place of their enunciation.[15] Moreover, the accentuated collage dimensions of the form (whether or not collaged video images are being used) manifest in its focus on the actual space and time in which the museum visitor is asked to interact with the installation's pictorial, sculptural, aural, kinaesthetic and linguistic modes of representation. In short, irrespective of the different material objects, images and sounds of the monitor(s) and sites used, video installations underscore the spatio-temporal passage which the body of the museum visitor has to traverse in order to negotiate them as complex, hybrid art forms. Therefore, video installations, as examples of the new presentational arts, manifest—regardless of whether they stress two-dimensional or three-dimensional features—a collage aesthetic, as Morse indicates, in that their plane of expression allows the museum visitor to experience physically more than one tense.[16] This is possible because video installations as a rule display two basic planes of language—a *here* and *now* (where people can be present to each other experiencing the art form's 'liveness' as a non-commodity art) and an *elsewhere* and *elsewhen* (where events and people are absent from the act of enunciation).[17] Thus, in video installations there is often a marked collage emphasis taking place where references to the past and the future can be made in conjunction with references to the present, on the condition that these references are rendered in the installation's experience of here and now.

Following this, as Morse says, it should be observed that there are two broad types of video installation art which can be distinguished by tense: (a) closed-circuit video installations which highlight 'presence' (as in the early video works of Dan Graham, Bruce Nauman, Peter Campus, Buky Schwartz and Judith Barry), where a 'live' camera relays images and sounds of the visitor's movements to one or more monitors, exploring themes of identity, power and voyeurism, and (b) the recorded-video art installation (the dominant mode of the genre), where the spectator can wander around the installation space encountering a bodily experience of various conceptual and imaginary worlds of anticipation, desire and memory.[18] A general conceptual world is foregrounded; this is a world where images, sounds and objects are connected to each other in many different sculptural and spatial ways.

But essentially, all forms of video installation display an enunciative mode that is either declarative or performative in character.[19] The many different referent worlds of video installations invariably suggest a propensity towards a non-mimetic form of representation. Characteristically, they stress abstraction as well as simulation. Central to the argument here is the fact that video installation art is a non-commodifiable genre with decisive links to other similar non-painting art forms—such as performance, happenings, conceptual art, earth works, body art and installation art in general—and that it therefore manifests a collage mise en scène in its conceptual and stylistic architecture. For Antonio Muntadas, video installations (in direct contrast to videotapes) are notable precisely because of their distinct collage features: 'Installation is cultural space. You cannot do an installation inside your television. Maybe in the station, but not on the air. I think an installation needs a three-dimensional aspect. Because I see an installation as a collage in three dimensions. It can therefore be installed. Mono-channel tapes can be screened on television or in a kind of a cinémathèque where the artist can discuss his work.'[20] This critical quality of the video installation yields many complex ideas relating to how the dramatic and psychophysical spaces of the form necessitate a period of adaptation, whereby all our senses are activated as we negotiate its three-dimensional spatial architecture. Concomitantly, as Anne-Marie Duguet notes, video installations resemble 'a sort of spatial collage' demanding (as we have already indicated) a profound interactive mode of aesthetic negotiation. From the beginning, interaction between the video image and the artist-constructed environment has been a vitally important feature of this genre, predicated as it is on a marked awareness of time.[21]

The various elements of an installation encourage perpetual engagement and exploration, to paraphrase Duguet, and spectatorial nomadism—a multiplicity of different points of view—in which questions of process, space, perception and viewer/object relations are constantly posed. We experience them as if we were mapping out an uncharted spatial topography of multi-dimensional audiovisual experimentation. The foregrounded collage characteristics of video installations—namely, their rhizomatic visual, sonic and kinetic qualities—compel the viewer to weave in and around their architectural spaces. Donald Kuspit's 1993 observation about Viola's sculptural installations holds true for the entire genre:

> Viola's installations are *Gesamptkunstwerke*, integrating architecture, sculpture, flat imagery, sound, theatre, and above all the individual spectator—the focus and center of these works, which really only exist when viewed by a participant/observer. Thus Viola returns art to an ambition of early avant-garde performance: he shows it rejuvenating itself by becoming 'impure'. For Viola, the *Gesamptkunstwerke* restores art to the grandeur of its original meaningfulness.[22]

In order to appreciate the collage concerns of installation video art, we must consider how the genre itself exemplifies the underlying idea of *Gesamptkuntwerke* and, as Shelley Rice has indicated, how there are two contrapuntal temporal systems operating in any given example of the genre.[23] In vivid contrast to other kinds of installations, video installations express a combination of stationary and moving media. This implies that the viewer's experience of a video installation is premised on its changing physical forms as well as its changing mobile images and sounds. This combination, according to Rice, reflects in graphic terms our common shared experience of the dynamic and fragmentary visual, audio and spatial features of everyday life.

It is interesting to note that the fundamental collage aesthetic of video installations was evident from the beginning of the medium's history: installations were virtually the first works in video. Any reasonable consideration of video art's 'origins' revolves around two pivotal figures: Wolf Vostell and Nam June Paik. Both figures are central to the development of the critical collage components of installation video art. In 1958 Vostell created an environment called *Dark Room (German point of view)*, consisting of a TV set (video's persistent shadow), bones, wood, barbed wire and newspapers. In 1963 he produced *6 TV dé-coll/age* for New York's Smolin Gallery. During the same year, Paik exhibited—at the Galerie Parnass in Wutterpal, West Germany—13 television sets with distorted images. These iconoclastic neo-Dadaist works epitomised the Cagean aesthetics of indeterminance and randomness. Both Vostell (as a de-collagist) and Paik (as a collagist) were concerned with the deconstruction and demystification of television.

It would be helpful at this juncture to differentiate between the role of de-collage in Vostell's numerous multimedia projects, actions and performances since the mid-1950s and Paik's use of collage in his far-reaching tapes, installations and sculptures, as both demonstrate a Fluxus-inflected desire to question the elitist nature of art as a socio-cultural institution and television's ideological and cultural meaning in everyday consumer culture. Vostell's publication *De-collage* defines what the artist meant by the term 'de-collage'. According to John Hanhardt, who has played a pivotal role in creating an informed and receptive curatorial and discursive ethos for video art (particularly as it applies to these two important figures), de-collage was a kind of a large scale happening event that took place in public spaces, constructing them as social environments.[24] In Vostell's text, de-collage referred to an artistic procedure where (as Hanhardt describes it) 'all manner of texts and information were erased in a technique that revealed different elements by tearing off the surface to reveal new combinations'.[25] Collage, in contrast, is a technique whereby different materials are added and joined together to create new combinations.

The critical point is that thanks to Paik and Vostell and the many others who were involved in the Fluxus movement and associated with the *Nouveaux Réalistes*, the recently accepted expanded forms of video installation can be recognised as an extension of the various ideas and techniques of collage into the spatial and temporal configurations created by video monitors and their multiple intertextual connections with other materials. Practically everyone who has contributed to video installation art has drawn upon either (1) certain strategies of image-making centring around video collage and then extended and refined them (see the work of Tony Oursler, the Vasulkas, Mary Lucier, Fabrizio Plessi and Rita Myers) or (2) ideas and processes inspired by the technique of de-collage pertaining to multimedia and performance in works that endeavour to deconstruct the ideological underpinnings of mass media (see the work of Joan Braderman, Paper Tiger Television, Juan Downey and Francesc Torres).

A few observations concerning how video installation, as a postmodern genre, extends the aesthetic, cultural and technological possibilities of the medium, and on the central role performed by the video monitor in an installation (as the central focal point of the genre's critique of representation and its complex, uneasy relationship to television), may be appropriate here.[26] Video installations represent an innovative search for new language forms of electronic image-making. Their underlying collage concerns express a basic urge to be different with respect to the foundational modernist principles of artistic practice.

Historically speaking, early video practitioners, such as Peter Campus, Lynda Benglis, Bill Viola, Joan Jonas and Nancy Holt, amongst many others, were preoccupied with questioning issues of ontology and Western representation. Video, for these artists, working in the context of minimalism and post-minimalism, was a medium with which to systematically probe the limits and experiences of the known.

Consequently, as artists creating new and complex mixed-means artworks encompassing a collage of different formal strategies and technological features of the video medium, all played a role in moulding the expansionist synthetic tradition of contemporary artmaking.[27] As installation artists working in the late 1960s and early to mid-1970s, they were involved in rejecting nature as a valid subject of art and instead emphasising the creation of hermetic languages as experimental languages.[28] In fact, they were interested in exploring—as stated earlier—live and delayed transmissions, so that they could generate different forms of dislocation and confrontation, expressed in a conceptually rigorous manner; they were interested in the idea of video as a temporal mirror. This signified a basic enquiry into the phenomenological sphere of consciousness and temporality.

In any discussion of video installation's distinguishing collage materiality—aside from the critical issues of electronic composition, which gives the image its fluidity, depth, speed and intensity, and its three-dimensional space—the significance of the video monitor itself should be taken into account.[29] The monitor as a central source of diffused light, electronic images and sounds remains a central component in the genre's collage interests. It is a strange, paradoxical object—tangible, yet at the same time somehow ephemeral. It is a captivating generator of infinite images and sounds. More to the point, it allows for many different imagistic and sonic compositions which contribute to the video installation's collage look and its intertextuality. For example, we can have images that are reversed, layered, accumulated, displaced. Over the decades, there have been various strategies to 'liberate' the image from the monitor. These have typically taken the form of using a video projector to magnify and project images on different surfaces, encasing the monitor in a wooden construction or in a wall, darkening the room so that only the image is visible, or having it partly visible by being reflected through glass, water or mirrors.

The monitor's presence in a video installation also embodies the medium's elaborate, shifting relationship to television since the 1960s. Television was a new object of furniture in the homes of the 1950s. Vito Acconci's perceptive reading of this underscores how the new medium was placed in the cultural position usually reserved for sculpture.[30] His incisive ideas on this subject are grounded in a cultural and existential analysis of what the genre signifies in respect to its hybrid imagistic and temporal structures.

Briefly, Acconci claims that the monitor's dominance in a video installation has to do with our perceptual habits and cultural expectations of television in relation to the rest of the sculptural objects that fill our living rooms: the monitor is representative of the future, and the rest of the installation is indicative of the past, and is in danger of fading away.

Since the emergence of the video image from its cuboid container, we have also now witnessed, over last decade, the development of modern film and video projective installations in the gallery space. These new moving image art installations and projections need to be seen in the context of the history of video installations. Indeed, as Païni notes in his account of projective installations, there were three cultural logics which shaped the image: (a) the formal, with painting, printmaking and architecture, ending in the 18th century; (b) the dialectical, with film, photography and the film frame, during the 19th century; (c) the paradoxical, with the creation of cybernetics, video and the holograph.[31] For Païni, what was significant was the 'concomitant appearance in the 1970s of projective installations in art and computers, the luminous expulsion and the coded implosion'.[32]

Therefore, by the 1990s, installation art in general—including video installations—was informed by the concept of the engaged viewer and the general notion of interactivity. The idea of the engaged viewer, as Catherine Elwes notes, came to dominate modern cultural theory and interactivity itself was established due to the rapid development of computer-operated delivery systems.[33] However, as we can all attest, there was a plethora of interactive video installations over the last decade and a half, and they had varying degrees of critical success. The reasons for this are complex—aesthetic, cultural, technological, and philosophical—but many interactive artists became sutured into the techno-hyperbole that heralded the new technologies of extraction and immersion, and also lacked a necessary self-reflexive approach to questions about art, culture, gender, power and technology.

However, this is not to say that all interactive video installations did little to engage the gallery-goer's imagination. Far from it. Artists such as Gary Hill, Luc Courchesne, Bill Seaman, Simon Biggs and Toshio Iwai, amongst others, have used interactive technology imaginatively in their installation works. One of the more memorable examples of interactive video installations is Hill's extraordinary *Tall Ships* (1992). This work uses sensors to allow the gallery-goer to activate the work's projected video images of 16 black and white, ghostly, silent individuals located in a darkened corridor-like space. As you traverse the space your movements—courtesy of the installation's computer-based interactive system—trigger the movements of the figures. These figures approach you, pause and then turn away from you, creating in you, in Chris Darke's words, the sensation of 'simultaneous distance and intimacy'.[34] This work, which was first exhibited at *documenta IX*, in Kassel, Germany, is one of the artist's key works, and typifies Hill's rigorous and poetic project, which is to define in his art, according to Chrissie Iles, a 'tension between detachment and absorption' and thus to position ' language (including silence) as the interface between the material and the immaterial'.[35]

Clearly, video installation, as part of video art's complex history, with its unique aesthetic, cultural and technological qualities, facilitated the introduction of time-based moving-image art into the gallery. As has been discussed above, video artists since the 1960s, such as Paik, Viola and Hill, amongst many others, have created—both in single-channel and installation formats—works that have shaped the contemporary audiovisual sphere. This includes the current focus in the gallery world on large-scale video projections and installations that directly highlight the complex connections between cinema, TV, video and digital media. Video now has become a major conduit between contemporary art and film. Artists such as Douglas Gordon, Mark Wallinger, Gillian Wearing, Tacita Dean, Mark Lewis, Isaac Julien and Stan Douglas, amongst others, have drawn upon the classic cinema and its attendant 'death of cinema' discourse to create installations that clearly evince the new willingness of galleries in the 1990s to engage with the moving image. All these artists deal with selected elements of the cinema: a certain scene or sequence, or the re-staging of a particular film, etc.—for instance, Gordon Douglas's slowed-down version of Alfred Hitchcock's film masterpiece *24 Hour Psycho* (1995) or Mark Lewis's recreation of Michael Powell's controversial film *Peeping Tom* (2000).

It needs to be remembered that many of these artists previously considered the gallery a cinematic tomb, functioning, in Darke's fitting words, as a 'repository for the splinters and debris of cinema'.[36] Classical cinema has fragmented into many different contexts, thanks to the proliferation of moving image delivery systems such as the Internet, video, surveillance, games and cable TV, and now it is becoming rarer to experience it in its traditional form, as a mass art form in a darkened auditorium.

Established filmmakers such as Chantal Akerman, Atom Egoyan, Harun Farocki, Peter Greenaway, Raul Ruiz and Chris Marker, to name a few significant relevant exemplars, have also made numerous film and video installations that centre on the moving image in the gallery context. Some of these filmmakers (Akerman, Ruiz and Egoyan) have also tried in recent years to 'exhibit projections'.

Interestingly, the installation space today is where the image operates as an object in time and space, as opposed to the conventional form of spectatorial suture with classical montage cinema. As Darke points out, the spectator of these modern moving image installations is asked 'to exercise a new skill, what one might call "three-dimensional montage"'.[37]

Relatedly, Bellour has also made a fascinating observation: that the notion of the installation has long been located in film sets, in the form of dramatised and stylised environments 'installed' within a film's narrative space.[38]

There always has been, as Mark Nash reminds us, a tension between advocates of 'single-channel' cinema—the traditional form of cinema where the viewer is looking at a single screen for a fixed period of time—and those of a multi-screen, multi-channel works of installation for a museum or a gallery.[39] For Nash this tension has always been a sign of a mistrust and misunderstanding of cinema itself. Regardless of whether or not one agrees with this, the point is that from the 1990s onwards, cinema—both narrative and documentary—has become a major influence on contemporary art practice, especially in the form of projective video installations.

Certain senior 'single-channel' filmmakers, such as Jean-Luc Godard and Chris Marker, have created a practice where the history and memory of cinema have been preserved thanks to digital technology. Nowadays artists and filmmakers creating installations for the white cube of the gallery can access cheap desktop editing programs and a range of digital video cameras to make their unique contributions to the cinematic arts.

To conclude, video installations have made a singular contribution over the last 40 years—because of their unique collage aesthetics—to the more recent introduction of the moving image in the gallery and museum. In many ways, video installations and projections have also played a substantial role in the convergence of film and video in our current 'post-medium world' (Michael Rush). Artists now make videos—in both single-channel and installation formats—and refer to them as film. In the process, there has been a displacement taking place with reference to a historical understanding of video art as a complex art form. More recently, certain artists have been creating video installations in the context of a reconfigured conceptual and minimal art tradition; others have been exploring the moving image for its cinematic history and genres.

Video installations and projections, in their far-ranging intertextual diversity, matter because they are playing a significant part in the articulation of a new world of seeing, as defined by Paul Virilio's aesthetics of disappearance.[40] When we encounter a video installation we are reminded that our increasingly mediatised world is saturated with certain kinds of images that contaminate us in our daily lives. These images, as Virilio argues, communicate to each other and consist of ocular images, mental images, optical images, pictorial images, as well as photographic, cinematographic, videographic and the infographic images. These images constitute an 'image-block' and we can't comprehend them, because we are blinded by their specularity.

The challenge remains to forge a critical language that is subtle enough to deal adequately with the aesthetic, cultural and epistemological features of video installations. Because what they are saying to us is yet invisible, yet unsayable, video installations are urging us to establish an art of seeing as envisioned by Michel Foucault: that is to say, an art of seeing that underlines the poetic capacity to see outside ourselves.[41]

NOTES

1 Andrew Benjamin, 'Matter and meaning: on installations', *Art & Design*, vol. 8, nos 5/6, 1993, p. 31

2 For information on installation art (and video installations in particular) as three-dimensional collage constructions, their major indebtedness to the historical avant-garde and their overall problematising of the material meaning and institution of art in late consumer culture, see Dan Cameron's 'The savage garden landscape as metaphor in recent American installations', in *The Savage Garden* [exhibition catalogue], Fundacion Caja De Pensiones, Madrid, 1991, pp. 16–48; John Conomos, 'Video installations: horizons unlimited', in Brian Langer (ed.), *Video Forms*, The Fourth Australian Video Festival, Sydney, 1989, pp. 9–17; Ann-Marie Duguet, 'Video installations' (trans. Sally Couacaud), *Scan +*, vol. 1, 1988, pp. 32–35; Dorine Mignot (ed.), *The Luminous Image*, Stedelijk Museum, Amsterdam, 1984; Margaret Morse, 'Video installation art: the body, the image, and the space-in-between', in Doug Hall and Sally Jo Fifer (eds), *Illuminating Video*, Aperture/Bay Video Coalition, New York, 1991, pp. 153–67; René Payant (ed.), *Video*, Artextes, Montreal, 1986; and Nicholas Zurbrugg, 'Installation art—essence and existence', in *Australian Perspecta 1991* [exhibition catalogue], Art Gallery of New South Wales, Sydney, 1991, pp. 16–21. For more recent critical literature on video installations, see Adam Geczy and Benjamin Gennochio (eds), *What Is Installation?*, Power Publications, Sydney, 2001; Nicola De Oliveira, Nicola Oxley and Michael Perry, *Installation Art*, Thames & Hudson, London, 1994; and Julie H. Reiss, *From Margin to Center*, MIT Press, Cambridge, Massachusetts, 1999.

3 Benjamin, p. 33.

4 Geczy & Gennochio, p. 3.

5 Zurbrugg, pp. 17–21.

6 ibid., p. 17.

7 On the conceptual difficulties of defining the genre of video installation in terms of its mutating material diversity of collage and intertextual concerns, see especially Duguet, pp. 32, 35; Morse, pp. 153–54; and Payant, p. 171.

8 Cited in Duguet, p. 32.

9 Dominique Païni, 'Should we put an end to projection?', *October*, 110, fall, 2004, p. 33.

10 ibid.

11 Payant, pp. 127–31.

12 Morse's claim that video installations belong to the so-called presentation arts (as opposed to the more illusionistic arts) is a valid one, meriting further critical attention. See Morse, pp. 156–61.

13 ibid., p. 155.

14 ibid., p. 156.

15 ibid., p. 154.

16 ibid., pp. 158–59.

17 ibid., p. 156.

18 ibid., p. 159.

19 ibid.

20 Interview with the author, 24 November 1993.

21 Duguet, p. 34.

22 Donald Kuspit, 'Bill Viola: the passing', *Artforum*, vol. 32, no. 1, 1993, pp. 145, 204.

23 Shelley Rice, 'Video installation 1983', *Afterimage* (special supplement), vol. 11, no. 5, 1983.

24 John Hanhardt, 'De-collage/collage: Notes toward a re-examination of the origins of video art', in Hall & Fifer, p. 76.

25 ibid.

26 On the concept that video installations extend the imaginative, cultural and sculptural possibilities of video, see Payant, p. 128. On the intricate shifting dialectic between TV and video—the literature on this aspect of video is appreciably extensive—see Vito Acconci's excellent article, 'Television, furniture and sculpture: the room with the American view', in Mignot, pp. 13–23; John Hanhardt, 'Video in Fluxus', *Art and Text*, no. 37, September 1990, pp. 86–91; Kathy Rae Huffman, 'Video art: what's TV got to do with it?', in Hall & Fifer, pp. 81–90; Rob Perre, *Into Video Art*, ConRumore, Rotterdam/ Amsterdam, 1988, pp. 52–62.

27 On video's genesis in the 1960s in relation to the historical avant-garde and American postwar time-based mixed-means arts, see Gottfried Hattinger, 'Introduction: a historical survey on the subject', in *Catalogue Ars Electronica '88 Supplement* (English translation), Festival of Art, Technology and Society, Brucknerhaus, Linz, 1988, pp. 8–15; Peter Frank, 'Postwar performance: mixing means and metiers', in *Catalogue Ars*

Electronica '88 Supplement pp. 33–45. Frank's article is exceptionally comprehensive and useful. For a much more succinct overview of the subject, see Silvio Gaggi, 'Sculpture, theatre and art performance: notes on the convergence of the arts', *Leonardo*, vol. 19, no. 1, 1986, pp. 45–52.

28 Of course there are numerous examples of video artists who have made landscape videos (Bill Viola, Joan Brassil, Rita Myers, Mary Lucier, Doug Hall, Dan Reeves, etc) in their explorations of nature. But the distinction that needs to be made here is, generally speaking, video artists since the 1960s (because of their postmodern concerns as image-makers anchored in the theoretical and stylistic currents of the historical avant-garde, Fluxus, and postwar European and American avant-gardism) have been critical of idealist and romantic representations of landscape/nature in contemporary art.

29 On the importance of the video monitor and its critical and sculptural implications for video installations, see Acconci, passim; Duguet, pp. 33–36; and Payant, pp. 128

30 Acconci.

31 Païni, p. 28.

32 ibid., p. 32.

33 Catherine Elwes, *Video Art*, I.B. Tauris, London/New York, 2005, p. 152.

34 Chris Darke, *Light Readings*, Wallflower, London, 2000, p. 181.

35 Chrissie Iles, " The metaphysician of media," in Holger Broeker (ed.), *Gary Hill: Selected Works 1976–2001*: Kunstmuseum Wolfsburg, DuMont Literatur und Kunst Verlag, Cologne, 2002, p.17.

36 Darke, op. cit., p. 160.

37 ibid., p. 168.

38 ibid.

39 Mark Nash, 'Wait until dark', in Robert Violette (ed.), *Tate International Arts and Culture*, Tate Gallery, London, 2002, p. 56.

40 Arguably, if we accept Virilio's dromological definition of our era as being one where audiovisual speed is replacing human perception and reflexes, and where the image is no longer so much interested in representation as it is in suggesting 'a kind of seeing without knowing; a pure seeing', then it is possible that video installations in their intertextual diversity are contributing to the construction of the new order of

seeing advanced by Virilio. See Jérôme Sans, 'Interview with Paul Virilio', *Flash Art*, no. 137, 1988, pp. 57–61; 'Interview with Paul Virilio', *Block*, 14, autumn 1988, pp. 4–7; Paul Virilio, 'Trans-appearance', *Artforum*, vol. 28, no. 10, 1989, pp. 128–29.

41 See John Rajchman, 'Foucault's art of seeing', *October*, no. 4, spring 1988, pp. 97–117.

Border crossings: Jean-Luc Godard as video essayist

The great musician seeks only music, the poet poetry, the painter painting—
Godard seeks only cinema.

Jean Douchet

Everything is cinema. Everything divided has always profoundly moved me:
documentary and fiction ...

Jean-Luc Godard

Jean-Luc Godard is, unquestionably, one of the most innovative and
searching image-makers in the history of 20th century art. Godard
always searches out new paths of creativity, thereby extending our
understanding of the image. Irrespective of the medium—film,
video, writing, television—Godard's dazzling, multifaceted oeuvre
suggests someone who is always prepared to start from zero in
order to make sense of the multiplying, mutating signs around him.
Godard is prepared to think aloud, to stutter, and to see what exactly
is taking shape in front of him. It is Godard's inventive transgeneric
experimentation that most clearly informs his peerless art.

To speak of the labyrinthine enormity of Godard's passionate
quest to create cinema, video, installation art, television, sound art and
multimedia as a 'writer–painter' (Raymond Bellour) is an extremely
difficult thing to do.[1] One is forced to state the obvious about his pivotal
role in postwar European cinema, simply because too often we tend
to ignore his presence as though he were an (in)visible given: we may
mistakenly think that his 'revolutionary' questioning of cinema's past,
present and future took place only in the 1960s, during the heady days
of the French New Wave and the events of May 1968. Nothing could be
further from the truth. For to discuss Godard's films, videos, graphic art
and television programs is to deal with a rhizomatic Godard.

Of which Godard do we speak? The Godard of the 1950s, at the
Cinémathèque and writing for *Cahiers du cinéma*? The Godard of the

1960s, before or after his collaborations with Jean-Pierre Gorin? Or the Godard of the 1970s, with his (then) collaborator–partner Anne-Marie Miéville, living in Grenoble? Or the 'solitary' Godard of the 1980s, living at Rolle?[2] To speak of 'periods' in Godard's work belies the intricate intertextuality and referentiality of his complex, multilayered oeuvre. Though we may characterise his life as image-maker into seven broad episodes, as Colin McCabe did over a decade ago, all of them are emphatically interconnected, and all ricochet off each other in terms of the complex thematic, textual and stylistic tendencies of the genres and mediums Godard has worked in: film criticism, feature films, essay films and videos, commercial videos, video art, installation art, sound art and television.[3]

There is no other filmmaker more intertwined with the fate of the image than Godard—no one so compelled to create a new poetics of image-making that is anchored in the dialectic between literature/writing and the cinema (and more recently, of course, video). From the beginning, Godard's involvement with cinema was with its other: and for him, cinema's constant other since the late 1950s and early 1960s, has been television. If we think of Jean-Paul Belmondo as a quasi-television host in *Breathless* (1960), then Jean-Paul Fargier's paradoxical observation—that perhaps Godard has never done cinema but has always in fact done television—may have a particular resonance apropos Godard's video work since the 1970s.[4] It is an interesting hypothesis, albeit one that does not quite match up with the evidence presented by Godard's always expanding corpus of transgeneric works. Bellour, commenting on Fargier's idea, gives an inflection that makes more sense of Godard's utopian drive to find ways of transforming the image, of giving it new powers of enunciation. He makes the observation that 'cinema must become the name of what we call television. Because that was the name given to a new passion of the image, to the mystery of its presence and its distancing.'[5] Thus television, for Godard (the exclusively contemporary filmmaker who, according to Serge Daney, is 'dedicated to the present'), represents new ways of seeing and hearing, new modalities of composition and decomposition (accelerating and slowing down the image), new strategies of mise en scène. In a word, television's alias—'video' or 'the electronic image'—signified, for him, an unexplored potential for locating new sites in the image.

Video is a whole way of being and thinking, as Philippe Dubois has argued, a way of writing electronically with images and sounds about image and sound, and of posing ethical, historical and theoretical questions about art, cinema, culture and society.[6] Video represents a way of breathing through, and being intimately associated with images, a means always within one's reach.

Since *Ici et ailleurs* (1974), Godard has expanded his experimentation with the new electronic image and sound systems, in order to 'redefine representation in reference to bodies, time, space and speech'.[7] Godard's 'border-crossing' activity over the last 30 or so years has taken us into the new forbidden zone between film and video—a new territory of imaginative possibilities, of 'in-between' forms, gestures and spaces (Bellour) that is predicated on Godard attempting ('essaying' in Montaigne's sense) 'to see not this or that, but only to see if there is something to see'.[8]

Godard's supple ability to locate new images and sounds in the 'in-between' spaces of cinema, video and photography suggests a markedly plural form of audiovisual writing which is contributing to the underlying concerns and methods of the hybrid intertextuality that characterises today's new media. With Godard's major essay-videos, such as *Scénario du film Passion* (1982), *Soft and Hard* (1986)—both tapes made in collaboration with Anne-Marie Miéville—and the Edgar Allan Poe-inspired *Puissance de la parole/The Power of Words* (1988), we are on the forefront of new anti-binary forms of electronic and digital mass communication.

These essay-videos—*Six fois deux/Sur et sous la communication* (1976), *France/tour/detour/deux/enfants* (1977-78), *Histoire(s) du cinéma*, and in more recent times, *The Old Place* (1999, co-directed by Miéville), *L'Origine du vingt et unième siecle* (2000), *Dans le noir du temps* (2002) and *Liberté et patrie* (2002, co-directed with Miéville)—constitute Godard's notable 'between method' (Deleuze) of image-making.[9] To make images and sounds as an open-ended, reflective form of creative stammering, and of analysing and making film, video and television in a different manner in order to be able to continue doing so, underlines the *utopian* character of Godard's art.

The 'writerly attributes' of the highly elastic video medium are ideal for Godard, and for other artists, including Robert Cahen, Thierry

Kuntzel, Chris Marker, Steve Fagin and Irit Batsry (to suggest a few), who seek to construct a Mallarmé-influenced approach to electronic image-making. These artists share a sustained interest in exploring the idea of *video-stylo* writing (following Alexandre Astruc's concept of the *camera-stylo* in cinema) in postmodern techno-creativity. This is a highly self-questioning, non-conclusive kind of electronic writing, uncertain of its own authority; it stops and starts in an intermittent narrative fashion, weaving a transgeneric hybrid.

For Astruc, who was one of the early promoters of the essay film, as Nora Alter reminds us in her resonant critique of Godard's 1994 essayistic self-portrait *JLG/JLG—Autoportrait de decembre, camera-stylo* image-making would:

> break free from the tyranny of what is visual, from the image for its own sake, from the immediate and concrete demands of the narrative, to become a means of writing, just as flexible and subtle as written language ... More or less literal 'inscriptions' as images as essays.[10]

Essentially, this form of videography is indebted to Michel de Montaigne's concept of the literary essay as well as to autobiography and the self-portrait: video as a personal, intimate cinema, trembling with experimental risk-taking, crossing generic boundaries without a passport; the film/video artist as a 'go-between' among cinema, literature, the visual arts and new media.[11] It means using video collage as an elliptical, fragmentary mode of image and sound writing exemplifying a 'Northwest Passage' aesthetic.[12] This is a discursive transmedia view of cultural production that criticises the constraints of modernism and official culture. Equally, it endeavours to capture the polyphonic indeterminacy of the new essay form (Theodor Adorno, Roland Barthes, John Cage, Friedrich Nietzsche and Paul Valéry).

It is important to remember that the Montaignian essay, as exemplified by Montaigne's *Essais* (1850), is recognised as the paramount precursive exemplar of the literary-philosophical essay form that had such an influence over the Enlightenment and the French Revolution, and advanced the more modern notion of the genre as a fragmentary, wandering, open-ended form of writing that fuses 'fact' with 'fiction' and is not explicitly concerned with defining absolute truth claims but is more interested in, to deploy Georg Lukács's expression, 'not the verdict ... but the process of judging'.[13]

Godard's form of *video-stylo* writing (which is indebted to Montaigne as much as to Astruc) permits him to transcribe rigorously and subtly his inner thoughts and feelings, thus formulating new fictions, new strategies of presenting information, new means of addressing the viewer. Perhaps the most recognisable textual trope of Godard's art is the mise en scène of direct address: where Godard's self-reflexive voice questions the work at hand, its fictionality, and cultural and/or production features. Godard's films and videos are thus linked to Jean Cocteau's Orphic-inflected autobiographical cinema of human creativity, with its sinuous narrating voice and wondrous, neon-like astrological drawings.

Godard's presentation of the act of seeing and hearing his own work as it takes shape before him typifies an oblique image writing, reflecting the wisdom of Montaigne's words: 'The world is but a perennial movement. All things in it are in constant motion ... I cannot keep my subject still ... I do not portray being, I portray passing.'[14] This is evident, for instance, in *Scenario du film Passion*, where Godard suggests that images are meant to render the invisible visible. Godard's stirring studio discussion, which takes place in front of his large TV screen (the 'white beach'), constitutes a grand search for the function and reality of today's images, predicated on the dictum '*voir-recevoir*' (see-receive). Referring to *Scenario*, Jean-Louis Leutrat persuasively argues how for Godard, in a fleeting and enigmatic moment, 'the relationship between the image to be made and the image already [made] ... contains the trace which belongs to the past'.[15] It is a prefigurative fragment. What makes the history of cinema possible, Godard maintains, is that there remain images which embody its traces, and these traces mysteriously resemble us. Godard is thus an author, 'the consummate essayist', who needs to create cinema and video as a continuous dialogue, a theatre of memory, infusing the image with language, with quotations.[16]

Godard's film and video essays, including his feature films, should be contextualised in relation to video art in the 1960s and new media in the last two decades, in line with Bellour's view that Godard's work has much to say about the 'crisis of the real' resulting from the emergence of the new 'in-between' forms of digital representation that are emanating from the ongoing computer-based collision of film, photography, multimedia and television.[17] Godard's essayistic practice of producing new anti-binary visual and sonic forms—Bellour's 'unspeakable images'—graphically echoes a similar crisis that took place in poetry (according to Mallarmé) in the 19th century.

Bellour argues that the divide between cinema and the new digital media is a very complex historical phenomenon obliging us to see Nam June Paik's first encounter with the Sony Portapak in the streets of New York, Christian Metz's first semiological essays on the cinema, and Godard's *Contempt* (1963) as all belonging to the same historical moment.

Video collage (particularly in reference to its organic and 'musical' aspects) offers the opportunity to write electronically—composing and decomposing images and sounds in a 'live' way. Godard's use of collage is structured by his obsession with harnessing the image to language. According to Bellour, this has four different modalities.[18]

From Godard's shorts in the 1950s to his current videotapes, we encounter the presence of books, heralding a concern to make art which is indebted more to language and writing than to music and painting. The second modality is quotation, issuing from characters and books like fragmentary traces pregnant with meaning, veiling and unveiling the image. The third modality consists of privileging text over image: ads, signs and graffiti are often foregrounded in his works, like Cubist collage elements. Lastly, there are the voices of characters and quotations, as well as Godard's own voice addressing his viewers.

In the three essay films of 1974 to 1976—*Ici et ailleurs, Numero deux* and *Comment ça va?*—Godard had already created essay-texts which (aside from their socio-cultural objectives) mix film and video. These particular works signify Godard's interest in making organic film/video forms and textures, ushering in the birth of new images and sounds through the use of the video mixer as an instrument of decomposition/composition.[19]

Godard's self-reflexive project of locating images and sounds in the 'in-between' gaps or spaces of cinema and video and television suggests a non-homogenous, mobile and plural audiovisual writing that is contributing to the current generation of new cultural technologies. However, it needs to observed that for Godard, working in video as an expression of montage represents, in Leutrat's words, 'a highly risky form of acrobatic thinking, a high-wire video artistry that not only jumps from art to art (painting, music, poetry, film) but also, within each art, attempts the most prodigious and precarious leaps'.[20] This essentially means that Godard, in his search for a new foundation for the image, walks a fine line between analogue and digital image-making. He sees the analogue image as the site for creativity, and as being 'threatened' by digital technology; therefore, Godard prefers to use the digital to seek new and unmapped horizons of analogue image-making. As Godard himself puts it:

> Invention, or creation, is always an analogical thing. Maybe that will change. Digital interests me as a thing in itself, or as a technique, but not as a ground for creation. Otherwise, the digital becomes the foundation and the analogical disappears.[21]

While we may not subscribe to Godard's emphasis on creativity being tied up with analogue image-making, what is evident is the artist's life-long aim: trying to make the image (in its forms, silence, movement, textures, spaces and stillness) capture life.

According to Michael Temple and James S. Williams, the complex issue of Godard's experimental approach to analogical cinema and the 'digital' is one of ambiguity and shifting attitudes, because for the filmmaker, since the invention of the magic lantern something called 'cinema' has always existed, though in a succession of different hardwares and related different discursive socio-cultural formations.[22] More to the point, as Peter Wollen notes, Godard's interests in the cinema, television and video centre not only around his perennial concern for experiment and technical change (viz. Godard's involvement with bounce lighting, the Anton camera, the technologies of video editing and digital enhancement); crucially, these interests 'should be seen as a form of resistance against a symbolic but real occupation, a way of infiltrating enemy-held territory in order to maintain the memory of cinema, to keep a desire for true cinema somehow flickeringly alive for the next millennium'.[23]

Moreover, as is evident in the 'writerly' meditative stylistics of *Scenario du film Passion* and in the pulsing collaged images and rhythms of *Puissance de la parole* (*The Power of Words*), Godard discovered that through directly manipulating and mixing images, 'seeing (with video) is thinking (live, with the image)'.[24] After the analytical video-scalpel of the mid-1970s and the slow-motion exercises (*France/tour/detour*) and video scenarios (*Scenario du film Passion*) of the early to mid-1980s, we have in the new complete and autonomous videos of the late 1980s and 1990s a 'video-vibration' whose collaged textuality operates 'like a cardiac pulsing that carries into and echoes throughout the whole universe the infinite marks of thought and speech'.[25]

However, more recently Godard has expressed certain misgivings that video, which for him has always been another name for cinema, is being overtaken by information technology. As he puts it, when he was interviewed by Youssef Ishaghpour, primarily about *Histoire(s)*:

> Video seemed to me one of the avatars of cinema, but it's become something rather different in broadcast television where there's no creation at all any more, just broadcasting. But video's going to be overtaken by information technology or some sort of hybrid mixture which will get increasingly remote from cinematic creation as it can still just about exist today. I'd say there was no very big difference between video and cinema, but you could use one like another. There are things you can do better with one, so with another you do something else. Video came from cinema, but you can't say now that IT comes from cinema.[26]

What matters is Godard's trans-disciplinary, essayistic approach to image-making as a form of transmedia creativity and thinking that resists the conventional binaries and boundaries of traditional film and video scholarship: fiction/non-fiction, documentary/avant-garde, and even film/video. When Ed Emshwiller, the late American computer animator/filmmaker, once asked Godard why he did not bother with specific technological questions, he replied: 'Video, film, writing—it's all the same to me.'[27] This 'Northwest Passage' approach to image-making questions our tunnel-vision fixities about art, ourselves and our socio-cultural institutions—located at the edge, always in the midst of things, incomplete.

Godard has shown us that it is possible to make films, videos, sound compositions, graphic art and TV, and still talk and write about them as if, as David Thomson aptly puts it, they are 'part of the same conversation'.[28] He has, time and again, demonstrated that films and videos can also be works of criticism. Godard is a supreme example of someone who has produced works that demonstrate Adorno's view of the essay as a consummate site for critique, and in relation to art, it produces constant new forms of presentation.[29] Alter's Adornian analysis of Daniel Eisenberg's trilogy of memory essay films in the 1980s and 1990s incorporates Edward Small's 'direct theory' of non-fiction cinema's growing essay-film genre: film theory is fundamentally flawed because it relies on words and written texts, and they are by their nature inadequate to theorise the ideas and elements of a medium which is audiovisual.[30] Small posits the view that a theory of film should thus be a film. This has also been Godard's position, throughout his career. For Small, 'certain kinds of film and video constitute a mode of theory, theory direct, without the mediation of a separate semiotic system'.[31] Small's 'direct theory' of experimental avant-garde production parallels, as Alter correctly points out, August Wilhelm von Schlegel's assertion that a theory about a novel should be a novel.[32]

Godard's view of himself as an essayist at work in a variety of media reflects his overall expanding oeuvre; it is only very recently, as Michael Witt has suggested, that he should be seen as a multimedia collage artist who works in multiple forms.[33] Take, for example, his magisterial *Histoire(s)*. Through its essayistic use of video to collage film clips, photographs, painting, drawings, voice, music, song and literary texts, it makes us rethink Godard as an essayist who sees creativity as an intertextual continuum across many different media. As early as in 1962, when Godard was interviewed by a *Cahiers* group that included Bertrand Tavernier, he told them:

> As a critic I thought of myself as a filmmaker. Today I still think of myself as a critic, and in a sense I am, more than ever before. Instead of writing criticism, I make a film, but the critical dimension is subsumed. I think of myself as an essayist, producing essays in novel form or novels in essay form: only instead of writing them, I film them. Were the cinema to disappear, I would simply accept the inevitable and turn to television; were television to disappear, I would revert to pencil and paper. For there is a clear continuity between all forms of expression. It's all me.[34]

Thus, *Histoire(s)*, which for Ishaghpour represents 'a memoir of the cinema and the century, a memoir of time inside time', is not only an eight-part, four-and-a-half hour video series; it is also four art books and a boxed set of audio CDs issued by ECM records in 1999.[35] But it has been circulated in various other forms as well: there have been published working documents, broadcast television (in France in 1999) and many different interviews, texts and public appearances throughout the series' long-term gestation period of 20 years. So *Histoire(s)*'s different perspectives of video art, graphic art, sound art and criticism indicate that it would be more rewarding to view Godard's work as a site of conceptual, formal and generic multiplicity.

The Godard corpus can therefore be profitably viewed as, to paraphrase Witt, an attempt to negotiate postwar technological change in terms of human and socio-cultural implications, and most significantly, to reinvent cinema in relation and response to successive challenges from television (during the New Wave and after), then deregulated neo-television and domestic video culture (including the video-art inflected art cinema of the 1980s), and, in more recent years, digital technology.[36]

Furthermore, Godard's complex mutating oeuvre—including his collaborative activities with Miéville during the last two decades under the auspices of their production company Sonimage—can be best described in the way Catherine Grant recently suggested, as the combination of expanded cinema and fine art: installation art.[37] In other words, all the various manifestations of their output—CDs, films, videos, interviews, and books—can be conceptualised as a kind of expansive large installation, always undergoing construction and in constant dialogue with its audience.

Concomitantly, in this specific context, Godard's fascination with André Malraux's notion of the museum without walls shapes the conceptual architecture of *Histoire(s)* as an audiovisual collage archive for the preservation of the traces of cinema during its 100-year evolution. As Witt opines, Godard and Miéville have defined the public cultural sphere as a vast gallery in which to create their project, using the mass media and other cultural forms.[38]

Godard always held fast to a profound, though paradoxical, attachment to the grand European traditions of art—as theorised by his early intellectual mentors, such as Élie Faure and André Malraux—as a source of classical great works, and at the same time, as a radical project of critiquing the norm.[39] This is clearly evident in the *Histoire(s)* and, broadly speaking, in all his essayistic experiments since the 1970s, which are graphically animated by the ghost of Montaigne. In 1985 Godard said to critic Alain Bergala that video 'taught me to see cinema and to rethink the working of cinema in another way'.[40] In this specific context Godard stands alone in cinema.

Godard's use of video suggests an artist who is constantly seeking uncharted creative sites within images. For Godard, video is a 'live' medium of images and sounds, where seeing is thinking and thinking is seeing. He leaves cinema and video as open questions. He remains, as always, one of the chief voyagers of the image.

NOTES

1   Raymond Bellour & Mary Lea Bandy (eds), *Jean-Luc Godard: Son + Image, 1974–1991*, Museum of Modern Art, New York, 1992. This excellent catalogue accompanied an exhibition of Godard's work since the mid-1970s and was a timely and fitting testimonial to his contribution to the concerns and direction of cinema, television and video.

2   I have used inverted commas around the word 'solitary' because of Deleuze's remarks concerning Godard's creative solitude in the context of the filmmaker's move in 1979 (after *King Lear*) to Rolle, Switzerland to live by himself: 'He's a man who works a lot, so he is, necessarily, absolutely alone. But his is not just any solitude.' Gilles Deleuze, '*Trois questions sur "Six fois deux"*', *Cahiers du cinema*, no. 271, November 1976. Reprinted in Bellour & Bandy, pp. 34–41.

3   Colin MacCabe, 'Jean-Luc Godard: a life in seven episodes (to date)', in Bellour & Bandy.

4   Cited in Raymond Bellour, '(Not) Just an other filmmaker', in Bellour & Bandy, pp. 217–18.

5   ibid., p. 218.

6   Philippe Dubois, 'Video thinks what cinema creates', in Bellour & Bandy, pp. 169–85.

7   ibid., p. 169.

8   ibid.

9   On Deleuze, regarding his characterisation of Godard's work as resembling a 'between' method of image-making, see Deleuze, 'Three questions about *Six fois deux*', in Bellour & Bandy, pp. 35–41.

10   Nora Alter, 'Mourning, sound, and vision: Jean-Luc Godard's JLG/JLG', *Camera Obscura*, 44, vol. 15, no. 2, 2000, p. 91. For Astruc's quote and idea of '*camera-stylo*' cinema, see Alexandre Astruc, 'The birth of new avant-garde: *la camera stylo*', in Peter Graham (ed.), *The New Wave: Critical Landmarks*, Doubleday, New York, 1968.

11   On the idea of Godard's oeuvre incorporating the open-ended, reflective tropes of the essay (as articulated by Montaigne's work) and the subsequent development of the essay-film and essay-video, see Michael Renov, 'Mekas as essayist', in David James (ed.), *To Free the Cinema*, Princeton University Press, Princeton, 1992, pp. 215–39. On Godard as a video essayist and the *video-stylo* genre, see also John Conomos, Video as Electronic Collage and as Writing, Sydney: University of Technology, [MA research thesis], 1994, chapter 7. And on the issue of autobiography and self-portrait in Godard's work—especially *JLG/JLG* (1994)—see Nora Alter & Kaja Silverman, 'The author as receiver', *October*, 96, Spring 2001, pp. 17–34.

12   On the idea of a 'Northwest Passage' form of anti-binary creativity in image-making and writing, see Michel Serres, 'Northwest Passage', in Timothy Simone et al. (ed.), *Oasis*, Semiotext(e), New York, 1989, p. 104.

13   For a succinct account of Montaigne's legacy on the film essay form and Georg Lukács's definition of the essay, see Nora Alter, 'Memory essays', in Ursula Biemann (ed.), *Stuff It: The Video Essay in the Digital Age*, Edition Voldemeer, Zurich/: Springer Wien, New York, 2003, p. 12.

14   Michel de Montaigne, quoted in Michael Renov, 'Lost, lost, lost: Mekas as essayist', in James (ed.), p. 217.

15   For the notion of 'the trace' in Godard's cinema, refer to Jean-Louis Leutrat, 'Traces that resemble us: Godard's *Passion*', *SubStance*, 15, 1986, pp. 36–51.

16   Wheeler Winston Dixon, *The Films of Jean-Luc Godard*, State University of New York Press, Albany, 1997, p. 5.

17   On Bellour's so-called in-between or unspeakable images that are surfacing in our post-computer epoch due to the convergences between film, photography and video, see (amongst numerous articles) Raymond Bellour, 'The power of words, the power of images', in *Camera Obscura*, no. 24, September 1990, pp. 7–9 and 'The double helix', in *Passages de l'image*, Fundacio Caixa de Pensions, Barcelona, 1991, pp. 48–75.

18   Bellour, '(Not) Just an other filmmaker', in Bellour & Bandy, pp. 219–20.

19   Dubois, 'Video thinks what cinema creates', in Bellour & Bandy, p. 170.

20   Jean-Louis Leutrat, 'The power of language: notes on *Puissance de la parole*,*le dernier mot* and *On s'est tous défilé*', in Michael Temple &James S. Williams (eds), *The Cinema Alone*, Amsterdam University Press, Amsterdam, 2000, p.185.

21   Godard, quoted in Bellour & Bandy, p. 231.

22   Michael Temple & James S. Williams, 'Introduction to the mysteries of cinema, 1985–2000', in Temple & Williams, pp. 20–21.

23   Peter Wollen, *Paris Hollywood*, Verso, London, 2002, p. 90.

24   Dubois, 'Video thinks what cinema creates', in Bellour & Bandy, p. 173.

25   ibid., p. 182.

26   Jean-Luc Godard & Youssef Ishaghpour, *Cinema*,: Berg, Oxford and New York, 2005, p. 32.

27   Godard, quoted in Constance Penley, *The Future of an Illusion*, University of Minnesota Press, Minneapolis, 1989, p. 104.

28   David Thomson, 'That Breathless moment', *Sight and Sound*, vol. 10, no. 7, 2000, p. 31.

29   Nora Alter, 'Memory essays', in Biemann, pp. 12–13.

30   ibid.

31   Small is quoted in Alter, ibid., p. 13.

32   ibid.

33   Michael Witt, 'Shapeshifter', *New Left Review*, 29, September–October 2004, pp. 73–89.

34   See Tom Milne (ed.), *Godard on Godard*, Secker & Warburg, London, 1972, p. 171. Godard's interview is profoundly prescient given the ground-breaking transmedia emphasis of his oeuvre over the years.

35   Compare this with Godard & Ishaghpour 2005, p. 20. And on the various manifestations of *Histoire(s)*, see Michael Witt, pp. 2–3.

36   Witt, pp. 7–8.

37   Catherine Grant, 'Home movie: The curious cinematic collaboration of Anne-Marie Miéville and Jean-Luc Godard', in Michael Temple, James S. Williams & Michael Witt (eds), *For Ever Godard*, Black Dog Publishing, London, 2004, pp. 100–117, p. 419, fn. 62.

38   On the importance of Godard's videographic montage as being indebted to Andre Malraux's imaginary museum and Henri Langlois's *Cinémathèque*, and also where Godard's cinema (including, most significantly, his videos) all represent radical mental spaces where artworks recover their aura through incessant comparison, see Antoine de Baecque, 'Godard in the museum', in Temple, Williams & Witt, pp. 118–25. Baecque's article underlines the critical idea that Malraux, Langlois and Godard are practitioners of what Baecque calls 'museum-montage' (p. 121). *Histoire(s)* is an excellent example of this concept. Further, the critic/curator Dominique Païni, who mounted the exhibition *Hitchcock and Art: Fatal Coincidences* at the Pompidou Centre in 2001 and is sympathetic to the interdisciplinary collage view of cinema in *Histoire(s)*, has commissioned Godard to do a

'museum-montage' project entitled *Collages de France*, which will incorporate live imagery from Godard's Rolle studio relayed into the Pompidou Centre. See Witt, pp. 86–89.

39   Wollen, pp. 90–91. On the representation of European art and culture as open questions of form in Godard's videographic montage, as in *Histoire(s)*, refer to James S. Williams, 'European culture and artistic resistance in *Histoire(s) du cinema* [chapter 3A], *La monnaie de l'absolu*', in Temple & Williams, pp. 113–39.

40   Temple & Williams. op. cit., p. 13.

Section 3

Liquid screens: art, culture, new media

Under the technocentric culture of the last century, particularly the last decade or so, 'interactivity' has come to underpin the techno-arts, with broad significance for celluloid cinema. If we accept that CD-ROMs, multimedia, video games and the World Wide Web helped computers become prevalent in our domestic life in the early 1990s, what becomes clearer by the day is interactive media's impact on the changing concerns of classical cinema.[1] The aesthetics of interactivity are emblematic of the video game paradigm itself, and interactivity has become ubiquitous in our art, cinema and culture.

Before we continue here, it is important to remind ourselves that the media arts have impacted on contemporary art practice in significant ways, not only in terms of the complex relationships between art and new technology and the cinema, but also in terms of the overall ideas and distinctive cultural phenomena they signify. When we speak of the 'media arts' we also need to be careful with our terminology, as Darren Tofts suggests, in order to avoid being reductive in our analysis of the media arts and placing too much direct emphasis on the computer as the central agency in the contemporary art-making process.[2] It is critical to understand that media art covers a very diverse range of ideas, forms and styles across a wide spectrum of artistic practices, and the computer itself has became the dominant medium, integrating and synthesising quite a range of media.

A critical point is consistently rehearsed across the individual essays in *Mutant Media*—there is a historical continuity between 'old' and 'new' media in terms of technological experimentation. To say that the newer forms of media art lack legitimate predecessors is simply incorrect; they need to be contextualised in relation to art, culture, time and space. In many ways, today's media art is linked to art forms of the historical avant-garde and beyond, and that suggests a need to examine the complex mutating relationship between art, media and technology.

In any discussion of how artists—including filmmakers—deal with the new digital technologies it is important to also look at how artists explore the diverse cultural and social implications and contexts of the technologies they are dealing with. The computer is—paradoxically—a Janus, a two-faced instrument, an instrument of both creative empowerment and limitation, and artists using computers need to use them in a self-reflexive questioning way so that they avoid making art that is literal, banal and derivative: art that lacks a critical dialectical awareness of its own anchorage in the socio-cultural fabric of our society, or art that is popular but not challenging—aesthetically speaking—and represents, as Siegfried Zielinski once put it, 'audiovisual pottery'.[3]

Therefore, computers still need to be used primarily as a source of self-reflective creativity that is substantially aware of the fragmentary character of knowledge and the lived experience of everyday life. This suggests using computers, with their rhizomatic possibilities of techno-creativity, to see and hear across the horizons of one's discipline in a constant lateral form of self-interrogation, for computers are tools of liberation as well as of repression.

Too often we ignore our cultural mindsets when we are dealing with computers and their attendant techno-futurist myths. In new media education, for instance, computers are still, despite the proliferation of new education networks and new forms of communication, being used in a sterile, conformist way. They are commonly thought of as tools for reconfiguring the binary banalities of modernism and formalism, and used in a context-free void of ahistorical learning. This is not a new problem. Fifteen years ago, Roy Ascott complained of the unimaginative way in which computers in art education were put to the service of the market: 'This has spawned a mechanistic, technocratic attitude and an abuse of what should be seen as an extremely subtle, complex and sensitive agent of perception, cognition and action.'[4]

Clearly then, as artists, educators, filmmakers and curators we need to be sensitive to what media art is saying to us today, to be open to the wisdom of Maurice Blanchot's timely statement that 'literature writes us', not the other way around. This means being attentive to the profound (but rarely described) dialogue that is taking place between analogue and digital media. It means locating, in an interdisciplinary and self-reflective spirit, the new audiovisual media in its evolving creative and pedagogic contexts within the larger circumstances of culture, history and technology.

The challenge today is to adequately address the emergence of postmodern techno-creativity in our art galleries, museums and contemporary art spaces by critiquing it in terms of its location within the intricate currents of the cultural, the historical and the temporal. And also, to be mindful of the contradictions and issues of control, deception and subjectivity inherent in the many new forms of computer-generated interactivity. Relatedly, we also need to be aware of how today's cybernetic virus of cultural amnesia is threatening to consume memory.

Thus, we have to ask ourselves, as Darren Tofts correctly does: what is media art?[5] Is it art that uses media? But do not all forms of art use a medium? Media art, by definition, involves contemporary art practices that deal with a substantial range of different media; it is art in which the computer is a critical agent. Media art is art that resists easy categorisation because of its complex hybrid forms and multifaceted temporality. Art in which the digital component constitutes just one layer or element of an intricate multilayered network of related media. Media art, therefore, refers to computer-mediated artworks that essentially involve the concepts of immersion, interaction and interface. Both interface and immersion are implicit in the very idea of interaction. All three essays in this section of *Mutant Media*, in their various ways, underline this important aspect of media art.

It is important that we clearly differentiate the different genres or forms that make up media art. We should not use 'media art' as a general catch-all term, because that would ignore the significance of distinguishing between media art genres such as hypertext fiction, net art, installation art, virtual reality environments, CD-ROMs, computer art and so on. All these media art genres involve different creative interpretations, techniques and explorations. Despite their differences, all these media art genres collectively share many attributes, and all draw on digital media to integrate diverse media elements.

It is significant to recognise the role of media arts in the 20th century evolution of art and technology. Indeed, as Frank Popper has emphasised in his seminal book *Art of the Electronic Age* (1993), the electronic arts of the 1950s and 1960s were explicitly a part of a general historical continuum that began with the dynamic conjunction of art and technology in the historical avant-garde in the 1920s and 1930s. Popper, amongst others, has emphasised how the connections between art and technology can be traced back to the Bauhaus, with its distinctive machine aesthetic, the seminal work of László Moholy-Nagy, and certain art movements central to the historical avant-garde, such as futurism and constructivism.

In a fascinating interview, Popper attests to his lifelong interest in art and the emerging new technologies of the 20th century, and discusses how art has become 'virtualised' through the evolution of the mechanical arts into electronic arts of the 1990s and beyond.[6] Popper describes his influential innovative work on art and technology in the context of (post)modernism as being influenced by 'the positive side of emigration and exile: a kind of creative nomadism' that abolished 'geographical frontiers and intellectual privileges' and cleared the way for 'such all-embracing creations as can be found in virtual art'.[7]

In many ways, late 20th century media can be viewed, as Tofts correctly points out, as an expression of the insatiable adoption of technological novelty into media art forms, and consequently, as Lev Manovich reminds us in *The Language of New Media* (2001), the term 'media art' itself is a kind of code word for the ongoing appropriation and reworking of the basic conventions of all existing media.[8] This crucial perspective on new media and its ongoing dynamic and multifaceted relationship to celluloid cinema informs this book. In any general critical negotiation of the aesthetic language of the media arts, it is essential to know, as Manovich puts it, 'what came before'.[9] Therefore, it is important to remember that the new media of today did not emerge as a cargo cult phenomenon; it is critical to ground them in the indispensable context of the cultural, the historical and the temporal.

Digitality has in essence much to offer to the cinematic legacy that is both critical and creative. To paraphrase Timothy Murray, digitality has stimulated much speculative thinking on the death of cinema, revived forgotten cinema histories, reinvented cinema form and sharpened theoretical reasoning.[10] What is emerging now in our image culture is the phenomenon of collaboration between artist and curator in articulating the memory of cinema through presenting it in exciting new interactive formats and milieux. Melbourne's Australian Centre for the Moving Image is one such digital venue where new media is defining the memory of cinema. Such a site demonstrates how artists working in new media have accepted the challenge to think of new creative, theoretical and craft horizons into the 21st century.

Murray has recently written about how new media, in the context of our visual and intellectual cultures, should be seen as 'the digital dialectic' (Peter Lunenfeld), as being aligned with both theory and practice.[11] In other words, new media can be seen as 'code and craft'; as Murray puts it, 'the digital dialectic' might ground the Platonic idea in the actual constraints of practice.[12] Citing Gary Hill's mysterious and playful digitised videotape *Site Recite (a Prologue)* (1989), a work whose elaborate horizontal pan of shells and skulls moves in and out of perspective, reviving the Baroque conventions of the still life assemblage of memento mori, and inventing the clarity of anamorphic perspective, he poses numerous engaging questions about new media as code and craft—for instance, does cinema itself provide the code of new media's craft, and does cinema, or the idea of cinema, in the wake of Hill's tape, 'provide the reference for the free floating hallucinations of new media's art'?[13]

Jean-Luc Godard mourns the passing of the cinema into the emptiness of the digital code. It is important to capitalise on Godard's nostalgia for the passing ontology of the cinema, and to, in Murray's words, 'carry on the legacy of cinema as the crypt of the twentieth century'.[14] This means to regard the cinematic code as something lingering in digitality as a carrier of loss, mourning and melancholia.

It is imperative, when discussing the so-called digital revolution, to remember that it is actually 'the flag-pole' (Alexander Kluge) around which many media gurus, politicians and pundits have rallied.[15] It is far too simplistic to categorise all the upheavals in our contemporary media landscape under this one term. The 'convergence' argument around the digital media and cinema necessitates an awareness that each medium itself had its own complex history, requiring its own cultural and technological 'archaeology'. This is salient to the underlying 'convergence' debates that inform both a number of the essays in and the overall framework of this collection.

Thus we need to ask questions, as Thomas Elsaesser does, relating to what cinema's early years have to teach us about media transitions and what 'pertinent facts' we have generally omitted in our histories of the subject.[16] What is essential to this challenging task is nothing less than rewriting cinema's history as, in Elsaesser's telling phrase, 'an archaeology of cinema's possible futures'.[17] When trying to understand the complex mutating connections between cinema, television, video and digital media—one of the critical objectives of this book—we need to ask (as Elsaesser does) whether they belong together at all. And when one compares them, what criteria do we use, and on what basis do we do so?[18] Equally importantly, we need to comprehend, in Elsaesser 's words, 'what are the bonds keeping them together as well as the feuds that keep them apart?'[19] It is crucial to understand that all named media differ widely in terms of their institutional histories, legal frameworks and social practice.

Characteristic of Godard's profound mournful probing of cinema's possibilities is the metaphorical Cain and Abel relationship between television and its eldest 'brother', cinema, thematised in his 1980 film *Sauve qui peut (la vie)*, with the slogan *'video et cinéma = Cain et Abel'*. That slogan is part of a dialogue Paul has with Marguerite Duras. Godard's confrontation between cinema and video was a critical move in his career as one of the great shapeshifters of late 20th century media.

The new technologies in the 1990s transformed the very basis of film, initiating a shift from celluloid to plasma. The image itself shifted from chemical registration of reality to electronic analogue. Laura Mulvey's new book, *Death 24x a Second* (2006), takes up the multifaceted challenge to critical thinking represented by the new digital media and the post-1990s propensity to reflect on the history of the cinematic medium itself.[20] Mulvey's title emanates from a phrase from—who else?—Godard's *Le Petit soldat* (1963), in which we are told that cinema is 'truth 24 times a second'.

Mulvey's main focus is not film's critical capacity to capture reality, but the specific relationship between movement and stasis that the cinema medium embodies. The images on the screen stem from the mechanised motion of a celluloid strip, while behind the general illusion of movement lies a series of stillnesses, each frame consisting of a frozen instant of action. Thus the cinema is divided into two parts, as Mulvey puts it, 'linked by a beam of light, split between its material substance, the unglamorous celluloid strip running through the projector on one side and, on the other, entrancing images moving on the screen in a darkened space'.[21] For Mulvey, the shuttling between animate and inanimate is related to the thematics of death and the uncanny, which is discussed in the earlier part of the book. The relationship between movement and stillness is the key paradox of the cinema.

This relationship is examined in terms of narrative flow and film form via the major examples of Alfred Hitchcock's *Psycho*, Roberto Rossellini's *Journey to Italy* and Abbas Kiarostami's Kroker trilogy, and the minor instances of Michael Powell and Emeric Pressburger, Douglas Sirk and Michael Snow.

The book's final chapters discuss the possibilities opened up by the new technologies—particularly video and DVD—which amplify the possibilities for delaying cinema. The new technologies have given viewers a new-found capacity to control both the image and the story: to freeze frames and move around within a film, producing new techniques of close reading and forms of fetishistic investment that had hitherto been limited. The new technologies have transformed the way we experience film.

At the end of the last century new technologies created new perceptual possibilities, new ways of looking, not only at the world, but also at the internal world of cinema. The new technologies allow the viewer to manipulate the image in two general directions: (a) towards a weakening of cinema's illusion, and (b) towards an enhancement of fetishistic investment. The new technologies, in effect, not only reinstate the aura that Walter Benjamin thought would be negated by mechanical reproduction, but permit the viewer to freeze the image and enter into the past. They also, significantly, make it possible for the viewer to perceive a Barthesian *punctum* in cinematic images.

Therefore, the 'possessive' spectator, as defined in Mulvey's landmark essay 'Visual pleasure and narrative cinema' (1975) can now be compared with an alternative spectator, the 'pensive' spectator (Raymond Bellour), who is not driven by voyeurism but by curiosity and, most importantly, by the ability (thanks to the new technologies) to assert control over the look within the fiction of a film and create new ways of looking at the inner workings of cinema. The 'pensive' spectator can reflect on the cinema with a dialectical awareness and passionate detachment.

Today's installationists working with avant-garde and classic cinema have become Bellour's 'pensive spectator' in that they can create in their gallery installations and/or DVDs new, engaging and thoughtful reflections on the cinema medium. This has been happening since the 1980s and early 1990s: artists were even then creating new ways of seeing into the screen images by stretching and manipulating them into new dimensions of time and space. Moreover, artists have also been producing 'in-between' images, forms and contexts (Bellour) that emanate from the collision of film, photography, TV and the computer.

Also, artists working with the camera-based art forms have been producing new relations and connections between them for the last two to three decades. Critically speaking, it is in the rise of the art-installation film that perhaps some of the more promising possibilities exist for cinema itself. This is one of the significant arguments informing this book. This uncertain speculative future of fragmentation is salient to the notion of how the new technologies can give life to cinema—in all its contexts and forms. What we are witnessing is the communal dimension of cinema being reshaped by DVD, TV, video and the computer into individualised forms of spectatorship.

For instance, one kind of 'pensive spectatorship' is epitomised by Douglas Gordon's art installation piece *24-Hour Psycho*— a projection work that slows down Hitchcock's original to two frames per second. This represents 'delayed cinema', and is created by the new radical possibilities of video technology and viewing. As Amy Taubin observes, *24-Hour Psycho* opened up a new Hollywood genre movie via the aesthetics of slow motion and the various traditions of the avant-garde film.[22] Gordon's installation is a meditation on new forms of private spectatorship in that the artist has shifted from collective voyeurism to, as Mulvey writes, 'something closer to fetishism and investment in repetition, detail and personal obsession'.[23] This self-reflexive shift in spectatorship represents also a new dawn, the beginning of an 'expanded cinema' which will grow in possibility, according to Mulvey, as the 'electronic technologies are overtaken by digital ones'.[24]

New ways of seeing movies in this new media age have meant the introduction of a new wave of cinephilia: what Elsaesser calls, in contrast to the 'classic' cinephilia of the 1950s to the early 1980s, 'cinephilia take two'. This is the new cinephilia of the DVD, the download, file swapping, editing and sampling, etc. The new technologies have allowed the cinephile to recreate images, sounds, and forms, and to create new storylines and textures. The new technologies have brought about a 'reinvention' of textual analysis, and with it a new wave of cinephilia. In many critical respects, *Mutant Media* attests to how the new technologies have impacted on all forms of cinephilia.

As a term, 'cinephilia' has been in and out of favour several times, particularly in the 1970s with the ascendancy of film theory and, in general, academic film studies—feminism, psychoanalysis, semiotics, structuralism, etc.[25] What took place with 'cinephilia take one', to adopt Elsaesser's terminology, during that decade was that film studies proceeded to deconstruct cinephilia by eliminating two important components—in Elsaesser's words, 'we politicised pleasure, and we psychoanalysed desire'.[26] Cinephilia is a multifaceted phenomenon as a discourse concerning the love of cinema, with all its contradictions, ambivalences and doubts. Classic cinephilia therefore is tainted with, as Elsaesser eloquently reminds us, unrequited love or disenchantment with Hollywood cinema. Moreover, it is important to note that cinephilia is never as simple as a love for the cinema; it is complicated (to paraphrase Elsaesser), as it tends to get caught in certain kinds of deferral—detours in place and space, delays in time and shifts in register. [27]

Classic cinephilia, 'cinephilia take one', does not merely refer to a love of cinema. It implies, as Antoine de Baecque notes, 'a way of watching films, speaking about them and then diffusing this discourse' which (most importantly) suggests the critical element of shared experience.[28] Today's technologically informed cinephile has become an astute media-savvy user, who interacts with the contemporary mediasphere with self-reflexive intelligence and instincts but at the same time nostalgically remembers and cares for outmoded media formats. It is precisely this experience of different technological formats and platforms, to cite Marijke de Valck and Malte Hagener, as well as affective encounters and subject positions, that describes the current practice termed 'cinephilia'.[29] For these authors, the contemporary cinephile is someone who is 'a hunter-gather as much as a merchant-trader, of material goods as well as personal and collective memories, of reproducible data streams and of unique objects ...'[30]

The new cinephilia recognises how the archive, the market and the filmic text, as unstable objects, are mutually dependent in the contemporary media landscape. Moreover, 'cinephilia take two' involves, as Elsaesser reminds us, converting the boundless archive of our media memory of unloved filmic bits and pieces, the overlooked or forgotten films and programs, into much desired and valued clips, bonuses and extras, thereby creating new forms of enchantment and probably new moments of disenchantment as well.[31]

The networked cinephiles of today are a testament to cinephilia's rejuvenated energy and transformative power, and suggest its enduring relevance for any fundamental understanding of the stylistics of a filmic text and the various practices of film viewing.

To conclude, the three essays that follow indicate in their own ways the complex shifting links that exist between cinema, new media, video and the visual arts. In short, the techno-cultural congruence of the camera-based arts—thanks to, amongst other factors, the computer—colours the theoretical architecture of these three essays as well as the remaining essays of *Mutant Media*.

NOTES

1 Darren Tofts, *Interzone*, Craftsman House, Melbourne, 2005, p. 7.

2 ibid., p. 8.

3 See Siegfried Zielinski, 'Time machines', in Annette W. Balkema & Henke Slager (eds), *Screen-Based Art*, Editions Rodopi B.V., Amsterdam/Atlanta GA, 2000, p. 174.

4 Roy Ascott, 'The art of intelligent systems', in Christine Schopf et al. (eds), *Der Prix Arts Electronica*, Veritas-Verlag, Linz, 1991, p. 28.

5 Tofts, p. 12.

6 See Joseph Nechvatal, 'Origins of virtualism: an interview with Frank Popper', *Art Journal*, vol. 63, no. 1, spring 2004, pp. 63–77.

7 ibid., p. 64.

8 Quoted in Tofts, p. 15.

9 ibid.

10 Timothy Murray, 'By way of introduction: Digitality and the memory of cinema, or, bearing the losses of the digital code', *Wide Angle*, vol. 21, no. 1, January 1999, p. 4.

11 ibid., p. 8.

12 ibid., pp. 7–8.

13 ibid., p. 8.

14 ibid., p. 9.

15 See Thomas Elsaesser, 'Cinema futures: convergence, divergence, difference', in Elsaesser & Kay Hoffmann (eds), *Cinema Futures: Cain, Abel or Cable?*, Amsterdam University Press, Amsterdam, 1998, p. 14.

16 ibid.

17 ibid.

18 ibid., p. 10.

19 ibid.
20 Laura Mulvey, *Death 24x a Second*,
Reaktion Books, London, 2006.
21 ibid., p. 67.
22 Amy Taubin is cited ibid., p. 102. See Amy
Taubin, 'Douglas Gordon', in Philip Dodd &
Ian Christie (eds), *Spellbound: Art and Film*
[exhibition catalogue], Hayward Gallery and
British Film Institute, London, 1996.
23 Mulvey, p. 103.
24 ibid.
25 See Paul Willemen, 'Through the
glass darkly: cinephilia reconsidered', in
Willemen, *Looks and Frictions*, British Film
Institute/Indiana University Press, London,
1994, pp. 223–57. See also Peter Wollen's
remarks concerning the disappearance
and reappearance of cinephilia in the film
academy, quoted in Christian Keathley's fine
analysis of cinephilia in the context of André
Bazin, *Photogénie*, the surrealists and the
French New Wave in Keathley, *Cinephilia,
or the Wind in the Trees*, Indiana University
Press, Bloomington IN, 2006, p. 28. Wollen
(in the guise of his alter ego, Lee Russell)
recently observed: 'I was attracted by the
element of cinephilia [in the early days of
academic cinema studies] and that's precisely
what got lost with the relentless expansion
of theory over the face of academe.' See
Wollen, 'Afterword: Lee Russell interviews
Peter Wollen', in Wollen, *Signs and Meaning
in the Cinema* (expanded edition), British Film
Institute, London, 1998, p. 155.
26 Thomas Elsaesser, 'Cinephilia or the uses
of disenchantment', in Marijke de Valck &
Malte Hagener (eds), *Cinephilia*, Amsterdam
University Press, Amsterdam, 2005. p. 40.
27 ibid., p. 30.
28 Quoted in Elsaesser 2005, p. 28.
29 See Valck & Hagener, 'Down with
cinephilia? Long live cinephilia? And other
videosyncratic pleasures', in Valck & Hagener
(eds), p. 22.
30 ibid.
31 Elsaesser 2005, p. 41.

Australian new media arts: new directions since the 1990s

Today in Australia, just as in any other part of the first world, new media arts are rapidly becoming embraced by the international art world. The present popular penchant for anything that speaks of interactivity is emblematic of the spectre of 'the frenzy of the virtual' that is impacting on our everyday lives in such graphically telling terms. This is virtually axiomatic in the context of late capitalist culture. Yet what needs emphasising is that here in Australia we are strategically positioned to appreciate the fundamental aesthetic, cultural and historical relationships that exist with the development of new media arts apropos of the curatorial, institutional and theoretical meta-narratives that are operating between the (post)modern metropolises of Europe and our peripheral shores of cultural reception and production.

To talk about media art in the context of contemporary Australian culture is a highly tricky thing to do because of the island continent's particular inversed geographical position in relation to the relevant global cultural and media vector flows. We shall discuss the reasons why this may be so soon, but for the moment, it is important to spell out some of the significant rhetorical strategies that this essay will use in order to come to grips with the more salient aesthetic, cultural, funding and technological factors that have been responsible for the current genesis and support of art and technology in the antipodean art world. This means that there is also the important attendant objective of looking at several important interactive art installations that embody certain essential aesthetic and textual tropes that are indicative of a fundamentally informed poststructuralist approach to the making of electronic art. The artists in question include Joan Brassil, Linda Dement, Phillip George, John Gillies, Stephen Jones, Brad Miller, Chris Caines, Jon McCormack, Patricia Picinnini, Bill Seaman, Ralph Wayment, Joyce Hinterding and David Haines, amongst many others. These artists are a relatively small sample of the numerous interdisciplinary artists, writers and technologists who are contributing

who still believe that the new media arts should not be quarantined from the major concerns of today's cultural criticism.[5] Nevertheless, there is also still a marked residual tendency to affirm in a naive, utopian way the novelty impact of the new immersive technologies and to be conveniently ignorant of their grounding in the emerging post-Reaganite/Bush 'new world order'. This, as we all know, was abundantly manifested in the cyberculturally-mediated pyrotechnics of Gulf War I—our first virtual war. (Needless to say, we now can also speak of Gulf War II [viz. Iraq].) In a critical sense, virtual technology as a technology of panoptic power represents how the language of the war machine is transforming the culture of everyday life. More than ever, Donna Haraway's words concerning the dubious epistemological, imperialist and masculinist discourses that are typically valorised by the contemporary digital technologies deserve to be cited:

Can these technologies be prosthetic devices for building connections? Can these technologies be part of producing the social agencies in the first-world cultures that are less imperializing? My hope [is] that the power, the visual and sensory power of the technology, can be a way of dramatising the relativity of our place in the world, and not the illusions of power.[6]

Haraway's words are directed at the shortcomings—idealist, ahistorical and logocentric—of the polemical techno-boosterism we often encounter when dealing with the new information and immersive technologies, and consequently her analytical and ethically driven questions resonate along many cultural, moral and theoretical lines.

How do we negotiate interactive media art without developing an adequate theory of representation that takes into account the problematic essentialist claims that are made in the art–science world on its behalf, and the multifaceted epistemological and phenomenological issues relating to how the user/reader navigates the relevant space of audiovisual interactivity in a truly dialogic manner? These questions have been raised before, but they still need to be reiterated, judging by recent interactive works that rely more on a one-way street of communication than an open-ended two-way form of interacting. Creative, discursive, interactive works are predicated on a dialectical, multilayered approach to experiencing their digital realms

of images, graphics, sound, text, music, etc., that transcends
the more limited Aristotelian model of cause and effect masquerading
as interactivity.

To say that interactive works challenge our most cherished beliefs
about the nature of art and the ingrained passive spectatorship that
is central to our major camera-based art forms (photography, cinema
and television) is almost axiomatic these days, yet when we peruse the
enormous breadth of the different ideas, media, attitudes, and practices
that constitute the expanding amorphous field we call 'interactive art',
one is conscious of how much we take it for granted that the creative
and transformative aspects of interactivity—as Roy Ascott recently
observed—reside more with the behaviour of the user than with
the artist's intentions.[7] Interactivity that merits its name, as Ascott
correctly demonstrates, is about self-directed creativity, connectivity
and transformability, not about cultivating a technophilic aesthetic
that centres the computer and the ocular-centric bias of our dominant
scopic regimes of modernity as epitomised by the prevailing hegemony
of the computer screen interface itself. Ascott's diagnostic acumen
in pinpointing the limiting way computers are used in education as a
means of reconfiguring the key concepts and strategies of modernism
and formalism should be noted.[8] Too often, art educators, artists, writers
and technologists do not question what is happening to their own
cultural mindsets when they are using computers.

Someone who agrees with Ascott's observations concerning the self-
imposed limitations of interactive media is the German theorist Siegfried
Zielinski, who has recently raised serious questions relating to whether
or not there is such a thing called 'media art', and whether or not artists
using media, computers and their programs need to bring something
else to their work, something that dramatises and self-critiques their
connections with techno-media.[9] Zielinski argues that now, more than
ever before, we need to 'address more critically what we like and what we
do not like'.[10]

In a word, computers are rarely used as a source of self-reflexive
creativity that is acutely aware of the fragmentary character of knowledge
and the lived experience of everyday life. Computers are a perfect
rhizomatic tool for creating non-linear aesthetic and cultural agendas
that centre around collaging, multilayering, networking and decentring.

In other words, the computer is not simply a tool—as evidenced by numerous works of mainstream 'computer art'—for advancing reconstructed airbrush versions of the literal-minded formal strategies of the rationality of technology and modern industry. Instead, as Ascott (amongst many others) has argued, the computer's increasing visibility in postmodern artmaking is suggestive of a new environment that exemplifies paradigmatic shifts in our aesthetic, cultural and political frameworks and formations.[11]

Moreover, in any informed analysis of the developing immersive and interactive environments, we need to de-mythicise their novelty value. The problem of articulating an adequate aesthetic for interactivity and all forms of the new media lies, as Peter Wollen has recently persuasively argued, in finding a constructive solution to the perennially artificially sustained schism between art and science, aesthetics and logic.[12] Wollen advocates the thesis that aesthetics and logic do have a place within the realm of reason, but that we need first to forge a new poetics of computer-generated art based on 'the development of a heterogeneous theory of meaning, open rather than closed, involving different types of sign, and bringing semantics together with hermeneutics, reference with metaphor'.[13] But what needs mentioning here is that despite whatever kind of theoretical perspectives we bring to the fore in analysing the creative potential of interactive artworks on a cultural and an individual level, the basic consideration to be mindful of here is our unquestioned propensity to import and apply complete theoretical paradigms from other fields, and explain their aesthetic, formal and technological specificities, histories and multiple effects without being *experientially* familiar with them as cultural artefacts.

Interactivity, with its constantly mutating heterogeneous concerns, techniques and operations, challenges us to become more 'empirical' and less theoretically certain of ourselves: that is, to forego the more dogmatic certainties of the Cartesian method of philosophising and instead start from an intuitive precept that is also mindful of Wittgenstein's statement: 'Don't think, look.'[14]

Before we proceed now to discuss certain Australian new media artworks of the last decade or so, I need to say that my remarks are related to (a) a certain number of different artists, amongst many others, who have consistently contributed to our local techno-media scene, and (b) Australia's fairly unique position in the global realm of transnational media and economic systems and its funding policies relating to the development of art and technology here. Also, it needs to be noted that when discussing the latest trends in Australian new media, the many prominent artists in this area include important video artists who have contributed to the new technical media in significant ways. They include the exiled Jill Scott (who works in Europe, as does the pioneering figure Jeffrey Shaw, who works in new media and interactive cinema), Stephen Jones, Joan Brassil, Phillip Brophy, Leigh Hobba, David Perry, John Gillies, Peter Callas, Geoffrey Weary, Ross Harley and Carol Rudyard, amongst many others. Further, as expected, some of our Australian digital artists are starting to return to video and related time-based art forms. Also, we can say, as do Zielinski and others, that after a period of 10 years or so, video art is becoming interesting once more in the international and local art world.

For over 200 years, Australia has been a phantasmic screen for European aspiration and anxiety. It has been given a variety of different names, as Ross Gibson points out in his book on the postcolonial narrative construction of Australia, entitled *South of the West* (1992), which describes the complex Eurocentric values resulting from this country's unique cartographic status and colonial past—the Great South Land, Down Under, the Antipodes, etc.[15] What becomes apparent, to paraphrase Gibson, in any rudimentary probe into the uneasy, complex dialectic existing between white Australia and the northern hemisphere (especially Europe) is how Australia has always been a nebulous receptacle for a succession of imported mythologies—nationalism, colonialism, rural romanticism, modernism and postmodernism.[16] But what needs to be noted is how, viewed from the Antipodes, the critical thing about its experience of modernity—and later postmodernity—is its regarding the globe as a digital space of ideas, matter, movement and strategy.

Consequently, the examples of current Australian interactive art that we are going to discuss manifest, in their own peculiar conceptual and textual directions, a common preoccupation with problematising either (a) the received cultural beliefs, icons and systems of representation from other cultures or (b) the (more fashionable) various postmodern theories of identity, gender and power coming from numerous sites abroad. In addition, most of the examples under review also manifest a certain commonality in their enunciating of a meta-commentary about the cultural politics of identity and techno-representation. Because of Australia's distinctive geopolitical status in the world of nomadic media flows (defined by the ubiquitous 'tyranny of distance' factor in her recent history), local digital artists are highly sensitised to the aesthetic, formal and theoretical issues concerning their electronic techno-culture and its indebtedness to the major Anglo-American sites of cultural and media hegemony. This awareness of what represents postmodernity being an expression of Europe's and America's relations to their many Antipodes (including Australia) rather than of what's happening inside these countries has (as McKenzie Wark cogently maintains) coloured many of the more recent instances of Australian multimedia art.[17] It is also evident in other recent forms of Australian cultural production, including critical theory, the cinema, installation art, painting and performance, which manifest other critical and cultural agendas that ironise the complexities of (mis)translation.

It is critical to observe that Australian media artists—including the more recent generation of artists, such as Adam Donovan, Mari Velonaki, Justine Cooper, Martin Walch, Lynette Wallworth, Jason Hampton, Oron Catts/Ionat Zurr and Rea, amongst others—are ideally conditioned to see and hear (through their non-binary interdisciplinary art forms) across the horizons of their discipline in a lateral, self-questioning spirit. They regard computers as a source of self-reflective creativity that is aware of the fragmentary nature of knowledge and of the lived experience of everyday life. However, there is also another salient concept that needs to be noted in relation to our general capacity to see things from afar, across our seas from our beaches: as Greg Dening suggests, our beaches represent (metaphorically speaking) 'spaces-in-between', 'spaces of defining rather than definition', and as such they are appealing for our artists and social thinkers.[18]

Although the new media arts do not necessarily imply, *ipso facto*, new aesthetic paradigms, artists working with these cross-disciplinary art forms are in position to glimpse—if they imaginatively question the personal, creative and professional horizons that surround them—Dening's apt expression 'beyond the ordinary limits of our vision'.[19]

Whether we are talking about Australian cyberfeminism (i.e. VNS Matrix, Linda Dement, Virginia Barrett, Lynne Sanderson, Anna Munster/Michele Barker, etc), Phillip George and Ralph Wayment's latest CD-ROM of interactive meditations on cultural displacement, *Mnemonic Notations* (1993–99), Troy Innocent's audacious virtual animation, *Iconica* (1998), Nola Farman and Anna Gibbs's photosensitive interactive installation, *The Braille Book* (1993–95) or Brad Miller's Deleuze-inspired hypermedia interactive installation, *A Digital Rhizome* (1994), we can observe a deconstructive, self-reflexive endeavour to question, in a non-authoritarian, hesitant style (something that approximates the 'reflective' open-end textuality of the essay [Adorno, Barthes and Nietzsche] and the essay film [Welles, Marker and Ruiz]), the cultural, media and theoretical discourses from elsewhere. This implies a flexible comprehension that the various complexities and issues concerning the contemporary Australian information landscape are a direct result of the country's passage from its previous colonial 'second nature' of highly abstract social spaces forged by the sea and rail transport, as David Malouf described in his 1998 Boyer Lectures *A Spirit of Play*, to the present postmodern information landscape shaped by the telegraph, telephone, television, satellite telecommunications and the internet.[20] It is in this context that we should locate the recent genesis of Australian new media art.

Malouf makes the interesting point that since white settlement, Australia has been a *continuing* experiment in which our institutions, narratives and values continue to be translations from one hemisphere to another. This has been crucial, I believe, to the idea of our digital artists as inventive experimental storytellers re-interpreting and giving shape to our shared experiences about identity, place and memory:

> We speak of these places we belong to as new worlds, but what they really are is the old world translated: but *translated*, with all that implies of re-interpretation and change, not simply *transported*. Our ways of thinking and feeling and doing were developed and tested over many centuries before we brought them to this new place, and gave them a different turn of meaning, different associations, a different shape and weight and colour, on new ground.[21]

If we shift our attention now, for a brief moment, to the funding agencies and policies responsible for the development of Australian new media artworks, we must note the central importance of the Australian Film Commission's New Image Research program, which was established in 1988.[22] Aside from the various funding grants and fellowships issued by the Australia Council's Visual Arts and Craft Board to visual artists who want to experiment with interactivity, New Image Research has been (on a federal and state level) the main funding apparatus that has allowed artists, filmmakers and technologists to pursue interactive media projects.

Furthermore, the Australia Council's New Media Board, in more recent times, has been a vital source of constant support for local new media art. In this context, the Council's two-year New Media Fellowship also needs to be noted, as it has provided critical support for mid-career artists who have contributed to the new media arts in significant ways. In the last decade or so, the Council has also been responsible for supporting local curators interested in doing new media exhibitions and programs.

Relatedly, there have been several key stakeholders in this context who have been central to the exhibition and distribution of new media in Australia. They include the Australian International Video Festival, Electronic Media Arts, Matinaze, Experimenta, and, more recently, the Australian Art and Technology Network (ANAT), Metro Screen and dLux Media Arts. And Melbourne's Australian Centre for the Moving Image, at Federation Square, has been, in the last five years, instrumental in promoting new media exhibitions and commissioning artists to create new works. Curators Alessio Cavallaro, Ross Gibson (who is also a prominent media artist and theorist), and Victoria Lynn should be acknowledged in this specific context.

Historically speaking, curator Brian Langer, in the context of the Australian International Video Festival and Electronic Media Arts since the mid-1980s, has been an important figure in the general promotion of art and technology in this country, as has been media artist and theorist Stephen Jones, whose archival and curatorial work in video and new media art (as well as his role as a prolific and pioneering video/new media artist) should be noted.

Let us now return to some Australian new media works created since the 1990s and briefly spell out some of their more interesting critical strategies, technological concerns and modes of interactivity in relation to the overall cultural and curatorial formations evident in our local techno-culture. Linda Dement's influential major post-feminist interactive piece, *Typhoid Mary* (1993), which was funded by ANAT, incorporates a wide array of different elements: manipulated photographs, theoretical texts, autobiographical narratives, poems, animations, sounds, and extracts from medical reports and books. Dement created a work with no apparent user interface, thereby allowing the user to move with more heuristic and playful freedom along the paths that had been determined by the artist. The links between the various texts follow the logic of dreams, intuition and reverie, in sharp contrast to the slick doxas of the mainstream computer world.

The already cited hybrid, computer-generated paintings created by Phillip George since 1990 have became the main focus of his collaborative interactive installations with Ralph Wayment: *Mnemonic Notations Interactive I–IV*. George's highly compressed collaged images of postmodern science, Orthodox Greek mysticism, cyberpunk mythology, tantric Buddhist symbols, Celtic mazes and Landsat photographs clearly denote his sustained postcolonial project to create art that comments on his own experiences as a bi-cultural subject living in postwar Australia.

Brad Miller's *A Digital Rhizome* (1994) is a multilayered computer-based screen and mouse interactive piece predicated on the key metaphor of the rhizome, as defined in Gilles Deleuze and Felix Guattari's 'schizoanalysis' philosophy—and particularly represented by their book *A Thousand Plateaus* (1987). The 50 images of this specific digital rhizome—which is based on sophisticated image-processing software—function as a fairly reflexive video collage.

Users are able to produce their own structure within the work as they form their own intricate associational connections and links and simultaneously trigger numerous sampled soundtracks and small QuickTime movies that depict the unpredictable kinetic formations of crowds (a motif central to Dadaist and 'primitive' cinema), amongst other images.

Miller's CD-ROM collaboration with media theorist McKenzie Wark, *Planet of Noise* (1997), is structured along the lines of a personal essay as it explores the fragmentary poetry of the aphorism as a way of examining our collective and individual complicity in being 'enframed' (Martin Heidegger) by the seductive aura of modern technology.

Bill Seaman's consummately designed interactive videodisk installation, *The Exquisite Mechanism of Shivers* (1992), combines modular music segments, poetic text fragments and image sequences. When navigating the work, users encounter a series of changing poetic audiovisual sentences. This engaging interactive work embodies Seaman's interest in exploring pluralistic meaning through the presentation of material in different contexts. The artist's playful response to the Duchampian legacy in 20th century art colours the work's overall critical and technological architecture. Hence, users directly navigate numerous imagistic and linguistic possibilities that express visual puns, humour, modular music composition, sense/nonsense, and 'canned chance'.

In the context of the last decade's Australian new media works, Mike Leggett and Linda Michael's critical survey exhibition of local and international CD-ROM art, *Burning the Interface* (1996), was a major curatorial development, illuminating the works of local media artists such as Michael Buckley, Leon Cmielewski and Josephine Starrs, Norie Neumark and Maria Miranda, Suzanne Treister, Debra Petrovich and Tatiana Pentes, amongst numerous others, all of whom have imaginatively investigated the CD-ROM's potential as an art form.

Jeffrey Cook, Gary Zebington and Sam de Silva's CD-ROM *Metabody* (1997) is impressive for its creative and recombinant technical imagination as it presents a rich criss-crossing array of biography, texts, videos and interviews with the world-renowned Australian media artist Stelarc and his oeuvre of golems, robots, automata and cyborgs.

Two digital animators who have significantly contributed to the immersive virtual worlds of digital art are Jon McCormack and the already mentioned Troy Innocent. McCormack's highly accomplished *Turbulence* (1995) is notable for its dazzling synthetic imagery of permutating flora, which is evocative of an Yves Tanguy or Max Ernst surreal landscape. *Turbulence*'s innovative atmospheric and virtual attributes clearly signal the possibilities of an emerging new digital aesthetic that speaks of artificial life, cybernetics and hyper-reality.

Innocent's inventive digital art represents his endeavour to create his own expressive visual language for the computer. Beginning with his early collaborative efforts with Melbourne's CyberDada (Dale Nelson and Elena Popa), Innocent has been creating highly poetic cyberdelic works, such as *Idea-ON>!* (1992–94) and *Ionica* (1998), that stress the unique iconographic signscapes, abstract virtual spaces and acoustic rhythms of computer games, computer graphics and virtual reality.

At the iCinema Centre for Interactive Cinema, College of Fine Arts, University of New South Wales (UNSW), Jeffrey Shaw and Dennis Del Favero have been, over the last few years, producing numerous groundbreaking interactive cinema installations, supported by the Australian Research Council. This centre (in conjunction with the Faculty of Computer Science and Engineering, UNSW) has been central to Shaw's continuing world-famous panoramic immersive work, which he has been producing at Germany's ZKM for over a decade. Shaw's collaborative piece *T-Visionarium*, created with Dennis del Favero, Neil Brown and the polymath Peter Weibel (ZKM), is an interactive virtual environment set within a large inflatable dome, with an electronic tracking system linked to the head movements of one of the viewers. This system allows the viewer to spatially navigate a database of some 24 hours of TV material recorded from 48 satellite channels, and apply a recombinatory search matrix to articulate emergent narratives from this database of audiovisual content streams. Shaw is a pioneer figure in new media (see the essay on Shaw's internationally acclaimed art) and related interactive and virtual environments.

Dennis del Favero's distinctive oeuvre cuts across a variety of media—installation, new media, performance, photography—and is concerned with a multifaceted exploration of history, narrative, trauma and memory. One of his most recent acclaimed works is *Pentimento* (2001), which utilises a vision-based motion-detection system allowing four different viewers to simultaneously interact with the work (which has two different modes of interaction: as a CD-ROM and as a multi-screen installation). *Pentimento* is typical of del Favero's multilayered documentary textured work, as it is based on a news story concerning an unresolved crime in the Blue Mountains (west of Sydney). Specifically, it relates to the discovered body of a young girl whose father and brother sexually abused her.

It should be reiterated that the works I have discussed here are only a small selection of recent Australian new media—and all of them in one way or another demonstrate a discernibly 'writerly' textuality that constitutes a meta-commentary on the way postmodern cultural and theoretical ideas and global media vector flows have been appropriated in the Antipodes.

To conclude, Australian new media empowers users to reconstruct the Romantic and modernist assumptions and constraints that inform the cultural politics of representation and meaning in everyday life. Further, many of the more recent new media works in Australia also attempt to connect interactivity with connectivity, ludic behaviour with thinking, and immersion with emergence and transformation. Beyond this, we can also detect certain key thematics and metaphors—artificial life, bi-cultural hybridity, cyberfeminism, identity, memory and postcoloniality—structuring these works. These are, one presumes, expressive of the artist's emerging telematic ethos in the Antipodes.

On another subtle level, there is a preoccupation with the ongoing interest among Australian media artists and cultural producers in redefining the idea of Australia in terms of the large 'building blocks' of the vocabulary of contemporary art theory and critical theory (viz. Culture, History, the West, Memory, Time, Space, Nature). Australian technological culture is witnessing an emerging sea change: a radical shift from the more conventional notions of mimetic and symbolic art to an accentuated desire to create new virtual worlds where the user is the active producer of cultural meaning and individual experience.

NOTES

1   See Timothy Druckrey, 'Feedback to immersion', in *Computer Graphics Visual Proceedings*, The Association for Computing Machinery, Inc., New York, 1993, p. 127 [annual conference series].
2   Peter Lunenfeld, 'Digital dialectics', *Afterimage*, November 1993, pp. 5–7.
3   Edward W. Said, *The World, the Text, and the Critic*, Faber & Faber, London, 1984, p. 35.
4   Martin Jay, *Force Fields*, Routledge, New York, 1993, pp. 1–4.
5   Contrary to the ongoing 'dystopic'

commentators on the limits of our late-capitalist digital culture, there have been numerous discerning and well-informed critics and theorists who have, since the late 1980s, written insightfully on new media. There are numerous such examples, but the ones who spring to mind include Donna Haraway, David Tafler, Simon Penny, Robert Fischer, Alfred Kroker, Norbert Bolz and Avita Ronell.
6   Cited in Druckrey.
7   Roy Ascott, 'The art of intelligent systems',

in Christine Schopf et al. (eds), *Der Prix Ars Electronica*, Veritas-Verlag, Linz, 1991.

8   ibid., pp. 28–29.

9   See Siegfried Zielinski, 'Time machines', in Annette W. Balkema & Henk Slager (eds), *Screen-based Art*, Editions Rodopi, Amsterdam/Atlanta, 2000.

10   ibid., p. 182.

11   Ascott, 1991, passim.

12   Peter Wollen, 'Modern times: Cinema/ Americanism/the robot', [in the author's new collection of essays], *Raiding the Icebox*, Routledge, London, 1993, p. 67.

13   ibid.

14   John Rajchman, 'The lightness of theory', *Artforum*, vol. 32, no. 1, 1993, p. 211.

15   Ross Gibson, *South of the West*, Indiana University Press, Bloomington, 1992, pp. ix–xii.

16   ibid., p. xi.

17   McKenzie Wark, 'Autonomy and antipodality in global village', in Alessio Cavallaro et al. (eds), *Cultural Diversity in the Global Village: The Third Symposium on Electronic Art*, The Australian Network for Art and Technology, Sydney, 1992, p. 99.

18   Greg Dening, *Readings/Writings*, Melbourne University Press, Melbourne, 1998, pp. 85–86.

19   ibid., p. 7.

20   David Malouf, *A Spirit of Play*, ABC Books, Sydney, 1998.

21   ibid., p. 26.

22   It should be observed that Gary Warner, who was instrumental in establishing the New Image Research program for the Australian Film Commission, has moved on: to work for the new Sydney Museum and as an independent innovator of museum digital installations and environments. Warner's brief at the Sydney Museum was to create new media exhibits to illustrate Australia's colonial history.

Vasulka at Buffalo University's Media Centre in New York state, and with polymath artist, educator and theorist Peter Weibel, who is now affiliated with COFA's iCinema Centre and is the current director of ZKM.

Shaw's research at COFA is significantly supported by the Australian Research Council, and Shaw's success (with Dennis del Favero and Neil Brown) in obtaining research funds for these unique explorations of different models of cinematic interactivity has proven quite an inspiring benchmark for other new media researchers working in the country at the moment. Furthermore, Shaw's work at COFA is a fine testament to the government's recognition of the need to attract world-leading expatriate artists, scientists and writers back to our 'fatal shores' (Robert Hughes) to redress the brain drain of creative talent leaving Australia for more rewarding horizons. The number of cultural theorists and academics who have left Australia in recent times indicates how severe the brain drain problem is in our tertiary education sector.

Shaw is a unique artist and researcher in new media in that he is a globally oriented investigator of high-tech virtual environments and systems who needs to probe different creative and technological opportunities and locales in order to continue making his world-renowned art. Consequently, Shaw's art and career have taken him to many different places to do his work: Japan, America, Europe, Canada. In many ways, Shaw is a fascinating figure in global terms because he has a brilliant conceptual and technical understanding of how interactive art, culture and technology interrelate in different cultural, historical and empirical contexts.

Shaw is, as art historian Oliver Grau reminds us, one of the leading proponents of working in immersive media in the context of the established tradition of the panorama in the visual arts.[2] No one else has Shaw's fine understanding and knowledge of pre-cinematic and cinematic panoramic technologies in the new media—he has vast empirical experience, having been working with these technologies since the mid-1960s. In this context Shaw's art is peerless.

Take, for example, Shaw's 1995 work *Place: A User's Manual*. Here we have the artist's consummate intertextual grasp of photography, cinematography and virtual reality working together towards a complex and dynamic aesthetic and technical objective. This work, since its creation, has had several different versions—which re-situates the old tradition of the panorama within the newer one of virtual reality. Shaw's art is based on his Paikian ability to create many different versions of the same work of art. In this way, Shaw's oeuvre is splendidly multifaceted and resourceful.

The first version of *Place: A User's Manual* surrounds the visitor with a 360-degree panorama screen whereby he or she can move through the landscape projected onto it, and in which further images of panoramas in cylindrical form are represented. All these elements, as Grau observes, form the panorama, and the visitor (located on a central platform in the installation) employs a video camera to zoom in on particular areas in the given virtual space.

The interface design of the installation facilitates navigation and allows the visitor to connect to the different individual cylinders, which feature panoramic photographs of such locales as Australia, Bali, Japan and La Palma. Shaw structured these deserted panoramas on a line drawing of the Sephitroth, a sign from the Cabbala, which is also discernible in the viewfinder of the camera. In the year 2000 Shaw restructured this work for an exhibition in Dortmund, Germany, to stress numerous locales and landmarks in the Ruhr, representing its social and economic history.

For Duguet, *Place: A User's Manual* is an engaging and complex installation that cleverly utilises some of the more fundamental concepts informing the original panorama genre by presenting 'surrogate voyages' like those that interested 19th century spectators. The eleven panoramas deployed in the work are not tourist sites, but rather deserted sites, memory sites, empty of actual movement.[3] So Shaw imaginatively uses photography in this context in order to exploit its capacity to record traces of existence and atmospheric detail, something which computed worlds cannot do very well. Consequently, Shaw creates hybrid techniques of representation that uniquely combine mechanical imagery with the omnidirectional mobility created through digitised space. For Duguet, *Place: A User's Manual* is an exceptional work in that it creates 'a certain euphoria, like that described by certain visitors to the earliest panoramas', generated by landscapes which move in a no-man's land region.

This work, in a way that is characteristic of Shaw's playful and imaginative ability to reinvent different forms of the same work, influenced his later Melbourne-based piece *Place—Urbanity*, which was itself based on the artist's earlier virtual reality installation *The Legible City* (1988–91). The latter installation is perhaps the most famous and critically acclaimed installation in Shaw's entire oeuvre.

The Legible City is an archetypal Shaw piece in that it converts the cities of Manhattan, Amsterdam and Karlsruhe into text. What we encounter are computer-generated three-dimensional letters forming words and sentences making up the buildings and streets of the installation's phantasmic city. As James Donald points out, *The Legible City* is 'an inversion and literalisation of Wittgenstein's analogy between language and urban space'.[4] Shaw's virtual Manhattan consists of various fictional monologues by ex-mayor Ed Koch, a con artist, Donald Trump, Frank Lloyd Wright, and a taxi driver. With the cities of Amsterdam and Karlsruhe, the scale of letters used reflects the scale of the buildings in the cities' actual streets. And the texts used are derived from archive documents about certain events that happened in those streets.

What is appealing about *The Legible City*, aside from its fascinating virtual cities and their immersive iconography of image, text and space, is its simple and very effective interface design of a stationary bicycle in which the visitor rides. The bicycle's handlebar and pedals are connected to a computer that gives the visitor control over direction and speed. There is also a small screen in front of the bicycle that shows a map of each city in the installation, thereby allowing the visitor to select which city to ride through, and to view where he or she is. *The Legible City* is a brilliant virtual reality installation that speaks of the artist's ability to connect art history, urban planning, philosophy, architecture, and installation art. In a word, for Shaw, the visitor experiences the urban space of the work as 'a journey of reading'.[5]

The Legible City is, as Duguet contends, a major instance of Shaw's 'virtual site-specific works', and each different version of it—Manhattan, Amsterdam and Karlsruhe—attests to the artist's fluid ability to make a work that subtly reflects the specific site and architecture for which it was produced (for example, a museum gallery).[6] Thus for each version of this installation a new database was built, as well as a new narrative, a new urban geography, and a new letter-architecture.

Shaw's approach to designing his interfaces has an ironic and critical role, in contrast to the more elaborate 'entertainment industry' interface modes for entering cyberspace. For example, with *The Legible City*, the bicycle interface requires the visitor to make a pronounced physical effort in order to traverse its virtual urban universe, or to slow down to read its streets. As Duguet perceptively notes, the more the image becomes immaterial, the more the visitor on the bicycle has to earn his or her perception of it.[7] This has a certain absurdist resonance to it that can be, for Duguet, traced back to the French pataphysicians: 'The effects of this approach could be inscribed in the pataphysical tradition of the velocipede, from the Quintuplette in Jarry's *Surmale* to Tinguely's Cyclograveur.'[8]

Place Ruhr 2000, a new version of *Place: A User's Manual*, is contextualised (geographically speaking) for the Ruhr region in Germany, a region which has been greatly transformed by heavy industry. This installation features traditional methods, enhanced by various interactive elements, not programs with evolving image spaces or agents, to achieve the desired immersive effects. The visitor can 'enter' various different places that show the profound effects of heavy industry on people and their culture. *Place Ruhr 2000* is a memorial to a time and space when once workers spent their free time at sites like the velodrome, which is now derelict, with trees forcing their way through the concrete. The overall atmosphere of melancholy is graphically enhanced by heavy industrialisation and is symbolic of many different similar regions around the world, regions that were once structured by heavy industrialisation and now are moving into new directions.

The hallmark feature of Shaw's oeuvre is his sustained experimentation with immersive image spaces, from his early work in expanded cinema to his *Extended Virtual Environment, EVE*, and his more recent installations, such as *Place Ruhr 2000* and *Place–Urbanity*, with its Melbourne suburbs, and the collaborative work *T_Visinarium* (with Dennis Del Favero, Neil Brown and Peter Weibel) for 2004–05. This work was commissioned by the Lille Cultural Capital of Europe 2004 year-long festival, and thus the first prototype was presented in France. It is an interactive immersive virtual environment located in a large inflatable dome with a mobile projection system connected to an electronic system that tracks the head movements of one of the viewers.

With this work the viewer can spatially navigate through a database of over 24 hours of television recordings from 48 satellite channels and use a recombinatory search matrix to extract emergent narratives from this database of diverse image–sound content streams.

Currently, at the iCinema Centre, Shaw is experimenting with *Conversations@the studio*, a project that continues his research into models of cinematic interactivity that aim to enhance the presentational flexibility of museum information delivery. (One of the great benefits of the so-called new media arts revolution of the last two decades has been the innovation made in digital museum installations and environments.) Shaw intends to use an immersive system of cinematic representation which incorporates three kinds of interactive narrative. As he puts it, 'We plan to work with a studio of glass artists and create a spherical cinematic visualisation of the activities in that studio that viewers can virtually enter and explore.'[9] It is intended that this final experimental application will be located in a major exhibition of the decorative arts at Sydney's Powerhouse Museum.

Place–Urbanity is a work of humour, wit and imaginative experimentation. It is a virtual reality installation, and so has (as is to be expected) distinct critical and technical links to *Place: A User's Manual*. Its overall sense of dislocation and disorientation is also, as Donald suggests, related to a situationist's notion of the fluidity and softness of experience, and the ambiguous zone between imagination and reality.[10] As Donald, Duguet and others have commented, Shaw's work is forged in the artistic and intellectual milieu of expanded cinema and performance art in the 1960s, and it is fundamentally concerned with the questioning of classical spectatorship and performance, creating new experimental realities and disrupting the connection between subject and environment.[11]

In contrast to the global focus of *Place: A User's Manual*, *Place–Urbanity* features video sequences of Little Italy, Victoria Markets, Chinatown and other recognisable Melbourne places central to Shaw's childhood memories. What comes through these various locales is the everyday life of the city itself. And then there are our encounters with various comedians and their stories about their own communities, etc. The question needs to be asked: why are they upside down? What are these images saying about being located in Australia as opposed to somewhere in the rest of the world? As antipodeans, do we have an inventive and sceptical wit and imagination when it comes to creativity, identity and place and seeing ourselves in the context of global cultural influences and vector forces? These are questions that the novelist and poet David Malouf eloquently poses in his 1998 ABC Boyer Lectures *A Spirit of Play*.[12]

Shaw is, unquestionably, at the forefront of the new media arts, especially in terms of working with virtual reality environments and installations and boldly experimenting with emergent digital modalities and narratives of interactive cinema. He is a pioneer in exploring the immersive spaces of media art and is absorbed in exploring the new possibilities of cinematic technology. Shaw's work at the iCinema Centre will allow him to investigate certain key drivers of new media technology—in particular, three models of interactive narrative: polychronic, transcriptive, and co-evolutionary. He sees his research work at the centre as creating new navigable, multi-user, immersive applications that will produce benefits for both the creative community at large in Australia and the country's economy.

In essence, Shaw's oeuvre exemplifies Mark Hansen's Bergsonian thesis that the virtual is a distinct quality of human and, generally speaking, organic life, and not to be equated with technology as such.[13] In other words, the virtual needs to be understood as that specific capacity, as Hansen puts it, 'to be in excess of one's actual state'.[14] Therefore, Shaw's art in general criticises Friedrich Kittler's post-human technical 'machinism' that defines the digital as transcending the human itself. According to Hansen's interpretation of Shaw's work, the work utilises technology as a means to trigger the virtual.[15] This means, to paraphrase Hansen, that in accordance with Bergson's appreciation of technology as an expression of intelligence, Shaw's aesthetic deployment of technology (from expanded cinematic environments to virtual reality) italicises 'the body's function as a center of indetermination'.[16]

Weibel sees Shaw's art as being relational in its technological emphasis on shaping the relationship between image and viewer, so it can be seen as a 'user's manual for the world itself'.[17] As Weibel puts it, 'To see the world [of images] as a user's manual ultimately implies a heightened ability to view and use the world according to one's own notions, more individually, more subjectively ... the world as a user's manual is a world of modality.'[18] Shaw's career parallels the development of technology over the last 35 years, but it also witnesses, as Hansen reminds us, 'a progressive deterritorialisation of the Bergsonist ontology of images'.[19] What Shaw accomplishes in his work is to place the body within a larger universe of images in order to stress (what Hansen calls) 'the body-brain's capacity' to generate image-events from inchoate information.[20] Ultimately, in contrast with Deleuze, who disembodies the Bergsonist definition of the centre of indetermination with the function of the cinematic frame, Shaw focuses on the bodily basis of the movement image (as articulated by Deleuze in his *Cinema* volumes)—and, later, the virtual image—by attacking the boundary of the cinematic frame.[21]

So in fact what Shaw has emphasised throughout his career, from his earliest expanded cinema works to the most current interactive cinema installations and environments, has been the space–image–body nexus, so that he may critique the body's subordination to the cinematic frame and free the space beyond the image as, in the words of Hansen, 'the correlate of the body's excess over the image'.[22] Shaw's work therefore also documents the substantial shift from seeing the image as a technical frame to trying to frame formless information, an issue which has become more and more salient to media art. Although Hansen's periodisation of Shaw's work into three partially overlapping stages is schematic in character, it is nonetheless quite useful to note how it encapsulates the innovative experimental breadth of his anti-cinematic project to break out of the frame of the image and to empower the body by attaching it to the image environment.[23] And, as Duguet correctly observes, perhaps one of the more innovative aspects of Shaw's work, from a cinematic point of view, is not his investigation of advanced techniques but his invention of varied interfaces, from the most traditional optical apparatuses such as mirrors and periscopes to the most sophisticated industrial processes, such as flight simulator platforms, virtual systems, etc.[24]

Clearly Shaw is disappointed with the commercial conservatism of mainstream narrative cinema and sees experimental cinema and video art (up to a point) as invaluable, in that it provides a historical and research context for media art.[25] His main interest now is in interactive cinema, which he sees as the future of the medium—he believes cinema now must reinvent its own technological capabilities so it can produce rich new interactive content.[26] Shaw's oeuvre is exceptionally complex and creative in its virtual architectures, spaces and narratives, and it is multifaceted in its symbolic structures and meanings. Shaw has given us interactive art that relies not only, as Duguet indicates, on the latest inventive use of virtual technology, but also on our most ancient eclectic representations of the universe.[27] His art is enduring because it questions the ever-present hyperbole of media art and it is steeped in a profound understanding of art history, critical theory and the various genres of the time-based arts and the postwar digital avant-garde. Above all, Shaw's oeuvre speaks of his liquid ability to sustain in a career of nearly 40 years a self-critique that is full of inventiveness, experimental wit and imagination.

NOTES

1 Anne-Marie Duguet, 'Jeffrey Shaw: From expanded cinema to virtual reality', in Heinrich Klotz (ed.), *Jeffrey Shaw—A User's Manual*, ZKM, Karlsruhe/Cantz Verlag, Ostfildern, 1997, pp. 21–23.

2 Oliver Grau, *Virtual Art*, MIT Press, Cambridge MA, 2003, pp. 240–42.

3 Duguet, p. 41.

4 James Donald, 'The world turned upside down: Jeffrey Shaw's *Place—Urbanity*', in Jeffrey Shaw (ed.), *(dis)Locations*, ZKM Digital Arts Edition, Karlsruhe/The Centre for Interactive Cinema Research, College of Fine Arts, UNSW, Sydney, Hatje Cantz, 2001, p. 76.

5 Jeffrey Shaw, cited in Donald, p. 77.

6 See Duguet, p. 44.

7 cf. ibid., p. 4

8 ibid.

9 Jeffrey Shaw, quoted in *COFA Magazine*, Issue 10, 2004, p. 16.

10 Donald.

11 ibid., p. 76; Duguet 1997, passim.

12 David Malouf, *A Spirit of Play*, ABC Books, Sydney, 1998.

13 Mark Hansen, *New Philosophy for New Media*, MIT Press, Cambridge MA, 2004, p. 50.

14 ibid., p. 51.

15 ibid.

16 ibid.

17 ibid.

18 ibid.

19 ibid., p. 52.

20 ibid,

21 ibid.

22 ibid.

23 Hansen's periodisation of Shaw's career trajectory into three phases is: (1) the expanded cinema and pneumatic architecture works (from 1966 to 1978); (2) works which explore the virtualisation of the image and use 'virtual slide projection techniques' and the computer (from about 1975 to 1995); (3) works that juxtapose image interfaces and conventions in order to catalyse bodily affect (1993 to the present).

24 Anne-Marie Duguet, 'Jeffrey Shaw's apparatuses: on the virtual, in situ', in Jeffrey Shaw &Peter Weibel (eds), *Future Cinema*, MIT Press, Cambridge MA, 2003, p. 381.

25 See *COFA Magazine*.

26 See Jeffrey Shaw, 'Media art and interactive media', in Annette W. Balkema and Henk Slager (eds), *Screen-based Art*, Editions Rodopi, Amsterdam/Atlanta GA, 2000, pp. 152, 154.

27 Duguet, 1997, passim.

The spiral of time: Chris Marker and new media

All I can offer is myself.

Chris Marker

In the last 20 odd years, certain artists have used video and new media (especially in its collage/montage techniques of representation) as a form of electronic writing. Commentators such as Raymond Bellour have written perceptively about video's 'writerly attributes' as a highly elastic time-based medium of representation-production. Arguably, certain artists, such as Jean-Luc Godard, Robert Cahen, Jean-Paul Fargier, Thierry Kuntzel and Irit Batsry, to name a few, have in their respective videotapes, installations and new media works articulated a Mallarmé-inspired approach to electronic image-making.

Chris Marker, like Jean-Luc Godard, uses video technology as a camera-pen or quill (after Alexandre Astruc's notion of a *'camera-stylo'* form of personal filmmaking) to create and think live, and to interrogate the image (often archival) of history, politics, time and memory. Marker's futurist enigmatic work—films, travel books, imaginary film scripts, photo–novels, videos, installations, photographs and travel essays—constitute a highly subjective voyage across the world and its Borgesian labyrinthine features of faces, landscapes, objects and animals in memory, time and space. He wanders the world recording his impressions as a furtive lyrical flâneur, reporting poetic meditative image–sound letters that are indebted to Montaigne as much as to Vertov, chronicling life as a vertigo of space and time linked by the insane impossibility and unreliability of memory. For Marker, fact and fiction intermingle in so many different ways, as do images, sounds and words; he is one of cinema's most elusive explorers, seeing it as a complex hypnotic kingdom of shadows—hence the apt title of part one of his homage to his friend the Russian filmmaker Alexander Medvedkin, called *The Last Bolshevik* (1993)—by stepping aside and looking at his themes from the margins, so to speak.

Marker's early essay films, such as *Sunday in Peking* (1955) and *Letter from Siberia* (1957), and his only fiction film to date (made almost entirely of still photographs), the science-fiction short *La Jetée* (1962), plus his more personal epistolary works, such as *Sunless* (1982), *AK* (1985) and *The Last Bolshevik*, constitute one of the more elaborate and haunting examples of film/*video-stylo* creativity as 'autobiographical documentary' in contemporary audiovisual media.

Today, all of us, are rapidly becoming, thanks to the ubiquitous presence of the new interactive media in our daily lives—like Homer's hero Ulysses in his epic poem *The Odyssey* or Jean Cocteau's night-voyager Orphée in his famous movie of the same name—familiar with journeys of ongoing self-definition into the virtual worlds of the human senses, new spatial awareness, memory, immersion and sensation. In other words, when we immerse ourselves in the cinema as a big-screen communal event (something that has been radically altering during the last three decades or so)—or television, or the Internet, or the telephone, or the radio, or installations like those by noted artists such as Gary Hill, Luc Courchesne, Bruce Nauman, James Turrell, David Haines and Joyce Hinterding, among others, in the 2001 exhibition *Space Odysseys* (Art Gallery of New South Wales, Sydney)—we are taking journeys from 'here' to 'there', from the past to the future, from actual space to imaginary space, from inner emotions to immensity.

Journeys across space, time, culture, light, genre and technology. Journeys that, to invoke Homer, again, echo Constantin Kavafy's wonderful line: 'Ithaca has given you the beautiful voyage' (1911). William Burroughs once described artists as 'space travellers'. Marker is such a person. Using today's digital tools, Marker represents a film crew of one. Like a shadow, he manages (as did the late photographer Henri Cartier-Bresson) to slip in and out of a given locale unnoticed. For example, in *The Last Bolshevik*, Marker, with his Video-8 camera, is unobtrusively filming Medvedkin's grave. I am not certain whether Marker knew it or not, but at the grave, among the many tourists milling around, was the leading Italian video artist and poet Gianni Toti—as irony would have it, he too was armed with a video camera and was shooting video.

The main aim of this chapter is to examine some of the factors that have led to Marker's turning to new media in the last two decades or so, and in the process to discuss these important aesthetic, cultural and technological considerations in the overall context of his diverse trans-generic oeuvre. I wish also to underline Marker's negotiation of the 'obsolete' interactive CD-ROM medium in *Immemory* (1997), a collaborative project between Marker and the Centre Georges Pompidou, Paris.[1] Marker's sustained interest in new media relatively late in his life is a testament to his life-long willingness to take risks by working across a variety of media in order to interrogate the image. Marker's artistic persona as an elusive, anonymous trans-media artist is equally at home with a typewriter, an Apple Mac computer, a 16mm film camera, a Rolleiflex still camera, or a Sony Handycam.[2]

Indeed, when in 1978 the world of media communications was irretrievably changed by the appearance of the first Apple computer, Marker entered the new world of video image-making with a 16-minute, two-screen video installation, *When the Century Took Shape*. By the end of the 1980s, as Catherine Lupton notes in her invaluable and timely study of Marker's oeuvre from the late 1940s to the 1990s, Marker was working with an Apple IIGS computer, creating primitive digital images for a 1989 television series investigating the legacy of ancient Greek culture in the modern world (*The Owl's Legacy*).[3]

Marker enthusiastically embraced new media, without any of the dystopic sentiments or reservations expressed by many others working in film when they first encountered the electronic media revolution in the 1980s. As Lupton observes, 'Between the installation and the television series, Marker began to diversify the media platforms in which he created work, under the impact of newly available technologies such as the Apple computer, the hand-held video camera and the domestic video recorder.'[4]

Before we proceed to look at Marker's new media works and their conceptual, formal and technical interests, which reverberate across his entire oeuvre (photo-novels, fiction, journalism, criticism, cinema, photography), it is important to state that till the early 1990s, Marker's stature as a major postwar French cineaste was only known by dedicated cinephiles—he barely amounted to, to use Chris Darke's apt expression, a 'cinephile's whisper'.[5] The initial critical reception of Marker's first essay films, in the early 1960s, was quite limited in its scope, but now there are increasing specialist dossiers, journal issues and monographs in French and German on his work, and just 2 years ago, *Film Comment* published a two-part dossier (the first of its kind in English).[6] Marker has now become, despite his fiercely guarded privacy as an artist—someone whose anonymity rivals the late Maurice Blanchot's—a common interest for many artists, writers and audiences across many different fields of contemporary audiovisual culture.

What distinguishes Marker's work from that of his contemporaries is his playful, erudite and literary approach to the paradoxical nature of the image and time's hallucinatory labyrinth. Marker's oeuvre— including his more current multimedia works, such as the installation *Zapping Zone* (1990)—evinces a growing concern with computer-based media and, more significantly, italicises the contradictory qualities of the image: its absence and its presence, its distance and its proximity, its reality and its virtuality. The image in its solitude, as memory, haunts us beyond our grasp.

Hence Marker quotes George Steiner's following words as an epigram in *The Last Bolshevik*: 'It is not the literal past that rules us: it is images of the past.' The six posthumous 'audiovisual' letters that form this work trace Medvedkin's life as 'the last Bolshevik filmmaker'. Characteristically, however, it is Marker's distinctive style of audiovisual writing, with its focus on a pliable mixture of reportage, autobiographical confession (echoing Philippe Lejeune's concept of the *autobiographical pact*, in which there are no visible traces of the author's presence in his own video work) and historical essay, that displays the open-ended, meandering textuality of the essay genre. Marker's typical emphasis on creating a visual writing that is always on the *move* is captured by his ability to freeze the image, as he does in *Sunless* or in the opening preamble of *The Last Bolshevik*, where we see Medvedkin beg Marker to write him a few words—just enough to fill in the space between Medvedkin's two foregrounded fingers.

Marker's oeuvre is notable for its indifference to the material specificities of media, and in this sense it evokes Godard's reply to the late Ed Emshwiller (who asked Godard why he did not bother to pursue technological questions in his video practice): 'Video, film, writing—it's all the same to me.' Above all, Marker's interest in audiovisual writing stems from his interest in making the spectator see and hear afresh and essentially doubt the reality of the proliferating images that shape our everyday lives. It is Marker's distinctive gaze, full of irony and engagement, empathy and criticism, that makes his work (across all media) so absorbing.

It is important to recognise, therefore, that the different media that Marker traverses with such innovative ease do not provide any kind of stability in our endeavour to classify him: they do not critically define him as much as his unique analytical and lyrical intelligence does. André Bazin, as Lupton correctly points out, in his celebrated essay on Marker's *Letter from Siberia* identifies Marker's intelligence as the primary feature of his work and the personal essay form as his preferred mode of image-making.[7] Bazin claimed that Marker departed from the conventional forms of documentary reportage to establish a new form: 'the essay documented by film'.[8] For Bazin, 'essay' meant a specific literary orientation in the sense that it should 'be understood in the same way as in literature: both a historical and political essay, though written by a poet'.[9] However, as Raymond Bellour points out in his excellent analysis of *Immemory*, Marker's understanding of the essay form had more to do with Henri Michaux's writings about the letter than with anyone else's writings.[10] Bellour's idea that Marker's multifaceted use of the essay across many media represents a particular strategy of mood should be cited here: 'Marker's essays have since taken many forms: they bear witness as much to a strategy of mood as to variations modulated by his subjects (countries, portraits, problems ...), his commissions, and his working rhythms (punctual engagements with "hot" material, long-term projects)'.[11]

Further, as Bellour suggests, Marker addresses the viewer as third party to what he himself sees and hears, and it is precisely this mode of address that enables Marker's subjectivity to speak to us so fluidly through a variety of different texts in *Immemory*.[12] In essence, Marker, who only appears behind his Rolleiflex camera, addresses us through his fetish animal, Guillaume-en-Egypte, the 'silent movie cat', his faithful double. Using this strategy in the CD-ROM, Marker speaks to us (through his texts) in a much more fluid capacity than the regular first person address 'I' allows, encompassing many other modalities of address—such as 'you', 'he', 'she', 'one', 'we', 'they'—before returning, as Bellour rightly observes, to 'I'.[13] By utilising this broad form of audiovisual writing, Marker is able to contact the other in all of us.

Marker's inimitable style—highlighted in *Letter from Siberia* and acclaimed by Bazin—hinges on its innovative structure as 'horizontal' montage, where meanings and associations are registered through a supple lateral relay between commentary and images, not through traditional editing, which stresses the relation from shot to shot over the length of the film.[14] Critically, then, Marker's editing style—which (according to Bazin) favours intelligence first, then the spoken word and finally the image—suggests that Marker's editing is, in Bazin's memorable short phrase, 'done from ear to eye'.[15]

It could be argued that Marker's willingness to experiment in his early writings, in the late 1940s and 1950s, indicates a breadth of interests, as well as a breadth of understanding of genres and contexts; as Lupton points out in her thoroughly researched book on Marker, there is also a substantial desire to go beyond writing to embrace other exciting forms of reflection and enquiry.[16] This trans-generic mode of creativity lies at the core of Marker's unique style of image-making. Indeed, as Lupton persuasively suggests in her illuminating first chapter on Marker's early career as a writer, editor, polemicist and filmmaker, he learned to scrutinise archival documentary images for hidden historical realities and created a unique editing style while working for the Catholic-Existentialist journal *Esprit*, the adult education cultural organisations *Travail et Culture* and *Peuple et Culture*, and, finally, working with Bazin himself at the cinema section of the former organisation.[17] Also, Marker's respect for Bazin's personality was such that he was also an early associate of the journal *Cahiers du cinéma*, which Bazin co-founded with Jacques Doniol-Valcroze. (It was Bazin who gave Marker, in 1945, his own 16mm film camera to begin his film on postwar Germany.)

During the 1950s Marker tried his hand at a new journalistic form by producing a series of travelogues that deployed impressionistic journalism with still photography; these were published by Editions du Seuil.

At the same time, Marker belonged to the so-called Left Bank Group of the French New Wave, an informal group of directors that included Alain Resnais, Agnès Varda, Henri Colpi, Armand Gatti and Georges Franju (the co-director, with Henri Langlois, of the Paris *Cinémathèque*). It was the American critic Richard Roud who gave these filmmakers this name in 1962/63, in contrast to the Right Bank Group of young critics-turned-directors associated with *Cahiers du cinéma*. The Left Bank Group had a shared background in the bohemian artistic and literary culture of the Left Bank, a dedication to innovation in cinematic and theatrical forms, and a desire to define political and social themes in their own work. They did not constitute an official movement but rather were united by a common sensibility and a camaraderie which led to helping each other with their projects.

One of Marker's closest friends is Alain Resnais, with whom he collaborated in the 1950s on a series of important essay films and short documentaries. One of these is the magisterial *Les Statues meurent aussi* (1950–53), which was banned by the French government of the time because of its scorching critique of the damaging cultural impact of colonialism and the devastating consequences of a white imperial gaze on African art and culture. Marker's sympathies have always been with ordinary people in the context of their everyday culture—the people, as curator Barbara London puts it, 'whose lives he turns into history'.[18] This is evident in his 1962 *cinéma-vérité* documentary *Le Joli mai* (co-directed with the film's camera operator, Pierre Lhomme), in which he elicits the views of Parisians in the wake of the Algerian war.[19] Marker's life-long identification with history from the bottom to the top is the direct legacy of his work with the aforementioned cultural groups in the 1950s—and, arguably, of his constant voyages to different cultures and places.

During the camera crew's day off during the shooting of *Le Joli mai*, Marker commenced photographing a new film which, as he stated in a very rare interview for the French newspaper *Liberation*, represented 'a story I didn't completely understand'.[20] This new work was finished during the ending of *Le Joli mai*, and it became Marker's most influential film, the highly acclaimed *La Jetée* (1962). Composed virtually entirely of still photographs, *La Jetée* is a moving and strange poetic film consisting of science fiction, psychological fable and photomontage. It is unquestionably one of the profoundest meditations on the nature of the film medium itself, particularly in terms of the complex relationship between still and moving image in the cinema. *La Jetée* has become a hauntingly beautiful cult film of world cinema, emblematic of the new media emphasis in postmodern audiovisual creativity. British author J.G. Ballard names *La Jetée* as his all-time favourite film—it is an extraordinary melancholic and potent film of indelible images of the inner landscapes of time.

The human perception of time and space and its transformation through memory are the critical themes of *La Jetée*—and all his work, as Jan-Christopher Horak argues in his discussion of Marker as a photographer-filmmaker who, in his personal essay films, takes his cue 'from a specific geographical place in the real world to create space and time coordinates for the construction of a subjective perception of the world'.[21]

La Jetée imagines the nuclear destruction of Paris after World War III, and follows the tragic destiny of its protagonist, whose life is, as the film's sparse, poetic voice-over informs the spectator, 'marked by an image from childhood'. The protagonist, as a survivor of the war, time-travels both into the past and into the future. He is granted an option by his captors and decides to live in the past, only to realise that by doing so he has chosen his own death.

Marker's and Godard's careers during the last three decades make an interesting comparison: Godard explores the 'death' of cinema and its history, as intertwined within the history of the 20th century, while Marker skirts across and through cinema in his risk-taking engagements with other media. More recently, as earlier noted, Marker has moved into art gallery installations that essentially recycle his own film work, anticipating the fragmentation of cinema and its traces into the 'white cube' space of the gallery. Other directors—as varied as Chantal Akerman, Atom Egoyan, Peter Greenaway, Isaac Julien and Harun Farocki, to name a few—have also created installation works that focus on the distinction between cinema and installation art.

Marker's oeuvre of the 1990s—including significant video and installation media works such as *The Zapping Zone* (1992–99), *Silent Movie* (1994–95), *Immemory One* (1997) and *Immemory*—are fine examples of artworks that can be shown in various forms. Marker's film and media art are crucial contributions to the expanding mixed-media Zeitgeist that prevails in the contemporary art world.

Let us now examine, in some detail, Marker's only negotiation of the interactive CD-ROM medium, *Immemory*. This medium is now all but obsolete, reminding us that contemporary media are in a state of transition. To some, like Brian Eno, the CD-ROM is a tedious and unexciting medium because it relies on the idea of moving huge blocks of data around.[22] But to someone like Marker, as a 'mutant' artist who is engaged in a constant trans-media approach to creativity, it was exactly the CD-ROM's unique 'branching' architecture that attracted him to the medium.[23]

Immemory, as mentioned before, was commissioned by the Centre Georges Pompidou Centre, Paris and it was originally planned as the first of a series of artists' CD-ROMs concerned with questions of memory. The work premiered there during 1997 as *Immemory One* (according to Lupton, the work was given this original title to allow subsequent modifications); it was then commercially released in 1998— the English version appeared in 2003.[24] As he does with the rest of his oeuvre, Marker explores in *Immemory* the geography of his own memory, as it can be traced through his lifetime's accumulated mementos, signs, photographs and experiences, and as it is germane to his inner life. Like Proust before him, as critic Kent Jones observes, Marker has fashioned a poetic, open-ended and engaging template for 'the working of memory itself as he's charting his own interior landscape'.[25]

Consequently, Marker, as he puts it in the accompanying essay to *Immemory*, inspired by Proust's *Time Regained*, claims 'for the image the humility and powers of a madeleine'.[26] Marker's wish is for the sympathetic 'reader-visitor' to use *Immemory* as 'a springboard for his own pilgrimage in *Time Regained*'.[27] Despite Eno's reservations about the limits of the CD-ROM medium, Marker has given us a highly inventive and positive definition of the medium's more resonant and playful possibilities, especially as they apply to the navigator working his or her way through large blocks of data. In his inimitable intelligent and playful style, he has thus given us in *Immemory* a work that self-reflexively questions the more predictable static and boring features of the technology itself.

Marker assembles his postcards, photographs, film stills and clips, written commentaries, collages, superimpositions, cherished objects, quotes and musical passages in a structure so that each of these elements is like a madeleine—that token shared by Alfred Hitchcock and Marcel Proust, the two figures who stand over the entry to the Memory Zone of the work—which, according to the artist, maps 'the imaginary country which spreads out inside of us'.[28]

Immemory's entry offers a welcome screen map with icons for seven separate zones: Cinema, Travel, Museum, Poetry, War, Photography and X-Plugs. Once you have entered its labyrinth, the pathways of *Immemory* are exhaustive, as they diverge into infinity, centred around these various zone topics and their autobiographically inflected materials, through which the navigators can go backwards and forwards across Marker's career as a writer, traveller and image-maker. When we say 'Marker', we refer to the person born of Russian and American extraction in July 1921 in Neuilly-sur-Seine, a suburb of Paris, who has adopted various disguises during his life as a global traveller with a camera—including Chris Marker, Sandor Krasna, Fritz Markasson, Chris Villeneuve and Jacopo Berenzi.[29]

It is as if Marker's whole creative career has anticipated the arrival of the new media technologies. As Lupton notes, though his early works in the 1950s speculate about cinema as the art form of the 20th and 21st centuries, by the close of the 20th century Marker was arguing: 'No, film won't have a second century. That's all.'[30] Whether we agree with him or not is another matter, but Marker's statement does clearly signal his role as a new media pioneer. *Immemory* is an interactive virtual collage that combines images, texts and sounds derived from Marker's sustained interest in the cultural memories of older media such as literature, cinema and photography.

As we navigate the work by entering any of its interlocking hypermedia zones, we navigate with a cursor in the form of a solid cross over a circle. The cursor changing colour signifies that there is a tangent to pursue. The circle becoming transparent (the crosshairs of a gun or a camera appear) indicates that there is yet another addendum to pursue (or not pursue).

Certain zones overlap with each other, as in the case of Memory, which overlaps with both Cinema and Travel. Marker's cartoon image of Guillaume-en-Egypte, the 'silent movie cat', sometimes pops up through *Immemory*, acting as a helpful tour guide by making various comments or suggesting that you take a detour to another place in the CD-ROM. In fact, Marker's cat character also appears in the Museum Zone to critique its high art connotations. Another key self-reflexive feature of *Immemory* is its instruction to the user: 'Don't zap, take your time.'

On an autobiographical level, the family album appears as a major leitmotif in the work, centred around a photograph of Marker's mother Rosalie in the Photography Zone. There are several significant tales relating to Marker's Uncle Anton and Aunt Edith Krasna, who appear as two seminal iconic figures in terms of Marker's life-long passion for travel and photography. Typically, Marker recycles old material into *Immemory*: for instance, the photo-text albums *Corennes* and *Le Depays* are contextualised as subsections of the Photography Zone, with slight layout modifications. Also, Marker deploys his *Vertigo* essay, 'A free replay', in the *Vertigo* segment, which is shared by Cinema and Memory.

Why was Marker attracted to the CD-ROM medium? Principally, because its distinctive technological features allowed him to map out a virtual model of his memory—he could combine text and image in open-ended, kinetic hypermedia configurations that books and films cannot do. One of the cardinal sources for *Immemory*'s philosophical model for memory is the writing of the 17th century English polymath Robert Hooke, whose ideas anticipated Newton's concept of gravity. For Marker, Hooke's ideas prefigured the CD-ROM. As he put it, 'when I proposed to transfer the regions of Memory into geographical rather than historical zones, I unwittingly linked up to a conception familiar to certain 17th century minds, and totally foreign to the 20th century'.[31]

According to Timothy Murray, the suitability of the CD-ROM technology for Marker lies in his experimental willingness to shift 'from the public screen of cinema to the private space of the multimedia book'; in doing so, Marker 'tracks 20th century visual history and its ambivalent relation to the electronic screen'.[32] Murray contends that it is the odd status of the CD-ROM as an electronic book which hovers over the threshold of the historical and the personal, the public and the private, that makes *Immemory* 'such a curious object of analysis'.[33] Marker's playful and resonant re-contextualisation of his personal and historical texts and images in *Immemory* neatly combine high art and popular culture, interactive media and an intellectual archive. Murray also makes the interesting observation that Marker, in *Immemory*, has given us a unique amalgam of what Jacques Derrida might term the feverous delirium of the digital archive; or, to quote Murray, 'similarly, as suggested by Raymond Bellour, "what Deleuze, speaking of Resnais's cinematic transformation of Proust and Bergson, called Membrane Memory, between inside and outside, actual and virtual" '.[34]

Finally, *Immemory* is not an essay like *Sunless*, as Bellour indicates; it is more akin to a self-portrait whose literary, filmic and video art traditions Marker has metaphorically located himself in.[35] The literary self-portrait, from Montaigne to Leiris, does not explicitly borrow the generic formula of the autobiography, even though it acquires many of its traits. In terms of filmic and video traditions, Marker's CD-ROM, like the rest of his more personal works, echoes the self-portrait films of Jean Cocteau, Federico Fellini, Godard, Jonas Mekas and Orson Welles, and in terms of video, certain works of Vito Acconci, Jean-Andre Fieschi, Thierry Kuntzel and Bill Viola, amongst others.

Marker once said that he needed the CD-ROM medium in order to do 'a flashback visit to my Cuban childhood' (via links to scanned family photos from the period).[36] But, in true mischievous form, this observation only hints at his reasons for doing *Immemory*; one could argue that they have more to do with his continuously trans-media approach to image-making across a variety of different media, and with how his characteristic 'horizontal editing' style of collage and montage has been boosted by the digital possibilities of juxtaposing, morphing and overlapping, as Murray suggests, elaborate sequences from visual and aural history.[37] In many ways, whether it is film, video, photography or new media, Marker has the capacity to enchant us in his quest, in exploring the cultural memory of our mutating audiovisual culture.

NOTES

1 See Catherine Lupton, *Chris Marker*, Reaktion Books, London, 2005, p. 205. Lupton's detailed and informative book on Marker is (so far) the only one in English that covers his entire career. I am indebted to Lupton for her excellent background details on Marker and her analyses of some of the rarer Marker works that are not so publicly accessible.

2 ibid., p. 10.
3 ibid., p. 148.
4 ibid., p. 149.
5 Chris Darke, ' The invisible man', *Film Comment*, vol. 39, no. 9, 2003, p. 32.
6 'The travels of Chris Marker', *Film Comment*, May/June–July/August 2003.
7 See Lupton, p. 55. For the Bazin essay,

refer to André Bazin, 'Letter from Siberia', *Film Comment*, vol. 39, no. 4, 2003, pp. 44–45 (English translation: originally published in *France-observateur*, 30 October, 1958).

8 ibid., p. 55.
9 Raymond Bellour, 'The book, back and forth', in Christine van Assche (ed.), *Que'est-ce qu'une madeleine? A propos du CD-ROM Immemory de Chris Marker*', Yves Gevaert (ed.), Centre Georges Pompidou, Paris, 1997, p. 110.
10 ibid., p. 111.
11 ibid., p. 110.
12 ibid.
13 ibid., p. 111.
14 See Lupton, p. 55.
15 ibid.

16   ibid., p. 44.

17   ibid., pp. 13–39.

18   Barbara London, *Video Spaces* [exhibition catalogue], The Museum of Modern Art, New York, 1995, p. 24.

19   See Lupton, p. 83. It is interesting to note Marker's objection to the term '*cinéma-vérité*' being applied to *Le Joli mai*, as he prefers the less problematic one of 'direct cinema'. See the interview (one of the very few that feature in this secretive filmmaker's career), Samuel Douaire & Annick Rivoire, 'Marker direct', *Film Comment*, vol. 39, no. 3, 2003, p. 40 [originally published in *Liberation*, 5 March 2003].

20   ibid.

21   Jan-Christopher Horak, *Making Images Move*, Smithsonian Institution Press, Washington/London, 1997, p. 31.

22   Brian Eno is quoted in Kent Jones, 'Time immemorial,' *Film Comment*, vol. 39, issue 4, 2003, p. 46. For the original Eno source see Brian Eno, *A Year with Swollen Appendices*, Faber & Faber, London, 1996, pp. 345, 308–309.

23   Douaire & Rivoire 2003.

24   Lupton, p. 205.

25   Jones.

26   Chris Marker, 'Immemory' [essay], accompanying *Immemory, a CD-ROM by Chris Marker*, Exact Change, Cambridge MA, 2002, [originally published in French by Editions du Centre Pompidou, 1998].

27   ibid.

28   Cited in Lupton, p. 206 [original source Marker, trans. Lupton].

29   ibid., p. 12.

30   ibid., p. 178.

31   Marker, 2002.

32   Timothy Murray, 'Debased projection and cyberspace ping: Chris Marker's digital screen', *Parachute*, 113, 2004, p. 93.

33   ibid.

34   ibid., p. 113.

35   Bellour, p. 120.

36   ibid., pp. 96-97.

37   Quoted in Murray, p. 98.

Conclusion: media in transition, or from montage to immersion

No matter what the new nature is, or what remains of the old, in the long run, we'll have to invent a name for this new art, or—why not?—simply go on calling it 'cinematography'. On the condition that *graphein* embraces the power of the voices as well as the physical quality of the words, and that *kinema* includes the touch of the hand and all kinds of time.

Raymond Bellour

Accumulatively, the essays that form *Mutant Media* endeavour to delineate critical debates about the convergence taking place between celluloid cinema and new technologies. The continuing fragmentation of cinema due to the ascendancy of the new audiovisual media in everyday life is a very complex and multifaceted phenomenon that merits long-term critical scrutiny. A significant aspect of this fragmentation of cinema is the way that, in recent times, visual artists have been resorting to cinema—in all its splendid multiplicity—to create film and video installations and projections for the art gallery world. This has been happening in significant ways during the last two decades. Artists have also been experiencing the cinematic image through the new electronic and digital technologies to create new media works like CD-ROMs, DVDs, computer-interactive pieces and art specifically designed for the Internet.

The essays gathered, rewritten and organised here into three sections, each with its own new introductory text, chart in their own complex 'criss-crossing' ways my own ongoing interests in art and film criticism and theory, video art and new media. The three sections register the many intricate, hybrid and open-ended connections that exist between cinema, video art and new media. The essays in *Mutant Media* collectively address the complex question of the convergence—including the continuities and discontinuities—between cinema, video and digital media. They constitute an argument that cinema and the screen arts, in general, have been engaged in a dialogue with each other for the last three decades. In *Mutant Media* I attempt to trace the mutation of the movie image via video and the new technologies across the contemporary mediascape.

On a certain level, the essays collected here constitute an autobiographical portrait of my life as an artist, critic and writer whose eclecticism has been substantially shaped by my own cinephilia. In fact, this book documents my role as someone who sees mainstream culture and society from a marginalised critical point of view: always at an oblique angle to the subject at hand. Thus, *Mutant Media*, metaphorically speaking, reflects my own bi-cultural identity and hybridity as a postwar Greek Australian who believes in the fragility and poetry of the moving image, self-reflexivity and does not subscribe to any notion of a grand, totalising film and media theory.

I need here to deal, for a moment, with the current state of play concerning academic cinema studies. In a significant sense, the essays collected in this book represent my own trajectory through the evolution of academic film studies from the 1960s and early 1970s. Although academic film studies started to flourish around 1968, today one can sense that it is in a state of disarray. My own interests in video art and new media began in the late 1970s and early 1980s, when I became tired of the imperialistic dogmas of academic film studies—these were reaching their zenith in the (post)structuralist 1970s and 1980s.

Dudley Andrew's 'three ages' characterisation of cinema studies in the Anglo-American academy deserves consideration, for it accurately diagnoses the many cultural, theoretical and pedagogic limits of academic film studies, particularly the way it was taught in the 1970s: as authoritarian dogma.[1] The 1970s was the era when Marxism, semiotics, feminist film theory and psychoanalysis together mobilised an 'iconophobic' spirit (Martin Jay), if you will, which treated cinema suspiciously. Drawing on Buster Keaton's film *The Three Ages* (1923), Andrew delineates three separate ages for academic film studies' evolution: (a) 'The Stone Age', (b) 'The Imperial Age', and (c) 'The Present Age'.[2]

Cinema studies in the Stone Age developed spontaneously in cafés, literary societies, parish halls and newspaper columns before it attached itself to the academy. This was the era of cine-clubs, chic journals and mimeographed notes for dedicated filmmakers and aficionados. It was the time for the appearance of certain important critics, such as Béla Balázs, Walter Benjamin, Siegfried Kracauer and André Malraux, whose seminal essays were read by a cultivated reading public. After World War II, Parisian art theatres sprouted, engendering discussion about films that gained their reputations at international film festivals—another postwar phenomenon. In 1950 André Bazin published the first 'auteur' study, a short study of Orson Welles, which was also introduced by Jean Cocteau. Auteur studies flourished and cinephilia caught on, infecting film journals, *Cahiers du cinéma* foremost among them.[3]

It was the rejection of Jean Mitry's two immense books—*Esthetique et psychologie du cinema* (1965) and *Histoire du cinéma* (the first of whose five volumes was published in 1967)—by Christian Metz, who criticised Mitry's aesthetics as being amateurish, and then Jean-Louis Comolli, who dismissed Mitry's linear historiography, that ushered in the Imperial Age, according to Andrew.[4] Semiotics, Marxism and psychoanalysis did not appreciate films, but rather 'read' them as hidden structures. The wholesale importation of French systems of thought, including textual semiotics, had systematically reduced the complexities of the cinema to its basic processes. By the mid-1970s students were engaged in going beyond the commonplaces of textbooks, Andrew argues, in order to 'theorise' 'the conscious machinations of producers of images and the unconscious ideology of spectators'.[5]

Today, cultural studies are deflating the basic force of films and the imperial spirit of continental critique. Film scholars are now roaming freely in a domain whose concerns and borders are highly flexible and cross-disciplinary: media studies, cultural studies and visual studies. Moreover, as this book I hope attests, this is an era of pluralism, where films and theories about films have become objects among other objects. This is especially evident now, as the original object of our attention—film—has mutated in its interactions with other visual media, art forms and technologies. This is one of the main points of my book: film's changing definition because of its convergence with digital media is a very complicated phenomenon that we are witnessing in the current mediascape. How best do we address this phenomenon? What critical languages do we adopt to adequately discuss cinema's ongoing techno-cultural mutation?

Indeed, when we talk about the cinema, what visual objects do we have in mind? As Andrew puts it, would either Mitry or Metz recognise cinema studies as it is practised today?—'does cinema studies recognise itself as it enters a new century?'[6]

Cinema is a transitional medium, which means many questions can be posed about its changing identity apropos of its highly complex interactions with digital media. What should cinema studies aim to be in the new century?

Cinema carries from the 19th century powerful traditions of narrative and visual representation, but we need to contextualise these traditions as new media and new functions in art and entertainment appear on the cultural landscape.

In fact, cinema represents, in Andrew's words, 'a century-long threshold', for it 'stands between'.[7] As Andrew writes, 'it stands between popular expressions (magazines, pop music, TV) and the more considered and considerable arts (novel, opera, theatre); between its old-fashioned nineteenth-century technological base (gears and celluloid) and its constantly renewed contemporary appeal (high-definition TV, virtual reality); between a corporate or an anonymous mode of production and the auteur mode it sometimes adopts from literature'.[8]

Ironically, universities are now expressing confidence in cinema studies, at a moment when cinema studies is quite anxious about the stability of its object. Will the loss of celluloid to digital formats, asks Andrews, signify the end of the field?[9]

As for the essays themselves, they represent my ongoing and varied interests in art, avant-garde, documentary and classic narrative cinema, art and critical theory, cultural criticism, new media, video art, and surrealism. In many different ways, the essays resonate off each other. For they reflect my fascination with the idea of cinema, new media, video and installation as forms of writing. The phantasmatic notion of film and video as a form of image and sound writing has haunted me since the 1960s (Cocteau, Jean-Luc Godard, Chris Marker and Welles).

In other words, I have always been interested in artists, video and filmmakers who create a highly self-questioning, non-conclusive kind of (electronic) writing that is uncertain of its own authority, and that is a trans-generic hybrid and mobile form of audiovisual writing.

In film, installations, projections, videos or theoretical texts that keep up a sustained and informed 'border-crossing' dialogue between the established and the more recent media forms. In producing transmedia work that questions the dualism and essentialism of modernism and Western thought.

Creating a work of film, video and new media art or a literary or a theoretical text that endeavours to capture the polyphonic indeterminacy of the new essay form (Theodor Adorno, Kathy Acker, Roland Barthes, John Cage and Friedrich Nietzsche). As an artist and writer working with the film/video essay form, I regard video as a cross-disciplinary medium that is anchored in the post-Astruc 'writerly' traditions of modern techno-creativity. In a significant sense, across *Mutant Media* I am most concerned with those works that seek to excavate new sites in the image in order to produce (ideally) a moving and intricate meditation on image-making itself.

It is important to note that we need to be suspicious of the 'border patrol' orthodoxies of official culture and monocultural thought, and instead embrace the transmedia possibilities of a pluralistic, collage view of the continuing long conversation that is taking place between cinema, video and the new media technologies. In doing this we need to go beyond the limits of traditional academic analysis of film as an aesthetic form and appreciate film alongside other media—video and the new technologies—side by side, as it were, in a non-mutually exclusive spirit. This has been happening with many artists, filmmakers and producers who are creating film, video and new media installations and projections for the art gallery world.

The rise of the art installation film is a testament to the creative value of appreciating images of all kinds—filmic, videographic and new media—as having highly intricate relations with each other in today's transformative image culture. This means we need to locate new ways of talking about the image and new ways of seeing.

One of the crucial concepts informing all the essays in this book and indeed all my writing in general is that all media are in a state of continuous cultural and technological transition. This applies to the cinema as much as it does to digital media. As Malcolm Le Grice puts it: 'Neither the range nor the limits of the digital media can be adequately defined—they are not only eclectic in content but continuously hybrid and in constant technological development.'[10] For Le Grice, artists can only continue to experiment, innovate and challenge existing concepts, forms and institutions; there is 'no security that they have found a crucial centre to the discourse—the heads of the hydra-media will continue to grow'.[11]

One other critical aspect of my argument here is the necessity for sustained support for the media arts to become a more integral part of culture generally. This suggests a long-term commitment to access, curatorial advocacy and exhibition, as well as to critical discussion and evaluation. We need to transcend the novelty factor in order to consolidate a culture of media arts. This means we require proper curatorial spaces for the exhibition of the media arts; the public will have a distorted appreciation of them if they are only ever exhibited in inadequate curatorial contexts.

All the essays collected in this book highlight, for me, the aesthetic, cultural and audiovisual importance of the essay form. In many different contexts, *Mutant Media* suggests the overall significance of the essay form as a subgenre located between major genres—the literary essay is situated between the philosophical treatise and the literary excursion—and is therefore, according to Nora Alter, in her very recent study of Chris Marker's cinematic practice, 'inherently transgressive, digressive, playful, contradictory, and at times even political'.[12] Alter, discussing Hans Richter, the German avant-garde director, who in 1940 coined the essay film as a new type of filmmaking and located it between documentary and experimental filmmaking, suggests that the essay film itself combines these two genres, thereby testifying 'to the inherent creativity of this new filmic form'.[13] It was Alexandre Astruc, a close colleague of Marker, who further developed Richter's concept of the essay film and emphasised the new genre's literary and philosophical antecedents.

Moreover, the essays gathered in this book register the many paths I have travelled over the years as an artist, critic and writer who, like a 'switchboard operator', shuttles between the cinema, critical theory, literature, video, new media and the visual arts. *Mutant Media* is the product of my role as someone who collages together the many different ideas, forms and genres from these different disciplines in order to create something different that stands outside official culture and its fixities. Thus, *Mutant Media* is not a systematic thesis as such but rather a work of speculative reflections and observations by someone who values the essay form as an experimental vehicle for open-ended lateral thinking aloud on a number of subjects that are interconnected in intricate and mobile ways.

I have observed that the ongoing convergence between cinema and other media has vast implications for contemporary art practice, especially in terms of the ascendancy of visual artists and filmmakers who have been producing art installations and projections for the performative space of the art gallery. Clearly, there are many aesthetic, cultural and technological reasons why this hybrid art phenomenon has been taking place during the last two decades or so. I have attempted throughout the essays collected here to address the complexity of these new developments in the international art world. These artists are drawing upon new concepts, forms, icons, passages and narratives from the cinema, which itself is undergoing a massive transformation due to the new technologies which are so ever-present in our current audiovisual landscape. Their installations and projections are quite mysterious as works of hybridisation and mutation. *Mutant Media* endeavours, in its own way, to contribute to an understanding of these new mixed-media artworks with their 'in-between' concepts, forms and styles.

To conclude, it is crucial to understand that today we are encountering a far-reaching complex transformation of the media, which is graphically impacting on contemporary art, culture and society. It is equally critical to appreciate that the media are always in a state of unpredictable transition; that complex debates continue to ebb and flow regarding convergence between cinema, video and new media; that we must continue to seek new ways of seeing and talking about the moving image as it cuts across other visual media; and that examination of how film and art are connecting to each other is crucial to the understanding of each. Why, for example, are artists and filmmakers today raiding the cinema to produce their installations and projections for the art museum world? This is the sort of crucial question I have attempted to address here—speculatively, in a non-definitive manner. As artists, educators and spectators, we need to see one media form through another in order to value the competing image delivery systems that make up our contemporary audiovisual landscape.

NOTES

1 Dudley Andrew, 'The "three ages" of cinema studies and the age to come', *PMLA*, vol. 115, no. 3, May 2000, pp. 341–51.

2 ibid., p. 342.

3 ibid.

4 ibid., p. 343.

5 ibid.

6 ibid., p. 345.

7 ibid., p. 348.

8 ibid.

9 ibid., p. 350.

10 Malcolm Le Grice, *Experimental Cinema in the Digital Age*, British Film Institute, London, 2001, p. 309.

11 ibid.

12 Nora Alter, *Chris Marker*, University of Illinois Press, Urbana and Chicago, 2006, p. 18. Alter's book appeared after I had written my chapter on Marker.

13 ibid.

Index